Hitchcock's Objects as Subjects

ALSO BY MARC RAYMOND STRAUSS
AND FROM MCFARLAND

*Hitchcock Nonetheless: The Master's Touch
in His Least Celebrated Films* (2007)

*The Dance Criticism of Arlene Croce: Articulating
a Vision of Artistry, 1973–1987* (2005)

Alfred Hitchcock's Silent Films (2004)

Hitchcock's Objects as Subjects

The Significance of Things on Screen

MARC RAYMOND STRAUSS

McFarland & Company, Inc., Publishers
Jefferson, North Carolina

LIBRARY OF CONGRESS CATALOGUING-IN-PUBLICATION DATA [new form]

Names: Strauss, Marc, author.
Title: Hitchcock's objects as subjects : the significance of things on screen / Marc Raymond Strauss.
Description: Jefferson, North Carolina : McFarland & Company, Inc., Publishers, 2016. | Includes bibliographical references and index.
Identifiers: LCCN 2015043781 | ISBN 9780786443086 (softcover : acid free paper)
Subjects: LCSH: Hitchcock, Alfred, 1899–1980—Criticism and interpretation. | Motion pictures—Setting and scenery.
Classification: LCC PN1998.3.H58 S83 2016 | DDC 791.4302/33092—dc23
LC record available at http://lccn.loc.gov/2015043781

BRITISH LIBRARY CATALOGUING DATA ARE AVAILABLE

ISBN 9781476622484 (ebook)

© 2016 Marc Raymond Strauss. All rights reserved

No part of this book may be reproduced or transmitted in any form or by any means, electronic or mechanical, including photocopying or recording, or by any information storage and retrieval system, without permission in writing from the publisher.

On the cover: Lighted candles, placed as they would be used on an altar, frame Sylvia Sidney in *Sabotage*, 1936 (Gaumont British/Photofest)

Printed in the United States of America

McFarland & Company, Inc., Publishers
  Box 611, Jefferson, North Carolina 28640
    www.mcfarlandpub.com

To my wife, Sarah Riley,
whose artistry never ceases
to inspire me

Table of Contents

Preface	1
Introduction	2
The Pleasure Garden (1925)	15
The Lodger: A Story of the London Fog (1927)	17
Downhill (1927)	26
Easy Virtue (1927)	27
The Ring (1927)	31
The Farmer's Wife (1928)	36
Champagne (1928)	39
The Manxman (1929)	41
Blackmail (1929)	44
Juno and the Paycock (1930)	47
Murder! (1930)	50
The Skin Game (1931)	51
Rich and Strange (1932)	53
Number Seventeen (1932)	57
Waltzes from Vienna (1933)	59
The Man Who Knew Too Much (1934)	60
The 39 Steps (1935)	66
Secret Agent (1936)	69
Sabotage (1936)	73
Young and Innocent (1937)	78
The Lady Vanishes (1938)	82
Jamaica Inn (1939)	86
Rebecca (1940)	88
Foreign Correspondent (1940)	92

Table of Contents

Mr. and Mrs. Smith (1941) — 96
Suspicion (1941) — 99
Saboteur (1942) — 103
Shadow of a Doubt (1943) — 105
Lifeboat (1944) — 108
Spellbound (1945) — 110
Notorious (1946) — 113
The Paradine Case (1947) — 120
Rope (1948) — 123
Under Capricorn (1949) — 126
Stage Fright (1950) — 128
Strangers on a Train (1951) — 131
I Confess (1952) — 134
Dial M for Murder (1954) — 137
Rear Window (1954) — 143
To Catch a Thief (1955) — 146
The Trouble with Harry (1955) — 149
The Man Who Knew Too Much (1956) — 151
The Wrong Man (1957) — 154
Vertigo (1958) — 156
North by Northwest (1959) — 161
Psycho (1960) — 164
The Birds (1963) — 168
Marnie (1964) — 171
Torn Curtain (1966) — 176
Topaz (1969) — 181
Frenzy (1972) — 184
Family Plot (1976) — 188

Conclusion — 190
Bibliography — 191
Index — 193

Preface

This book is about the objects in Alfred Hitchcock's films that are treated as subjects, equal protagonists to the human actors. Every detail that is visible on Hitchcock's screen carries with it information that impacts the audience; the importance of objects as subjects, while noted from time to time in other writings on the director, has not been given comprehensive attention until now.

I became interested in these elements while studying Hitchcock's films, realizing that his objects seemed to move about the frames like human characters, with human characteristics and qualities that impacted those people and my responses to them. I cover objects such as lamps, staircases, chairs, sculptures, tables, cars, and buildings that recur in many films over the director's fifty-plus years of filmmaking, to help the reader better appreciate their place in moving an audience.

I screened all 52 extant Hitchcock films numerous times as well as many of the major texts on the director and his work written since 1957 by the French critics-directors Eric Rohmer and Claude Chabrol. These important published works are essential to developing a richer context for this book, but mine is the first to focus solely on objects as subjects in Hitchcock's canon.

Introduction

> One idea, for instance, is that I'd like to do twenty-four hours in the life of a city.... It starts out at five a.m., at daybreak, with a fly crawling on the nose of a tramp lying in a doorway. Then, the early stirrings of life in the city. I'd like to try to do an anthology on food, showing its arrival in the city, its distribution, the selling, buying by people, the cooking, the various ways in which it's consumed. What happens to it in various hotels; how it's fixed up and absorbed. And, gradually, the end of the film would show the sewers, and the garbage being dumped out into the ocean.... Thematically, the cycle would show what people do to good things [Hitchcock; cited in Truffaut, 1967, p. 241].

The 52 extant, full-length films of Alfred Hitchcock remain as fascinating today as when they were released—and then re-released, transferred to video (Betamax first, for those who remember, and then VHS), videodisc (or laser disc, a short-lived format), DVD, Blu-ray, and now streamed. They can be played again and again with slow motion, pause, rewind, and fast forward. Their popularity remains high nearly forty years after his death, resulting in books and articles still published annually at a steady rate. Twentieth century geniuses like Hitch—Pablo Picasso, George Balanchine, Igor Stravinsky, Martha Graham and the Marx Brothers come to mind, too—are palpably stimulating, endlessly compelling, and as bottomless as a well always full of fresh spring water. And lovers of these kinds of people feel compelled to return to the source for periodic sips and swallows.

Because of this never exhausted well, the director's characters, plots, music, actors, use of colors, silences, suspense, camerawork, *mise en scènes*, montage, exacting precision, planning, and artistry have been

Introduction

identified and analyzed to the nth degree. And yet, there still seems to be something new to spot and discuss in a Hitchcock film. That really is the definition of genius: Their work truly never dies. It persists, lasts, and in fact *welcomes* repeated scrutiny. Alfred Hitchcock's films— miraculously, happily—keep going and going and going, after the tenth or hundredth viewing.

And so, after that hundredth viewing, one naturally wonders: Can we whittle these elements down to one overarching quality that makes so many viewers, critics and movie lovers return to his films time and again? The answer is actually within the director's own comments and understanding of the potential power of film: Hitchcock's goal was to find the best ways to capture, keep and emotionally move the viewer as if he/she was a participant in the story on the screen, right alongside the other actors. In François Truffaut's groundbreaking 1963 interviews with the director, *Hitchcock/Truffaut: A Definitive Study of Alfred Hitchcock* (Simon & Schuster, 1967), Hitchcock himself speaks about his imperative to evoke audience emotion. Here are just four:

- Whichever way you choose to stage the action, your main concern is to hold the audience's fullest attention.... [One] might say that the screen rectangle must be charged with emotion [p. 43].
- Technique should enrich the action. One doesn't set the camera at a certain angle just because the cameraman happens to be enthusiastic about that spot. The only thing that matters is whether the installation of the camera at a given angle is going to give the scene its maximum impact. The beauty of image and movement, the rhythm and the effects—everything must be subordinated to the purpose [p. 71].
- Planting the camera in the countryside to shoot a passing train [in *North by Northwest*] would merely give us the viewpoint of a cow watching a train go by. I tried to keep the public inside the train, *with* the train. Whenever it went into a curve, we took a long shot from one of the train windows [p. 202].
- My main satisfaction is that the film had an effect on the audiences, and I consider that very important. I don't care about the subject matter; I don't care about the acting; but I do care

Introduction

about the pieces of film and the photography and the soundtrack and all of the technical ingredients that made the audience scream [in *Psycho*]. I feel it's tremendously satisfying for us to be able to use the cinematic art to achieve something of a mass emotion [p. 211].

If, indeed, the effect of "mass emotion" on audiences is the most important thing in a Hitchcock film, everything that appears onscreen must therefore be subordinate to that dictum: actors, narrative, set design, art direction, sound, all that we see and hear and feel. All these carefully chosen details must also necessarily include every *object* that appears in the frame. Immobile objects that we repeatedly and deliberately find carefully placed within Hitchcock's frames are highly charged: house-bound items such as chairs, stairs, walls, lamps, bedknobs, candles, windows, pictures, desks, glasses, and cups, as well as more public ones, both immobile and mobile, such as buildings and homes in towns and cities, the cities themselves, and trains, buses, cars, planes, boats, etc. Carefully placed alongside the actors and art direction and sound design, these objects have an equally powerful effect on an audience in Hitchcock's hands.

> [The] term "vehicle" seems to be the only one to account for all the trains, planes, automobiles, skis, boats, bicycles, wheelchairs, etc., which haunt [Hitchcock's] universe. We receive them not only as a sign of passage from one world to the other but especially as a sensation. A sensation of being carried off ... [Deutelbaum and Poague, 1986, p. 14].

A train, of course, is just a train, as is a lifeboat, and a staircase, and a pair of eyeglasses, and they do not have to mean or represent anything but what they usually do in our everyday world. But, on Hitchcock's screen, these objects are also much more than just trains, boats, staircases, or glasses. If we look and listen carefully, they take on human characteristics in his films, as if they, too, were actors playing their parts.

Another way of putting this is that everything on the screen, subjects *and* objects, are there for the purpose of influencing that which is not on the screen—us, Hitchcock's audience. Objects do indeed help fulfill the director's imperative:

> In Hitchcock movies, where nothing appears just because it happens to be in the shot, everything is calculated for the single purpose of induc-

Introduction

ing emotions. Naturalistic details are not included to show us the real world for its own sake. There is an ulterior motive: to make us feel (whether or not we think) that we are watching things relevant to our own experience. Hitchcock is fond of scenes in ordinary places like shops, offices, or restaurants, and in this he is capitalizing on the complacency he attacks with *The Birds*. In familiar, safe places, where we spend large parts of our lives, nothing ghastly is likely to happen [Cameron and Jeffery; cited in Deutelbaum and Poague, 1986, p. 265].

These everyday and ordinary places, microcosms of the bigger world at large, resonate most deeply with audiences who live and work in them, just like everyone else. Especially homes.

Homes have many thematic associations Hitchcock routinely trades on: the safety of a place of shelter or refuge, the stability and security of long-standing assumptions, the basis for self-definition through family relationships and a genetic sense of identity.... Home is thus a goal both desired and deferred as the end of narrative, and audiences' ambivalence toward this goal—they want the principals to arrive home safely, but not just yet—opens the space for an ambivalence toward home ... [Leitch, 1991, p. 25].

Likewise, the screen itself, that "flat" repository for these all-important details—objects, subjects, and carefully shaped negative spaces—become subjects, too, in a way that allows for the characters onscreen to breathe, and thereby affect the proceedings.

You see, the point is that you are, first of all, in a two-dimensional medium. Mustn't forget that. You have a rectangle to fill. Fill it. Compose it. I don't have to look through a camera for that. First of all, the cameraman knows very well that when I compose I object to air, space around figures or above their heads, because I think that's redundant. It's like a newspaperman taking a still and trimming it down to its essentials. They have standing instructions from me—they never give me any air around the figures.... I follow the geography of the screen. I can only think of the screen. Most directors say, "Well, he's got to come in that door so he's got to walk from there to there." Which is as dull as hell. And not only that, it makes the shot itself so empty and so loose that I say, "Well, if he's still in a mood—whatever mood he's in—take him across in a close-up, but keep the mood on the screen." We are not interested in distance. I don't care how he got across the room. What's the state of mind. You can only think of the screen [Hitchcock; cited in Bogdanovich, 1963, p. 4].

INTRODUCTION

The clear implication with this Hitchcock quote is that whatever is placed within the composition of the screen image—outdoor objects both mobile and immobile, indoor objects and, yes, human beings— are all equivalent and controllable, detailed objects that conspire, via the director's will, to manipulate an audience's emotions. "Things, then, are as important as actors," Hitchcock said (1965; cited in Gottlieb, 1995, p. 214), and all those things have been placed there deliberately to increase their impact on us. "I make it a rule to exploit elements that are connected with a character or a location; I would feel that I'd been remiss if I hadn't made maximum use of those elements" (Hitchcock; cited in Truffaut, 1967, p. 163).

Film critic Andrew Sarris called these objects "visual correlatives" (1968, p. 58), literal and figurative subjects that act like protagonists: "Hitchcock's objects are never mere props of a basically theatrical *mise en scène*, but rather the very substance of his cinema. These objects embody the feelings and fears of characters as object and characters interact with each other in dramas within dramas" (Sarris, 1968, p. 59). Likewise, Robert Yanal (*Hitchcock as Philosopher*, 2005), in the 2008 DVD special feature for *The Lodger* entitled "The Sound of Silence: The Making of *The Lodger*," called these film details and objects "cinematic equivalents for expressing a character's state of mind."

Conversely, human beings onscreen are often treated by Hitchcock as protagonistic objects. Are they not, after all, merely two-dimensional images of people, and not the people themselves? "Expressionist inwardness, it seems to me, necessarily makes objects seem like characters and characters seem like objects" (Deutelbaum and Poague, 1986, p. 152).

As two-dimensional representatives of people on the screen, certain recurring objects in Hitchcock's films truly carry an equal amount of subjective weight. For example, film professor Lesley Brill notes the impact of the director's oft-employed stair motif in *Blackmail* (1929):

> As [Crewe and Alice] walk up the shadowy staircase, the music on the soundtrack ascends as well, in a faintly comic aural emphasis of the rising action of the characters and the camera. Alice's ascent to the artist's room seems at first to be leading to something like a prince's castle.... [But as] she creeps out of the artist's studio after stabbing him, Alice recrosses the landing—its heavy shadows having been foreshad-

Introduction

owings indeed—and begins to descend the stairs. The stairs are now photographed from above, the camera looking straight down the stairwell to the black and white tile floor of the entrance hall [1988, p. 151].

Beginning with a foreboding medium distance shot of the staircase as seen by the lodger through the open doorway and misty haze of the London fog in *The Lodger: A Story of the London Fog* (1927), Hitchcock's third film, and continuing through Roddy's descent on an escalator the next year in *Downhill* (1927), and in the three most horrible montages involving staircases in all of Hitchcock's oeuvre—*Psycho* (1960), *The Birds* (1963), and *Frenzy* (1972)—Hitchcock's use of stairs as a conveyance that allows characters to travel between landings *and their own emotions* is as integral to his cinematic plots as the human actors themselves.

> The most common staircase shot is downward through a seeming spiral, which leaves the impression of stairs within stairs.... The occasional round staircase, as in *The Pleasure Garden* and *Secret Agent* [and *I Confess*], also suggests a plunge through layers of one's self.... Hitchcock's stairs image both man's composition and the rigors and fears of his rise or plunge to awareness [Deutelbaum and Poague, 1986, p. 18].

In other words, stairs are the handmaidens of the films' travelers, literal characters that carry people from one place and one emotion to another.

> Whether upwards or down, Hitchcock's stairs take his characters and his audience to the fears, dangers, and rewards of self-discovery.... [For example, in] *Shadow of a Doubt* Charlie's home has two parallel staircases, the clean public front and the dangerous, steep, private back, the latter which Uncle Charles uses to escape and threaten Charlie. The two-staired house works as an image of the human psyche and as an image of a societal ideal, both of which project a front that is more attractive and safer than their hidden natures [Yacowar, 1977, pp. 258–259].

Brill, in his earlier analysis, and Donald Spoto, in his analysis of *Frenzy*'s famous shot—"the camera backs away from the door of Foster's upper-floor flat and descends, seemingly without a cut, to the ground level" (1983, p. 314)— rightly assert that those sequences move the narrative along, up or down, in anticipation of the next emotional "landing." But Brill and Spoto may have missed at least one other aspect of Hitch-

Introduction

cock's intent for stairs. It turns out that these objects are themselves characters that require negotiating, obstacles to movement and forces to overcome, and they demand a response. They are real protagonists equal to their human counterparts. "Stairs compel movement and with it, fear, as in Constance's ascent to Murchison's office in *Spellbound*, and [Arbogast's] in *Psycho*" (Yacowar, 1977, p. 259). They are dangerous places to spend any time in Hitchcock's films, beginning with the silent films as in Mrs. Bunting's imagining of the lodger walking down hers in *The Lodger*, Roddy's seemingly endless descent on them in *Downhill*, Samuel Sweetland's in *The Farmer's Wife*, and Pete's in *The Manxman*, on through Scottie's problems with them in *Vertigo* and Melanie's harrowing experience at the top of a staircase in *The Birds*.

Likewise, objects such as lamps play a more than significant role, as when the testosterone-filled encounter between Keane and Latour in *The Paradine Case* (1947), becomes increasingly tense due to the cunning intrusion of a ceiling lamp. The way Hitchcock films the scene, the lamp never actually moves, of course, but it *seems to move* from place to place as he shifts the points of view (POVs) of the characters from angle to angle, from close-up to medium shot. Its bright glow deceitfully darkens, not illuminates, their agon.

> As always in such cases, the viewer has to decode the positioning of the characters.... The impact of the images comes ahead of such a rationalization, and the impact is strong; it has the modality of a surprise, intriguing yet visceral and at the same time mystifying.... The incitement to attentive watching is one of [Hitchcock's great] achievements [Sharff, 1991, pp. 243–244].

Filmmaker-author Stefan Sharff notes above how important it is for an audience to pay attention to all of Hitchcock's films with both vigor and rigor, in order to have half a chance at full comprehension. And if, as in the abovementioned *Paradine Case* scene, there are three characters vying for our attention when only two are human, our efforts to richly respond to Hitchcock's films can become even more delicious.

Lamps—normally brightening objects—do not always behave the way they should in Hitchcock movies. Ostensibly, items such as lamps and candles are meant to light a room and/or provide a certain ambience. The word "illuminate" is a variegated and powerful one. Its obvious definition means "to light up," both literally and figuratively, as in

Introduction

"a flash of lightning illuminated the house" for the former, and "his face was illuminated by a smile" for the latter (*The New Oxford American Dictionary*, 2001, p. 847).

But there are two other, no less valid definitions that are apropos, as in "to decorate a building or structure with lights" and, perhaps most significantly, to "help ... clarify or explain (a subject or matter), [as in] "a most illuminating discussion" or to "enlighten (someone) spiritually or intellectually" (2001, pp. 847–848). These last definitions, of course, are the ones that apply most to Hitchcock's films, particularly to the metaphorical, almost human characteristics of his lamps, lights, and candles.

> In Hitchcock's films, lamps have their conventional association with enlightenment, with literal and metaphorical vision: it is in the light cast by [lamps], after all, that the truth about [characters] will be revealed. But lamps become such a familiar feature of the Hitchcock world and the Hitchcock frame that they too become private symbols, yet another signature of Hitchcock's authorship. They are associated with illumination, but also with a mysterious, private realm that the light of reason cannot penetrate [Rothman, 1982, p. 35].

When Hitchcock employs this definition of "illumination" by using objects to *obfuscate or compound* a situation, the tension in the film viewers' minds between their intended use and an inverse application can be potently felt. The reader will frequently find discussions of illuminating object protagonists such as lamps throughout this book, particularly in the chapters on *Sabotage, Spellbound, Notorious, The Paradine Case, Dial M for Murder,* and *Vertigo*.

Similarly, objects such as works of art are carefully employed as actors, too:

> The laughing clown in *Blackmail* provides the neatest statement Hitchcock makes about art. Coherent with the fertility of silent montage, the portrait gains new meaning from each juxtaposition, each context, yet it maintains the same detached, ironic stance regardless of its changing set. When all about are noisy, loud, ambiguous, Hitchcock's mute jester remains silent. Yet the portrait is eloquent in its accusatory stare, its lively eye, its shameless traditional garb [Yacowar, 1977, pp. 266–267].

Rebecca, Foreign Correspondent, Suspicion, Notorious, The Paradine Case, The Trouble with Harry, Topaz and many other Hitchcock films feature artwork that powerfully impact human subjects.

INTRODUCTION

Like lamps and artwork, another of Hitchcock's most potent objects that cloud situations is crowds. While made up of people, obviously, *masses* of people wedged tightly together invariably act not with many minds but one. And they often act mindlessly. Hitchcock crowds are skillfully moved about like chess pieces on a board, blocking our view here, hiding characters there, and disrupting our sight in myriad ways. This is true from the silents on up through his final film, *Family Plot* (1976).

> In most Hitchcock films, humans acting in concert very quickly begin to degenerate into mobs. Three or four seems to be an upper limit for morally coherent behavior. The opposing political sides in *Secret Agent*, *Notorious*, and *North by Northwest* are ethically indistinguishable.... It is broadly true that Hitchcock shows humanity as fallen collectively and redeemable in pairs [Brill, 1988, pp. 68–69].

As with their use in mobs, many of Hitchcock's individuals are treated as commodities, further blurring the line between object and subject on his screen. "In general, in Hitchcock the human body is the first vehicle," states Deutelbaum and Poague (1986, p. 14). If subjects are treated like objects, then they can be more easily directed onscreen. Again, this idea is consistent with the "placement" of human beings within Hitchcock's frames in ways that first objectify them and then make them into objects of control. Not surprisingly, "Hitchcock consistently has his villains regard ordinary people as foolish animals" (Yacowar, 1977, p. 305), as in Uncle Charlie's reference to humans as swine in *Shadow of a Doubt*, a truly dehumanizing, objectifying perspective.

One way the director "objectifies" humans is by zeroing in, usually via close-ups and, more often, with extreme close-ups on body parts, not the whole body. Arms and legs—and their respective subsets of hands and feet, forearms and calves, etc.—are given especially privileged moments throughout Hitchcock's oeuvre. Eyes, too, when "disembodied," can act "as offensive weapons," says film studies Professor Thomas M. Leitch (1991, p. 53), in his *Find the Director and Other Hitchcock Games.* For example, "throughout [*Easy Virtue*, 1927], Larita (Isabel Jeans) is defined by the gaze of others" (p. 53). Even shadows or footprints of body parts count as characters in the director's films, the power latent in the realism of their detail. "[F]or audiences, the

Introduction

wilder the storyline is, the more realistically it must be told. It's like a nightmare. When you have a nightmare you use the word 'vivid.' Well, that's what the film has to be so that you're glad when you wake up on your way to the guillotine" (Hitchcock, 1974; cited in Gottlieb, 2003, p. 187).

In other words, body parts may indeed represent the entire person but, by focusing closely on one part rather than the whole, Hitchcock universalizes arms and legs and hands and feet by allowing the parts to "speak" for themselves. In *The Lodger*, for example, an "overhead shot of [Daisy's] legs in the tub, toes twiddling securely, tempts us … to imagine a whole image on the basis of but a part" (Yacowar, 1977, p. 34). Likewise, in "*North by Northwest* (and in Hitchcock's films generally), hands are an emblem of intimacy," a "delicate detail" that speaks for the entire person and, in fact, all people, states Brill (1988, p. 21). "Situation follows situation at a leisurely pace, and it is only the amount of detail which I pack into each sequence that makes my films appear to move so quickly" (Hitchcock, 1938; cited in Gottlieb, 1995, p. 197).

Hitchcock's use of symbols and images via objects fulfills the same purpose as all his various characters, primary or secondary. They signify something other than themselves, one more point of view (POV) or thought to consider. Furthermore, his use of subjective and objective characters helps confuse the audience's identifications, giving us a surfeit of viewpoints on display.

> But suppose we *could* make really artistic films for the artistically minded minority. Could we not then make as beautiful a film about rain as Debussy did a tone poem in his "*Jardins sous la pluie*"? And what a lovely film of rhythmic movement and light and shade we could make out of cloud studies—a sort of film interpretation of Shelley's "The Cloud" (Hitchcock, 1927; cited in Gottlieb, 1995, pp. 166–167).

The character of the places people live in—a city, building, home, or apartment—is likewise essential in establishing the proper feel for a situation and narrative. Longtime Hitchcock production designer Robert Boyle, in films such as *Saboteur* (1942; the Statue of Liberty scene), *North by Northwest* (1959; Mount Rushmore and crop-dusting sequences) and *The Birds* (1963; extreme overhead bird-gathering shot), said as much:

INTRODUCTION

> If [the set] doesn't have any meaningful application to the story, it's never a great shot.... [Films] start with the locale, with the environment that people live in, how they move within that environment.... I'm all for construction, because we're dealing with the magic of movies [and] I always feel that if you build it, you build it for the dream rather than the actuality. We make up our own truth [William Grimes; "Robert F. Boyle, Designer for Hitchcock, Dies at 100"; August 3, 2010; http://www.nytimes.com/2010/08/04/movies/04boyle.html?_r=1&hpw; retrieved on August 3, 2010].

The most important object of all in Hitch's world, the one always implied and invisible but which lives and breathes in spite of the fact that it is never seen—*the camera itself*—must also be treated with close attention. It is, after all, the stand-in for us, Hitchcock's primary actor to be directed.

> In *Hitchcock—The Murderous Gaze* [1982], William Rothman argues that Hitchcock's films are meditations on the camera's nature, perspicuous critiques of the camera's active and passive aspects.... [The] camera's nature is fundamentally active *and* passive. As Freud argues against separating the active and passive forms of an instinct, so [Stanley] Cavell and Rothman argue ... that the ways they inform one another lie at the heart of the medium itself.... It also performs a number of gestures that constitute declarations about the camera's nature and its power [Marian Keane; cited in Deutelbaum and Poague, 1986, pp. 239–240].

As yet another character to be reckoned with, the camera is treated by Hitchcock through "the power of his consummate technique [and, through it,] he directs not the actors but the audience" (Bogdanovich, 1963, p. 7). The camera itself, then, becomes Hitchcock's consummate objective subject, representing both the director and us, his audience's eyes (and ears). In other words, we are talking about "the fact of the camera itself, which always exists in two worlds at once—the real world, wherein 'the camera is the instrument of a real relationship between author and viewer,' and the film world, in which 'the camera has the power to penetrate its subject's privacy, without their knowledge or authorization'" (Deutelbaum and Poague, 1986, p. 84; quotes from Rothman, 1982, p. 102).

Pertaining to the eye of the camera—or the subjective "I" of the camera, as cinema professor William Rothman argues in his *The "I" of*

Introduction

the Camera (1988)—we must assume that there is a face that holds within it that "eye" (or two, in our case). If the camera is indeed a subjective "I," it necessarily embodies *both* the director and us, his audience. "Anne Baxter saw the liveliness of Hitchcock's camera while shooting *I Confess*: 'He did not care so much that the actors acted—he wanted the *camera* to act'" (Pomerance, 2004, p. 290; referencing Spoto, 1983, p. 361).

In Hitchcock's emotionally manipulative hands, one can readily argue that the subjects *not* on the screen—the audience itself—are the actors most carefully directed by the director through the camera, and his technical prowess with it. The camera is "a leading protagonist for me," Pomerance affirmed Hitchcock saying (2004, p. 219).

The purpose of this book is to help the reader identify and take a closer look at the way objects act as protagonists—true subjects themselves—in each of Alfred Hitchcock's movies.

The Pleasure Garden (1925)

> Hitchcock knows that there is no such thing as an innocent object because an object in film works exclusively in context. If the context is sufficiently elaborate, you can make the most inoffensive object look menacing [Guillermo Del Toro; "The Master's Touch: Hitchcock's Signature Style," 2009 *North by Northwest* DVD bonus feature].

While the chorus girls in the dance hall called the Pleasure Garden look like real human beings, the mostly male patrons treat them as the non-human objects they will sadly turn out to be—mannequins, actually—in Daisy's more dangerous world of *The Lodger* (see next entry). Conversely, when a lecherous old man remarks that he has fallen in love with one of Patsy's kiss curls (our heroine's name is Patsy Brand, played by actress Virginia Valli), she pulls it off and gives it to him, saying, "I hope you two will be very happy together." The shattering of his fantasy illusion about her, and not a pleasurable possession of her kiss curl, is immediately reflected upon his face. Patsy's strong, subjective character follows up his reaction with, "Your love wasn't very lasting, was it?" This proves that she is no gullible patsy in this picture but a real woman with real feelings and her own thoughts. Her kiss curl does indeed turn out to be the object of the lecher's affection, object becoming subject.

The Pleasure Garden of the film's title, then, is not just a repository for objectifying women in particular and dehumanizing people in general but an actual subject in itself that encourages such behavior. Maurice Yacowar clearly articulates the character of not one but four separate settings in this, the first film of the director:

> Hitchcock develops his story in terms of four contrasting settings, each with its own character and moral values: the Pleasure Garden, the showgirl's modest flat, the honeymoon setting at Lake Como, and the

jungle proper. The Pleasure Garden is a false image of the jungle, as the Lake Como scenes will provide a false image of romantic harmony, and as the ambitious showgirl's palace is a false parallel to the modest girl's homey flat [1977, p. 20].

And that "ambitious showgirl" Jill's lack of character is embodied in an often hovering prop, a cigarette holder she waves about as stand-in for who she believes herself to be. (A similar holder will "carry" within in Larita's bereft character two films hence in *Easy Virtue*.)

> Jill ushers Ivan off with a theatrical cigarette holder—because she is carrying into her real life the falsity and shallowness that on stage pass for theatre.... The basic irony of the film is that the Pleasure Garden is neither a garden nor a pleasure. The real pleasure is what one finds with someone like Patsy in a flat like Patsy's. The delights which lure clients to the Pleasure Garden are illusory, like the detachable kiss-curl on Patsy's blonde wig.... The Pleasure Garden only plays at life and nature. It is a false pretender to the fertility of a garden, as lechery and greed are false pretenders to passion [Yacowar, 1977, pp. 26–27].

Younger lechers soon put the moves on our second protagonist, Jill Cheyne (actress Carmelita Geraghty). Hitchcock has her and Patsy look and dress so much alike that we must work hard to tell them apart. But we realize that when Jill smiles back at the boys, she hasn't the purity of heart or character that Patsy will continue to demonstrate throughout this film. In fact, Jill will turn out to be more the mannequin and in need of learning lessons than anyone else. (Hitch fakes us out about Jill—as he does so often with characters throughout his oeuvre—for our initially sympathetic identification with her is soon tested.)

Jill's disdain for all things human becomes clear when she yawns over a picture of Patsy's fiancé (who she'll soon steal), throws away Patsy's dog's bone, kicks the dog off her foot, and blithely takes Patsy's best pillow for herself in their shared bed. The world is hers for the taking, an object to be owned, as she even weasels a dancing job away from Patsy the next day (having never danced before) and argues the manager up from £5 to £20 a week through bald-faced *faux* flirting. This is no real person at work here. The Pleasure Garden itself is a metaphor for Jill's vacuity of character, notes Hitchcock scholar Ken Mogg: "The theater's very name ... suggests both the sensual delights

The Lodger: A Story of the London Fog (1927)

it offers and the false Eden it represents—and which the film shows may be a microcosm of the world at large" (1999, p. 4).

Of course, the very act of acting in a theater brings into question the veracity of people's lives: From *The Pleasure Garden* to the theaters in *Downhill, Murder!, Sabotage,* both *Men Who Knew Too Much, Stage Fright,* and many others, real character is a quality hard-earned in Hitchcock's films:

> What Hitchcock is primarily interested in is not illuminating the process whereby the truth is established but dramatizing the application of the metaphor of acting to normal human behavior. As in so many films beginning with *The Pleasure Garden*, Hitchcock's characters have a public side produced by acting, theatricality, or conscious misrepresentation, and a private side beneath [Leitch, 1991, p. 67].

In other words, the real character that Hitchcock's protagonists largely lack—particularly near the beginnings of his films and for which they work so hard to gain or recapture by the end of them—have been cleverly usurped by or transferred into the inanimate objects of architecture such as these theaters. Or cigarette holders. Or kiss curls.

Or staircases.

The Lodger: A Story of the London Fog (1927)

A staircase is just a staircase ... but in Hitchcock films, staircases are never just staircases. Something as simple as someone walking down a staircase becomes, in The Lodger, an act full of menace and potential horror ... just as at the end of Notorious, in which two characters who walk down a staircase become full of suspense and drama and romantic meaning and complexities of all kinds [Jonathan Freedman; "The Sound of Silence: The Meaning of *The Lodger*"; 2008 *Lodger* DVD bonus feature].

Mobs, car windows, arched wall portals, handcuffs, banister bars, fireplace pokers, and yes, staircases ... *The Lodger* is loaded with objects that not only stand in for other characters but affect us as if they were characters themselves. Rohmer and Chabrol alerted us early in the canon of Hitchcock criticism to these icons:

> Certain themes or details that are frequently to be repeated in later works are already present in this film ... handcuffs, symbol of lost liberty; objects (in this case a poker) on which suspicion confers an erroneously menacing role. We also note an obsession with Christian iconography: the hero, attached to a railing by his handcuffs and hooted by the crowd, suggests the image of Christ on the cross [1957, p. 8].

Almost immediately in *The Lodger*, from the two minute forty-seven second mark until three minutes in, Hitchcock pressures us to peer in vain through a mass of onlookers. His penchant for imbuing mobs with a disruptive claustrophobia frustratingly blocks our view of a murdered girl at the river's edge. We are meant here to feel as if we are part of this crowd, just as Hitchcock shoots a similar milling about at the Thames River at the start of *Frenzy* nearly fifty years later. By shooting masses of bodies constantly pressing in on one other, Hitchcock makes it next to impossible for us to identify with individuals within the crowd. Even with close-ups on the faces of bystanders, we are made to feel we are trapped in the mob, anonymous and ignorant. "Hitchcock often has dark figures partially obscuring the foreground or framing the foreground. Or how he shoots past an obstacle course of legs, hats and shifting bodies" (Patrick McGilligan; 2008 *Lodger* DVD audio commentary).

As with his use of telephones in, say, *Dial M for Murder*, that tests our patience and increases our suspense, Hitchcock makes us wait seemingly endlessly (a full minute of unmoving screen time) as his 1920s onlookers gaze at a teletype machine while it inexorably taps out the murder narrative. The next shot is of the director himself, from behind, alerting us to both his presence and power. More shots ensue of the long, slow work of newspaper presses rolling out their stories in pre-dawn darkness, conveyor belts and trucks carrying copies to the city and back into crowds—the city's character on display. More close-ups on darkened, scared faces reacting to news on the radio are contrasted with a humorously played bright shot of masses of models taking off their blond wigs and laughing, briefly unaware of the horrors outdoors. "Anyone could be killed any time," Hitchcock seems to be telling us, the cheery scene turning creepy as it catches in our throat.

The Lodger: A Story of the London Fog (1927)

In fact, before Hitchcock allows us to meet the protagonists of this film—Daisy, her parents Mr. and Mrs. Bunting, the lodger himself, and Joe the policeman—the first ten minutes are intercut with shots of anonymous bodies one after the other scurrying across the screen, destabilizing any sense of security or individuality that we might gain from them as people. In first a dehumanizing and then reanimating way, people in Hitchcock's crowds are objects that embody characteristics the director wants them to have.

Two unnerving "eyes" stare back at us (6:30–6:40) through the rear windows of the *Evening Standard* cab as it races away from the camera, distributing its hot-off-the-presses, still-wet news of the drowned girl. Whose "eyes" are they? Perhaps they belong to the city streets themselves. As seen through the cab's oval glass, the driver and passenger's heads are dark, rocking irises, daylight far in the distance the translucent whites of their pupils. Hitchcock himself claimed that the scene did not work (in his book with Truffaut), but I disagree:

> Lend me your pen a moment. I want to show you a shot, though we were never able to get it right. I showed the back of a small London news van. The back windows are oval. There were two men sitting in the front, the driver and his mate. You see them through the windows—just the tops of their heads. And as the van sways from side to side, you have the impression of a face with two eyes and the eyeballs moving. Unfortunately, it didn't work out [Hitchcock; quoted in Truffaut, 1967, p. 45].

In a 1970 interview with Emerson Batdorf for the *Cleveland Plain Dealer*'s Sunday newspaper magazine, Hitchcock spoke less disparagingly about the same shot, granting the van's subjectivity in gazing back at us, the film audience, with real power:

> It was the back of a newspaper van.... A back view like this, and it had back doors, double doors. Just like that. [He rapidly sketched on the back of a menu the drawing.... He started his career doing art work.] It had oval windows. And sitting in front were two men and I put black caps on them and the result was that the black caps make the windows look like eyes. As the thing moved side to side, so the black caps move from one side to the other [cited in Gottlieb, 2003, p. 81].

Ken Mogg likewise pointed out the importance of the van's "eyes" as stand-in for both the audience (us) and the city of London itself:

Hitchcock's Objects as Subjects

"[W]ell before the end of the film, London becomes a major character. Something that helps establish this is the visual gag that Hitchcock later described to Truffaut, in which the back windows of a careering London news van appear like two rolling eyes. In turn, there's a faint suggestion that those eyes are mirroring our own—that the city *is* the viewer" (1999, p. 6).

The Lodger's mob returns with a vengeance for another twenty seconds at exactly seven minutes in (as it will recur many times in this director's films), its members hungrily grabbing for a newsman's papers, then staring blankly at the scrolling newsletters on a building's wall of "another avenger crime." There are actually two chases in this film: the early one of the crowd grabbing for news and, of course, the killer mob at the end racing after the wrongly accused innocent, the lodger himself, played by Ivor Novello, in his first of two Hitchcock films. The director noted the importance of the masses in both instances in a 1950 interview with David Brady in *The New York Times Magazine*:

> In that particular movie you just started with the people who were doing the chasing instead of the man being chased. The chase was in the mind of the onlooker seeing the picture, you might say.... [W]hile the Ripper is how shall we say it always on the run psychologically, he really goes on the run in the last reel. That's when the whole thing is crystallized into the final physical chase.... You see, as the picture approaches the climax of the tension, everything should begin to move faster. The threads of the plot become tauter and I even change the style of acting, broaden it. The tension is then released into the final physical chase, which must be short and breathtaking, to avoid the error of anticlimax [cited in Gottlieb, 1995, pp. 127–128].

Both scenes, especially the last, literally propel us into the crowds alongside the rest of the bodies, a skill Hitchcock would wield throughout his career. It is easy to feel blind rage when one is running with a pack of dogs and not watching from the outside. The vertigo induced by Hitchcock's loss-of-the-individual crowd shots was often quite palpable and unnerving.

The subjective power of lamps to affect other characters appears soon. When we first spy our heroine, Daisy, just past the ten-minute mark, we see her in a medium long shot dressed to the nines as she descends a short flight of stairs. She moves through one of two high-

The Lodger: A Story of the London Fog (1927)

arched portals, themselves framed by two glowing lamps; these four objects plus Daisy are also framed by two fair-haired cherubs. They all stare disconcertingly back at us, like the earlier cab's "eyes." "Placing symbolically charged objects in the frame is a means of expression first systematically exploited, in film, by Griffith.... In Hitchcock's films, lamps have their conventional association with enlightenment, with literal and metaphorical vision: it is in the light cast by [a] lamp, after all, that the truth about the lodger will be revealed..." (Rothman, 1982, pp. 34–35).

When Daisy reaches the bottom stair, darned if she doesn't step into what can only be described as a dirt-covered circus ring within which she and the other models strut their wares, just like horses on display, led by a rather butch-looking, cigarette-wielding ring leader. (In early 20th century England, and even today, models were called "mannequins," hence its usage in the titles.) As retired professor of film studies Maurice Yacowar notes, circles such as these and, especially, triangles (particularly the latter in this film) are also treated as geometric "characters" in Hitchcock's films:

> The title art emphasizes the triangle, as the shutter effect makes a triangular flare. The Avenger's "A" signature is a bottomless triangle. The policeman's map of the Avenger's crimes traces a triangle. [The lodger's] arrival in the Bunting household represents the intrusion by the "Avenger" into the complacent Bunting family circle, which includes Joe. The circle, associated with order and completion [look for its resurgence with a vengeance in both *The Ring* and *Easy Virtue*], is despoiled by Joe's expressions of romantic tension: "When I put a rope around the Avenger I'll put a ring around Daisy's finger" [Yacowar, 1977, p. 38].

Hitchcock scholar Charles Barr makes special note of the subjective power of shapes as detailed objects:

> The film takes over and develops this triangle motif, incorporating it both into the design of some of the title cards and into the dramatic structure. One triangle ... is the obvious romantic one: Daisy, Joe, lodger. Another is formed by three strong-willed men: Joe, lodger, the Avenger.... The triangle structure is made complete by the link between the Avenger and Joe.... It is not only the triangle of male protagonists who are "keen on golden curls," but also the theatre audience at whom the show is directed, and the film audience at whom *The Lodger* is directed [1999, pp. 39–40].

Hitchcock's Objects as Subjects

Cut to the rest of the mannequins scurrying about backstage like rats in a maze awaiting their doom, yet another cluster of characterless subjects as masses for the Avenger's picking. Already one can see in this film how Hitchcock found ways to give subjectivity to inanimate objects and, conversely, *lifelessness* to human subjects.

Soon, the director's oft-favored over-the-shoulder shot (in this case, from behind the lodger's back) has us staring at a "screen left" bright hallway, foreboding-looking stairs "screen right" leading to a "to let" sign on the Buntings' home—the same stairway noted in the Freedman quote at the top of this chapter. Stairs, of course, recur with ever more commanding frequency in Hitchcock's films. They are, in biographer Donald Spoto's view, endlessly evocative:

> The staircase is the quintessential device of German expressionist cinema, especially in the films of Fritz Lang and F.W. Murnau ... and may thus reflect Hitchcock's admiration for these directors. It is one of his recurrent devices and is filled with both moral and theological significance. It is, first of all, apt for the theme of ambiguity—ascent and descent, attempts at achievement and regressions in failure, the forces of right and the forces of evil, the way up and the way down.... Hitchcock ... describes relationships in terms of ascent and descent along a staircase. From *The Lodger* there is a direct line to *Vertigo* [and, of course, *The Birds*, for the] power of the image [of the staircase] has a real yet tenebrous quality, breathtakingly beautiful [yet] mysterious [1976, p. 8].

Christ-like iconography is clearly intended by the lodger's handcuffed hanging at the end of the film. The cross-like shadow lines on his face as seen through window panes nineteen minutes in are similarly potent religious imagery—recapitulated in spades 26 years later throughout *I Confess* (and *The Wrong Man* and *Topaz*). The mix of jail-like entrapment and seemingly intolerable anguish wrought on actor Ivor Novello's visage when he closes that window, as filmed from the outside in a medium shot looking in, afford us genuine empathy towards this man. Motion pictures professor William Rothman rightly notes Hitchcock's skill in using parallel vertical (or diagonal) lines throughout his pictures—bars of banisters, shadows on walls, etc.—as signifiers of confinement.

> I call this pattern of parallel vertical lines Hitchcock's //// sign. At one level, the //// serves as a Hitchcock signature: it is his mark on the

The Lodger: A Story of the London Fog (1927)

frame, akin to his ritual cameo appearances. At another level, it signifies the confinement of the camera's subject within the frame and within the world of the film. Like the profile shot, it announces that we have arrived at a limit of our access to the camera's subject; we might say that it stands for the barrier of the screen itself. It is also associated with sexual fear and the specific threat of loss of control or breakdown [Rothman, 1982, p. 33].

Scenes shot through framing and restraining rails of stairways and bed headboards and wooden cross panes of glass frequently occur in this film, seeming to entrap *us* as well.

Hitchcock constructed a four-storied open staircase with the same double function. It visually expresses what the character hears, in this case, Mrs. Bunting in bed hearing the lodger slink out for his midnight deeds. But as well the image works as a non-realistic projection. It does not express the fact of the lodger's leaving so much as Mrs. Bunting's heightened state of mind, in which she omits everything else within her range of awareness to concentrate on the man upstairs. The shot suggests the vision of sound, true, but also the landlady's extreme disposition.... Hitchcock's poetic imagery has a literal basis in the novel but the richer meanings of the image involve the way they project the impressionability of the senses [Yacowar, 1977, p. 36].

While not technically objects in his films, isolated or tightly framed body parts—wrists, hands, forearms, faces, legs, etc., that are "anatomized"—also stand in as symbols of complete subjects, and are often treated as mere objects placed upon this director's canvas. "You will see that, whenever possible, Hitchcock anatomizes his two leads into body parts, latticing his shots of them with shafts of light or blocks of shadow.... *The Lodger* would be full of hands reaching [as in *Blackmail* and *Torn Curtain*], stretching, clutching, giant lips, wide, darting eyes and Cubist ears, treading feet, and naked limbs" (Patrick McGilligan; 2008 *Lodger* DVD audio commentary).

In fact, if we can treat Novello's eyes, so very haunting and haunted and held by the camera throughout this picture, as gateways to the soul—or at least repeatedly immobilizing, Olympia-like gazes back upon us—stares such as these (like other stairs) are themselves motifs throughout the picture; i.e., the aforementioned pairings of cab windows, dual portals, lamps, and, especially, oval-shaped wall hangings liberally sprinkled throughout the Buntings' home.

Hitchcock's Objects as Subjects

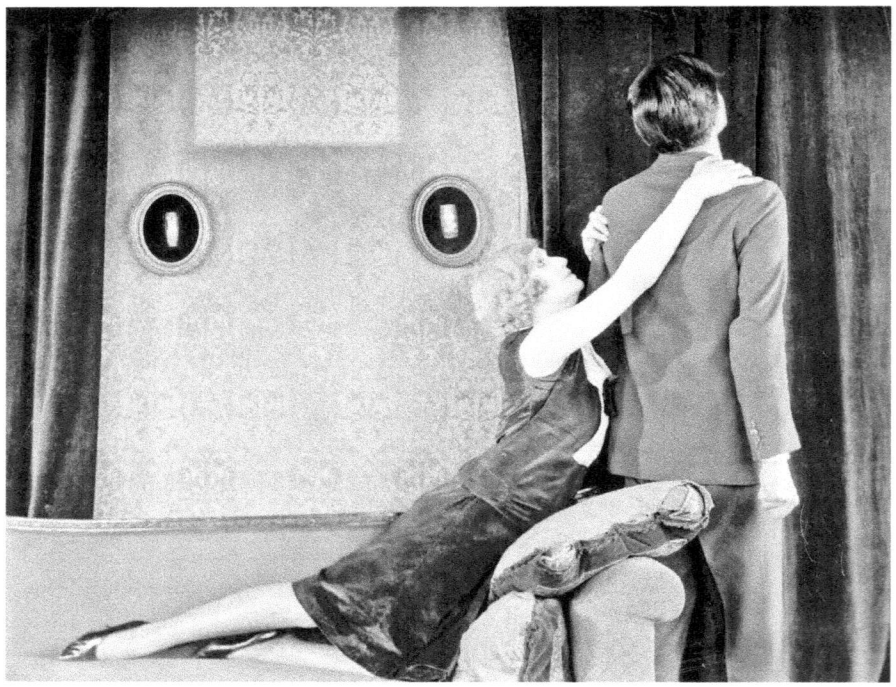

The Lodger (1927): Oval-shaped portraits on the lodger's (Ivor Novello) wall unnervingly peer back at us as Daisy Bunting (the actress with just a first name, June) strains for his love.

Not surprisingly, after the lodger turns all the portraits of gorgeous, golden-curled women around to face the walls of his room—and they are subsequently removed—the blank spaces eerily take up their gazing back at us and him. Stand-ins for his murdered sister (and, we later find out, their heartbroken dead mother), Hitchcock keeps the blank walls and remaining oval-shaped portraits peering back at us throughout the picture.

A lovely moment during the chess game between the lodger and Daisy highlights the positive power of objects, in stark contrast to the fearful suggestions about Novello's use of the fireplace's poker by numerous critics: "Hitchcock sets a delicate symbol of the intimacy growing between the Lodger and Daisy. During the scene in which they play chess, the hero and heroine face each other over a small table.

The Lodger: A Story of the London Fog (1927)

Behind the table the arched opening of a fireplace rainbows between the two players and expresses, in contrast to the opposition of the chess game, a joining, a coming together" (Brill, 1988, p. 88).

Conversely, Rothman rightly notes that profile shots such as this one of two characters facing each other deny the viewing audience full entrée into their thoughts and feelings. Their faces become like sculptures, immobile and inscrutable. (See, especially, *I Confess* and *The Wrong Man*.)

> It is characteristic of Hitchcock to frame a figure in profile at the moment of his or her most complete abstraction and absorption in an imagined scene to which we have no access. In such a profile shot, the camera frames its subject in a way that does not allow that figure's interiority to be penetrated. Indeed, such a shot declares that impenetrability; it announces that we have come to a limit of our access to the world of the film [Rothman, 1982, p. 22].

The half-drunk bar crowd near the end of the picture is particularly gullible and frightening—director Fritz Lang's mindless mobs in his harrowing 1936 *Fury* come to mind—as Hitchcock tracks his camera rapidly forward in an effort to catch up to its blind fervor. "Quick— before they tear him to pieces!" screams the almost-too-late Joe, concern finally breaking through the jealous rage that has driven him to pursue and blame the lodger for most of the story. Shot from behind and below and above and alongside and above, the mob is imbued with a Hitchcockian forward-propelled power that clearly overcomes any one individual's strength of character. In fact, within Hitchcockian mobs lie stereotypes of individuals that make them pawns of mass hysteria, not real characters with thoughtful and concerned human characteristics:

> Only after [the lodger] has been all but torn to bits by a lynch mob is it revealed that his sinister perambulations resulted from his tireless attempts to avenge his sister on the man who killed her. The misanthropy lies not only in his murderous intent but in the film's study of upright citizens who like the heroine's mother and father ... and her detective fiancé ... jumped to conclusions and all but condemned an innocent man to death.... For the film's theme is panic as a social network—[and the] angry crowd is its final, climactic "crystallization...." Which way the moral balance dips depends also on the degree to which one is prepared to identify with the mob [Durgnat, 1974, pp. 69–70, 73].

Barr (1999), too, highlights the insanity implicit in crowd consciousness:

> The public itself is ready to become a violent, avenging mob, pursuing the lodger through the streets and only saved, it seems, from lynching him by the fortuitous last-minute news of the arrest of the real criminal. We all have violent and vengeful potential in us. *The Lodger* is an early, very rigorous, working out of a theme with which Hitchcock will come increasingly to be identified [p. 41].

Brill (1988) notes Hitchcock's "less well known but more consistent demophobia. In a Hitchcock film any group of people larger than roughly half a dozen members registers as a mob—conformist, unimaginative, inhuman. [Their presence suggests] the counterpull of a corrupt social mode against which is set the love and struggle for innocence of the central pair" (p. 94).

These mobs transcend individuality and become single objects that then become—ironic full circle—one individual with just one character quality: blind hate.

The lodger, barely saved from the masses, recovers in a hospital bed near the end of the picture. One last frame that appears empty above the lodger's bed reminds us of his own dead family members. Hitchcock leaves us with a warning and an entreaty: Beware of mindless mobs and the unfeeling, unthinking bodies that inhabit them.

Downhill (1927)

> Roddy comes home to cold, large rooms and massive furniture.... [E]verywhere, Hitchcock's use of the details of the physical world serves his primary interest in the fertility of the imagination [Yacowar, 1977, p. 43].

As Ivor Novello did at the end of *The Lodger* the previous year, the actor's Roddy looks downright frightened when yet another mass of mindless people, this time fellow athletes in his school class, charge toward him after his winning rugby score. It's almost as if Hitchcock had carried the murderous mob's energy over into the start of *this* film. Roddy will truly have something to fear when his so-

Easy Virtue (1927)

called best friend does not stand up for him against a vamp's vindictive tirade.

"The Headmaster" wants them in his study. Imposing arches seen in long shot at this prep school impart a foreboding of gallows. Likewise, the shop girl wears an accusatory dress with lines like jail bars on it (see Ingrid Bergman's Alicia in *Notorious* nineteen years hence for a similar look), and the whole room is shot with a claustrophobic feeling of pressing in on Roddy, continuing through the many downhill descents he makes in the film. Back outside, we see his long walk once again in long shot, a minuscule figure wholly dominated by those arches.

He is soon seen walking down staircases that themselves have jail-like bars as banisters on them. Shortly, we feel that he is descending to Hades as he rides the London underground escalator down, down, down for a depressingly long thirty seconds of screen and real time. An extreme long shot of Roddy leaving the school for good prefigures any number of similar high overheads, Thornhill's leaving of the United Nations in *North by Northwest* and the birds amassing in *The Birds* foremost in our minds.

The chess set floor patterns back home imply his part as a pawn in this film's narrative. As Roddy sits dwarfed in long shot in a huge living room chair, his father's entrance seems like a looming totem pole towering over his head. "All those baronial halls and Gothic fireplaces ... express the solidity of tradition" (Durgnat, 1974, p. 76), and Roddy will have no place to escape to in this dark and harsh cinematic look at how humans can choose to beat down fellow humans into literal objects of scorn.

Easy Virtue (1927)

> Hitchcock told the press that he built excitement, quote, "not by quick cutting or by incessant camera movement but by packing every sequence with incident and small details of characterization" [Leonard Leff; "Mystery Train"; 2007 *Lady Vanishes* DVD bonus feature].

The film opens in a court of law, the rabble seen in long shot sitting beneath arches reminiscent of a church altar. A flashback sets up Larita

HITCHCOCK'S OBJECTS AS SUBJECTS

Filton (Isabel Jeans in her second of two films for Hitchcock) as an object not only of desire—her husband treats her as something to be owned—but as an art object, for artist Claude Robson (Eric Bransby Williams in his only Hitchcock appearance) is painting her portrait. A small sculpture of a woman sitting on a dresser behind Larita mimics-mocks her pose.

Hitchcock's reverse angle shots in this film frequently place us squarely in the line of sight of his main characters—especially the husband, Aubrey Filton (played by Franklin Dyall), Larita, and Robson—effectively working against this early subject-as-object treatment in a highly charged way: "Might we the audience be similar objects of desire and rejection?" Hitchcock seems to ask us. The director increasingly presses this object-subject conundrum into our minds with a startling medium four-shot of Larita's portrait itself looming "screen left," Robson talking with Larita (both art object and human being) center screen, and the small sculpture in the distance "screen right." As Hitchcock cuts between close-ups of her account of her husband's physical abuse to the artist intimately rubbing her wrist, our hearts are made to go out to this half heroine, half mannequin (shades of *Lodger* imagery with Daisy).

Claude offers up his love to Larita, and the husband is shot catching them in the act, seen standing beneath a smaller version of the courtroom's chapel-like arches in a doorway to the studio—his own religious icons of arbitration, perhaps. When Claude actually shoots Aubrey, both maid and butler appear beneath their own separate arched doorways, two more accusatory church frames. Christ-like, Larita cradles her husband's body like Michelangelo's "The Pietà" (1498–1499), prefiguring a similar shot forty-one years later in the *Topaz* jail scene with the Mendozas.

Hitchcock's concerns, typically, are for his protagonists' (and audience's) emotional growth. In this case, we wonder if Larita can learn to transcend the shame of a divorce and become a healthy adult in spite of the trappings of wealth and surface happiness. Sadly, objects such as pearls, a mink coat, the paparazzi, and the ability to travel the world all conspire to hem her in. Larita is quite literally the silent screen version of Tallulah Bankhead's Constance Porter seventeen years later in *Lifeboat*, stuck with everything money can buy ... except wisdom. In

Easy Virtue (1927)

this film, as in *The Pleasure Garden*, Hitchcock's subjects must first transcend objectification in order to become true protagonists.

By the twentieth minute of the film, Larita has gone to the Mediterranean on holiday, hiding "her scarred heart, but not her magnetic charm," reads a title card. Even the hotel lobby she arrives at mimics the look of a church—always judging, in Hitchcock's recovering Catholic style—as columns grandly rise on the left and right to frame the arched altar of the center screen elevator.

When John Whittaker (Robin Irvine in his second of two Hitchcock films) first chats with Larita after accidentally slamming her in the face with a tennis ball gone awry, Hitchcock shoots them both in close-up profile facing each other—a kinder version of harsher counterpoint shots of Larita and her husband from the courtroom earlier. Later, when they flirt in her room (which has more than a striking resemblance to the one back home), their close-up profiles include yet another sculpture of a woman in the background, larger than the earlier one but now standing and gazing over their shoulders. Could Hitchcock be implying that Larita is some kind of "trophy" sought after by any number of eligible men? Most certainly. As John moves in for their first clinch at nearly the thirty-minute mark of the picture, they share a palpably intimate kiss that Hitchcock fades out on below the cool stare of that same leering sculpture. Things will not go well for these two.

John professes his love to Larita and Hitchcock cuts to an extreme long shot of their horse-drawn carriage traveling over an immensely tall bridge, huge altar-like arches holding it up. Once they are married, Hitchcock shows us the vast amounts of conspicuous consumption that each of them carries around by way of trunks and objects (compare, for example, Pengallan's booty in *Jamaica Inn* twelve years hence), a striking contrast to the vulnerable tenuousness of their earlier carriage upon the lofty bridge. "What lives and meaningless objects the rich carry with them," Hitchcock seems to say. In this melodrama of manners, a typical narrative of bon vivant author Noël Coward that was adapted for the screen, the film's characters never have to struggle with any of the baser needs of humanity except, perhaps, the luxuries of love. Soon their car, loaded down with enormous amounts of all their belongings, pulls up to an even more imposing mansion.

Hitchcock's Objects as Subjects

We meet John's mother, Mrs. Whittaker (Violet Farebrother, who is the spitting image of Claude Rains' mother in *Notorious*, actress Leopoldine Konstantin). Her immobility recalls the earlier staring and judgmental statues. A smaller gong than the one in the upcoming *Ring* announces dinner as Round One of this family battle approaches.

John's old girlfriend Sarah (Enid Stamp Taylor) begins to fill out the rest of the trophy women inhabiting this house; two younger sisters, the mother, and two maids add up to lots of female choices. When everyone sits down to supper, and Hitchcock cuts to a medium long shot of the proceedings, darned if church imagery doesn't make yet another appearance. Four huge and imposing Christ paintings loom over them like the tallest of sculptures, leering characters indeed. "Much of *Easy Virtue* can also be taken as the Cockney Hitchcock's vision of the upper class, with their cavernous dining room—its massive murals of saints cold and towering over the diners..." (Yacowar, 1977, p. 57).

Interestingly, as the only woman who smokes—incessantly— Larita's act of 1920s independence feels more like a distancing object in Hitchcock's hands than an assertion of burgeoning equality. To lend us a stronger sense that Larita does not belong alongside the other trophies in this home, Hitchcock's next title card objectifies her in an even baser manner: "John—who is this woman you have pitchforked into the family?" queries the mother. The question, spit out with venom, treats Larita as if she is a pile of pig manure, a truly macabre image (and, of course, typically Hitchcockian in its black humor). We have now arrived at the 45-minute mark of this 80-minute film.

The mother's suspicions, written all over her face with perfect derision by the excellent Farebrother, continue to recall the immobile features of not only the earlier sculptures but the four guilt-inducing Christs. In another startling foreshadowing of an upcoming film, we see that she wears two baroque, twisted bracelets on both her upper biceps, shades in spades of the serpent bracelet that will trouble Nelly so much in *The Ring* later this same year.

Larita keeps smoking, then knocks back a stiff shot of alcohol. Again, these actions are all manners of a certain type of independent woman, but not a real person. "Will she achieve personhood," we still wonder, "through all of these trials set before her?" The cigarettes are

***The Ring* (1927)**

literally burning her up, and the guilt brought on by her earlier divorce becomes harrowing as she spots a camera on a dresser aimed right at her (the paparazzi even pursue her in this house).

Once the mother finds photos proving Larita's scandalous past, Farebrother stares directly into Hitch's camera to accuse *us* of her shame, an always unnerving move on the director's part and done at exactly the right moment to bring *our* character as his audience into the proceedings. Cut to a reverse angle shot of Larita, frozen by Mrs. Whittaker's stare; again, merely a sculpture herself. The father, like Sarah, attempts some voice of reason, but even he succumbs when Larita's photo, posed in the artist's studio again like an art object to own, stares back at him.

With no real character(s) to the lot—only empty characteristics—all the mother can think about is the disgrace Larita's presence brings to the family. Perhaps Larita's dawning understanding of these close-minded family members will give her the impetus to become more of herself finally, and not merely an object of disgust.

When she decides to come downstairs to join the party, Hitchcock shoots Larita carrying a huge feathered fan, a bird of prey now. More assertive by the minute, she soon reveals a dawning truth to the Plaintiff's Counsel (a friend of the family, of course): "I think marrying John was the most cowardly thing I ever did ... poor boy!" She pulls one of her bird feathers off Hunter's coat. Arms bare and buff in this scene, actress Jeans assumes for the first time in this film a strikingly strong persona. And when Sarah makes one more attempt to help John and Larita stay together, Isabel kisses her on the cheek, yet another subjective and warm act.

Hitchcock will not allow Larita any easy emotional growth, however, for after her second divorce, we see her descend the steps outside the courthouse. The paparazzi press in as she exclaims, "Shoot. There's nothing left to kill." The film fades to black.

———————

The Ring (1927)

[In Hitchcock's] silent era boxing film, The Ring ... he films some of the fights seemingly from the last row so that film-

Hitchcock's Objects as Subjects

goers have to crane their necks and peer past all the partial obstruction in order to follow the main action.... It piques the audience interest, makes them join the action [Patrick McGilligan; 2008 *Lodger* DVD audio commentary].

Objects are of particularly potent import in *The Ring*. It opens on a still photo of a boxing ring. After the superimposed credits finish, the photo fades into a circular, oversized gong being hit (later, we realize it is the "bell" that is struck between fight rounds). The gong then segues into an old-style carousel rope swing with seated bodies whirling around ... all symbols of the wildly curving arc of this hour-and-a-half film, a complex love circle–ring that is far from a joy ride. Hitchcock then privies us with shots of a laughing woman enjoying the vertigo of the huge carousel as it rocks back and forth, hammering home the disruptive nature of the film's coming narrative. Cuts to two extreme close-ups of the round mouths of live carnival barkers are followed by a close-up of large, round, and painted full mouths of cardboard "teeth" as they are shot down by rifle-wielding sharpshooters. Another huge carousel swing is visible in the background. In just under two minutes, the director has established beyond a shadow of a doubt *The Ring*'s theme of dizzying rotation that boxing, carousels, and subsequent wedding rings represent.

Next, Hitchcock's macabre wit makes an early appearance as two mischievous boys throw a couple of rounded eggs into the face of a seated dunking clown. A policeman laughs at his misfortune before a barker pulls him up short. "Circular objects are not only meant for fun and games," Hitchcock's not-so-subliminal message says, "but can harm us."

Crowds once again run rampant in *The Ring* as we are forced to look hard for The Girl Nelly (actress Lilian Hall-Davis in the first of two films for Hitch) and Bob Corby (actor Ian Hunter in his third of three), the challenger to "One-Round" Jack Sander (Carl Brisson in the first of two), both in and out of the ring. Hitchcock cleverly jumps among frequently alternating close-ups of our three protagonists with a mix of medium and long shots of obfuscating carnival mobs.

When Corby takes the bait to fight Sander, Hitchcock cuts to close-ups of the unwinding ticket rolls Nelly is selling to the hordes—again, more dizzying circles before our eyes. The director next cuts to

The Ring (1927)

Nelly's view of the fight, an extreme long shot as she opens a tent flap to look far into the distance beyond the mass of patrons at the barely visible, mostly obscured battle. Except for a quick close-up two-second reversal of Nelly's peering face, Hitchcock gives us a pleasurably frustrating thirteen full seconds of this extreme long shot in order to test our visual acuity. Even the two preview bouts prior to the Jack and Bob fight had been seen in medium shots, crowd members crowding out our clear view of the ring. Hitchcock brilliantly turns the tables on us by following a quick three-second close-up shot of Jack as he steps into the ring for his go at Corby with Jack's reverse angle extreme long shot view of Nelly as spotted through the flap far past the crowd. Again, the director makes us work for that satisfying moment, the fight's audience a challenging impediment to our gaze and Jack's gaze.

Needless to say, Hitchcock replaces the dirty old sign stating "1," as in "One-Round Jack," with a spanking new card, a fresh and no doubt never used "2" painted on it. The director brilliantly withholds *any* view of the ring now by thoroughly blocking Nelly's (and our) gaze through the flap for a solid twenty seconds of suspense. Who is winning? It doesn't matter. The fight has now been so effectively implanted into our minds that we do not have to see it at all. Finally, the crowd parts just enough for us to watch the referee count Jack out. A mere fifteen minutes of this full-length feature film has now passed. And to leave no doubt in the viewers' minds that Corby's win will complicate all the relationships in this circuitous story, Hitchcock has him disappear into the crowd in a medium shot in between two separate, whirling carousels—the first one shot in day time, the second segueing into the mysterious night.

The first jeweled ring of the film's title makes its appearance at the twenty-two minute mark when Corby gives Nelly a present he has bought her with his fight earnings—a coiled snake bracelet. Danger, Will Robinson, danger! Deals with a handshake are made between the agent and Jack as Hitchcock fades into a corresponding close-up of Corby seductively sliding the serpent all the way up Nelly's forearm to end on her bicep. It works: Hitchcock now stays on the couple in extreme close-up for a solid eighty-plus privileged seconds of sexual, intimate tension, deep kisses and heaving breasts in our face. The bracelet sealed the deal (albeit for most of the film) as Nelly succumbs to the seduction. Upon returning alongside Sander, she surreptitiously hides the bracelet from his view with her other hand. "This bracelet carries great emotional weight throughout the story. It is a snake bracelet, and I think Truffaut is right to see it as one of the film's references to the biblical story of the serpent and the fall in Eden" (Spoto, 1976, p. 12).

Shortly, the gypsy fortune teller's huge round earrings mimic the circular pattern that her cards make on the table as she tells Nelly her future. Will it involve the King of Diamonds (money) or the King of Hearts (love)?

The next day, Nelly causes eddying waves in the stream where Jack washes his face. Hitchcock lovingly shows us their features in reflection, a fantasy quite at odds with the previous distraught scene. Surprising us yet again, he cuts to a medium shot of the serpent bracelet suddenly sliding off her arm and splashing into the water, arcing ripples rushing outwards. Hitchcock's macabre wit returns as Corby slides the bracelet disconcertingly onto Davies' left ring finger, a mock and grotesquely huge wedding ring.

Hitchcock shows us in medium shot a bunch of circular circus tents followed by the arc of the inside of a church in preparation for their marriage. With the giant, dwarf, fat lady, and Siamese twins all in attendance (prefiguring a similar scene fifteen years later in *Saboteur*), actor Gordon Harker's (in the first of four films for Hitch) best man barker makes a humorous and non-stop botch of handling the wedding ring, at one point proffering a coat button instead. Of course, when Jack slides the real wedding ring onto Nelly's ring finger, Corby's present of a serpent bracelet immediately falls down her arm into view. Then, an oval horseshoe falls off a wall and bops the gypsy woman on her head, more convoluted circles causing confusion through their protagonistic forces.

As two drunken female dancers teasingly cavort around the room, an apartment party recapitulates the dizzying, characteristic nature of carousels and rings. Close-ups of revolving records on a player are juxtaposed with elongated mirror images of the dancers among a crowd of drinkers, guitar players and not-so-stolen kisses between Corby and the now-married Nelly. Prefiguring similar uses of rotating objects in *Secret Agent* and both versions of *The Man Who Knew Too Much*, music

The Ring (1927)

from the records record trouble in paradise as, in extreme close-up, Hitchcock superimposes the spinning disc and wildly playing fingers on the rounded curves of guitars over Jack's forehead. And, after Bob wins his final bout necessary for him to challenge his wife's lover to a rematch, we watch first one and then all six round glasses filled with champagne go rapidly flat (foreshadowing similar glasses in *Champagne*).

Jack awaits a wife who will not come home until too late while Hitchcock puns us with signs outside the cross-hatched apartment window—shades of the boxing ring ropes—flashing "Every Sunday watch this spot" and "Rivoli," as in the round watch. Jack tracks Bob down at a club and slugs him, and we see the rounded end of a trombone (from a jazz band in the room) maliciously crossing and uncrossing in front of actor Ian Hunter's face as he lies on the floor.

The final fight reveals the disruptive hordes once again. Nelly, seduced by the stronger and richer man and the trappings of his wealth, has unconsciously left her serpent's bracelet at home on a dresser. Perhaps she may yet learn something about love caused by the memory loss of such an annoying object. The square boxing ring frames the circle of fate surrounding these two fighters, but Hitchcock again prevents us from seeing the fighters clearly until the referee brings them together for his pre-fight admonishments.

The last ten minutes are taken up with the fight, intercut with shots of hungry women munching snacks in their seats. When Jack spots Nelly, "Wham!" he's slammed by a hard right, and the ropes of the boxing ring intersect with the bright, blinding circles caused by flashing camera bulbs, embodiments of his painful experience. (See Jefferies' use of flashbulbs in *Rear Window* 27 years hence for an updated use of these objects.) Jack is saved by the round gong.

Nelly sheds her mink coat (again, an object as a meaningless trapping of wealth) and moves to get a better look at her husband, figuratively and literally going behind his corner for the first time in the film. There are three minutes left in the movie. Hitchcock shoots a stunned Jack in close-up gazing into a round pail full of water, gentle ripples from his sweat in the bucket recapitulating the idyllic husband and wife moments by the water months earlier. While all the rings in this film have come full circle, it's hard to tell how much the humans have learned from their dizzying roundelays.

HITCHCOCK'S OBJECTS AS SUBJECTS

The Farmer's Wife (1928)

After Noël Coward's melodrama of manners in *Easy Virtue*—wherein the mansion felt like an oppressive weight on all of its repressed members—farmer Samuel Sweetland's (Jameson Thomas in his first of two films for Hitchcock) house in *The Farmer's Wife* is shot from so many angles, with housekeepers running to and fro and the camera constantly in pursuit, that it is clear that Hitchcock is opening up this story with the character of its architecture. The director's whirlwind mix of extreme close-ups, cuts, dollies, zooms, pans, long shots, and numerous reverse angles give real personality to this home, an energetic and charming contrast to the earlier claustrophobic *Easy Virtue* "cathedral."

Just look at those bodies filling up and milling about the farmer's cottage during his daughter's pre-wedding dinner, everything brightly lit and mobilized. Strikingly, such active business surrounding the human characters intentionally highlights the two immobile and empty chairs by the hearth and open banister. These chairs are prominently in sight during so many medium distance background shots that they literally cry out for human habitation. Such a *cri de coeur* is the kind Sweetland himself so desperately invokes in his search for the right kind of replacement for his recently deceased wife. His land may be sweet but his home and hearth feel bereft and bitter.

Our heroine, housekeeper Araminta (Minta) Dench—played by the gorgeous Lilian Hall-Davis, Nelly from the previous *Ring*, whose character then had required an entire film to grow emotionally—does the most scurrying about in the early going of this film ... and already has her act together. Hitchcock does little to privilege her in the film until a full two-thirds of the way in, exploiting our focus on her regardless of the camera's movements. She has, apparently, already and obviously begun *The Farmer's Wife as* his wife, at least in spirit and wholly unbeknownst to Sweetland, until the end.

On the way to his first of four "failed" conquests of the local available spinsters—all of whom are set up to look ripe for the picking

The Farmer's Wife (1928)

during the practice dinner—Hitchcock shoots Sweetland from such a distance that his significance is literally lost within the naturalness of his verdant countryside. The false assumptions he makes about these potential spouses reflect yet another incorrect and wholly improper objectification of women in Hitchcock's richly constructed silent films. "I am not the sort of woman for you—I am far too independent," reads the card for Louisa Windeat (Louie Pounds in her only Hitchcock film)—a sound rebuff. She laughs in his face and, when he goes outside to leave, even the horses and dogs hanging about seem to join in her derision. Upon arriving home, his own horse humorously follows him into the house as if *he* were the owner, not Sweetland.

He fares equally poorly with Thirza Tapper (Maud Gill in her only film), his assumption about her as just an old biddy (encouraged in us quite well by Hitchcock during another dinner) thoroughly dashed by her rejection of him. When he abruptly stands up, crushed, Sweetland's disregard for all but his own selfish concerns causes all the lovely objects on Thirza's piano to go tumbling down. Before the other guests arrive, his clumsy wooing continues to knock over all sorts of foodstuffs on a table. Like the hilarious episode around the couch between Francie and her mother in *To Catch a Thief* twenty-seven years later, Sweetland's entreaties are cleverly stymied by this infernal table full of food between them. His marriage proposal at one point elicits a riotous shaking-of-the-Jell-O reaction on the plate in her hands. (*Airplane* [1980] used real breasts for this same kind of humor fifty-two years later!) Likewise, the iced desserts that have melted away when left by the fire are quite the metaphor for Thirza's fiery haranguing of Sweetland. With the entrance of the pastor's wife in about as large a wheelchair as one could imagine, another scene from a future film is humorously anticipated: the overcrowded stateroom scene in the Marx Brothers' *A Night at the Opera* (1935). All the objects in Thirza Tapper's house have truly conspired against him.

More comedy ensues as Mary Hearn (Olga Slade in her one Hitchcock film) turns him down a third time because of his age. (Her character, too, is living under a false illusion, we may think, as Sweetland is stunned by such a proclamation. Although she is at least a decade younger, convention to marry was and still is harder on middle-aged women.) She gets so wound up, Hitchcock makes her look like a freaked-out rag doll during her hysterical arm-waving, blathering reaction. We see Thirza Tapper faint into Churdles Ash's arms (our old friend character actor Gordon Harker, the barker from *The Ring*)—her own kind of rag doll—as the maid goes berserk, too. By this time it's a loony beehive of bodies buzzing all about the living room, a hysterical tour de force in this Hitchcock silent.

Sweetland's final slap in the face is disrupted by the sardine can crush of drinkers in the pub where Mercy Bassett bartends. Actress Antonia Boroughs more than holds her own as she physically jokes around with him, a rough-and-tumble gal with great manhandling skills. To supplement the large number of people in the bar, Hitchcock rented what appears to be at least a hundred hounds (Bassett's hounds?) that lead the hunters out into the fields seeking their prey, another metaphor for Sweetland's cruel yet ultimately futile wooing escapades.

When he returns home from that effort, confirmation of his fourth and final rejection is cleverly withheld until as late as possible. First we see Minta and Sweetland sitting as happy as can be in the once empty hearth chairs. With no other takers, Hitchcock knows that our payoff—Lilian Hall-Davis' long-delayed, privileged camera moments and, for the story, the lead protagonists' long-awaited consummation in marriage—must come soon. But, finally, at the one hour thirty-six minute mark in this over two hour-plus movie, Hitchcock gives us a satisfyingly long and loving subjective medium shot of Davis as she gently runs her hands along the top of the tall back of Sweetland's chair, then poignantly sits in the other one directly across from his. In his (and our) mind, her objective status as housekeeper is finally changed to a subjective one as an equal wife. The first and only truly happy, intimate scene in the whole film—and only one, for the love Sweetland had for his wife at her death bed was sadness, not elation—shows us Sweetland as a crushed man with Minta looking on, hoping against hope that he has learned something. Critic Robin Wood called this kind of film-long emotional growth Hitchcock's always challenging "experience-therapy" (Wood, 1965, p. 59; see also Barr, 1999, p. 60). Sweetland's classist attitude—primarily in his treatment of his housekeeper as not worthy of marriage, let alone more than passing attention, but also towards his four single-women neighbors—took nearly the entire film to be broken and shown, to him, as the dehumanizing act of objectification that it was. Not until Minta herself sits in the place of his deceased but imagined spouse are his illusions finally shattered. Sweetland's hard-earned humility prevents him from speaking, so he writes her name now at the top of his list of human objects to "own," all others crossed off.

More gorgeously lit close-up shots of Davis aglow in the fire's light finally puts "sense in a man's heart," says Hitchcock's title card. Few directors could better privilege his leading ladies via close-ups than this one. And his last shots of Sweetland's oft-parodied look of desperation and anger finally soften actor Jameson Thomas' face in ways that literally transform him from a caricature to a real human being. They warmly hug each other, and—wait for it—rather than kiss, he offers up his wife Tibby's party dress for her to wear. Gorgeously lit on her body, she descends the now inhabited stairway. The house has become a real home again.

Champagne (1928)

> It was time to pop a champagne cork or two—something that Hitch was seldom averse to doing. The sparkling liquid flows freely in Champagne, one more symbol of the sexuality and spirit that is the true subject of all his films right up to the last, *Family Plot* [Mogg, 1999, p. 17].

Champagne, like any other type of alcohol, enhances one's mood at the time, whatever it may be. Happy, your happiness increases; sad, ditto. *Champagne* opens with a champagne bottle cork popping directly into our eyes and, once here, once in the middle, and once at the end of the film, the camera "drinks" it down out of a convex glass that eventually reveals what goes on beyond—dancing, partying, and two lovers' kisses respectively. The evolution of relationships moves from frivolity to hints of maturity.

Frivolity, thy name is money, conspicuous consumption, peacock feathers molting off gowns, fickle love, and the dizziness of surface happiness (*Easy Virtue* themes again). On a slowly rocking ship or upon

HITCHCOCK'S OBJECTS AS SUBJECTS

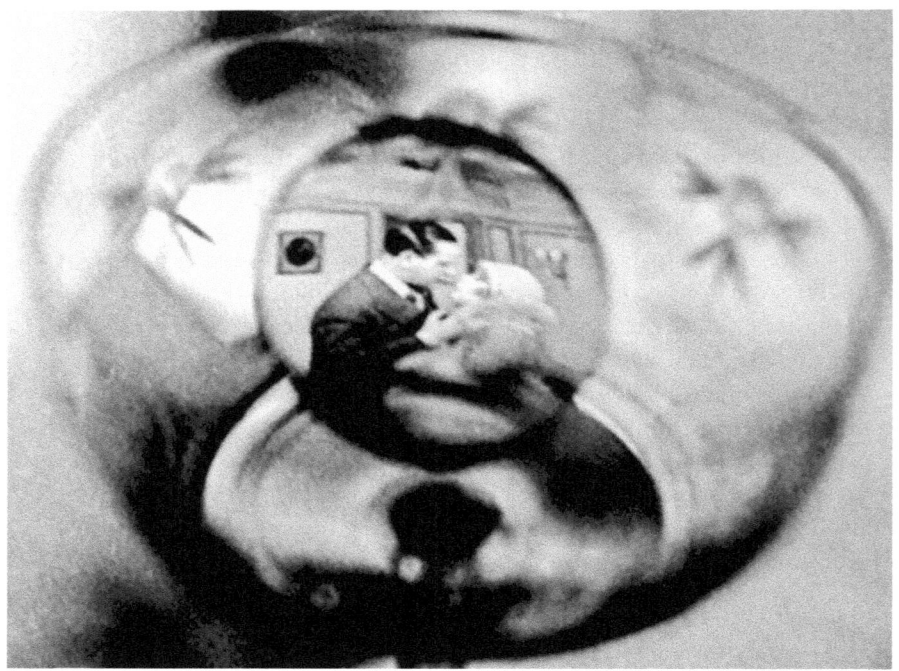

Champagne (1928): The camera literally "drinks" down the bubbly.

learning one may be broke, however, that dizziness becomes sickening to watch as girls prance in mock pleasure, drunk, during an Apache dance that causes a whirlwind of skirts flying. Rooms starting to spin are metaphors for the enhancement in either direction that alcohol brings to people (shades of *The Ring* again).

Champagne's visual metaphors prefigure the sickening vertigo Elsa feels from repetitious Swiss songs and swirling coins in a bowl from *Secret Agent* during the next sound decade. They might as well be the spinning dancers waltzing in that film and in *Shadow of a Doubt*, or the rocking of the ship that makes Henry Kendall so ill in *Rich and Strange* a few years hence. Such movements caused by liquids that inebriate people or disturb their inner-ear balance are, indeed, the result of objects that literally move our protagonists from the inside out. *Champagne* is fun on the surface but ... its true character really gets underneath the skin.

The Manxman (1929)

> The shot of a lighthouse with its rotating beam serves a triple function: It reinforces the coastal *mise-en-scène*, marks a transition to evening, and establishes a source of expressive imagery. Pete asks his more educated and articulate friend to speak on his behalf to Caesar, requesting Kate's hand in marriage; the on-off light effect behind Phil's head is an image of his anguish, torn between love and friendship [Barr, 1999, pp. 68–69].

Loyalty, friendship and honor between friends are sorely tested in this film's triangular complications of two men in love with the same woman. While *The Manxman* is an unremittingly sluggish melodrama about a love triangle that goes from bad to worse, there are several interesting objects in it that are given subjective status by Hitchcock.

After raging waves crash on a shore (intimations of the following decade's opening of *Young and Innocent* and *Jamaica Inn*), Hitchcock shows us a strange geometric image in the shape of three splayed legs connected at their shared "hip," all walking separate ways—a perfectly iconic representation of our three protagonists' coming predicament. Known as a *triskeles* or *triskelion*, it is a symbolic three-legged figure indigenous to Great Britain's Isle of Man, where the story takes place.

When soon-to-be Deemer (Judge) Philip Christian (actor Malcolm Keen in his third of three films for the director) begrudgingly walks into the Cregeen parlor to speak on behalf of his close friend Pete Quilliam's (Danish actor Carl Brisson in his second of two) love for Kate Cregeen (Czech actress Anny Ondra in her first of two), Hitchcock withholds our view of his entire body behind a stone wall, allowing us to see only the family's responses to his entreaties through a cross-hatched inner window. Its prison-looking glass panes will reappear several times throughout the film. All the while, the flashing and circling beams of a lighthouse's floodlight cross the screen left to right, frequent portents of trouble in this tragic tale of love. Similar emotional uses of a lighthouse's "rotating beams" occur eighteen years later on Alicia's apartment deck in *Notorious*.

Likewise, mill wheels provide similar foreshadowings of danger ahead, their round shapes harkening back to the ubiquitous circles that inhabit *The Ring*:

> In *The Manxman* Hitchcock makes his best use yet of settings. Kate and Philip consummate their love in an empty mill.... [It] has the idyllic associations but without the sinister omen of the mill in *Foreign Correspondent*. Kate is excited by the sight of the mill wheels, but the image—wheels turning wheels turning wheels—is an image of their own lives run by forces beyond their control [Yacowar, 1977, p. 93].

Hitchcock typically uses his mobs as framing devices for nearly hidden individuals, or stand-ins for the stupidity of mankind, and this film is no exception. In the first pub scene, the director makes it unusually difficult for Phil to spot both Kate and Pete far across the room. Not only are drinkers tightly crushed together between camera and subjects but an inordinate amount of smoke from the patrons' cigarettes swirl about (see a similar use of smoke in *Mr. and Mrs. Smith*, *Shadow of a Doubt*, *I Confess*, and *The Birds*, among other films). Later, just before the thirty-minute mark in the film, Philip's point of view of a bereft Kate is an extraordinary composition shot from behind at medium distance, tightly framed through and constrained by three foregrounded patrons *and* two door frames.

After Philip and Kate clinch for the first time (thinking Pete's dead, after we've just found out he's not), Hitchcock cuts to the mill wheel in the background spinning slowly, ever so slowly, silently mocking their brief hopes. "Their walk takes them to a millhouse.... Inside, Kate turns a handle to set the millstones rotating, and they go on and on turning, as if to underline that a process embarked upon is difficult to stop. The pair embrace solemnly, the millstone grinds on, and an ellipse evidently marks their first love-making" (Barr, 1999, p. 71).

Shortly, Kate asks to meet Philip in their "usual place," and Hitch shows her in an extreme long shot walking right to left, with her figure foregrounding a huge storm cloud that nearly blots out the sun. The next shot is a similarly stunning extreme long shot of her entering the frame of a huge arched rock at the beach, its encircling shape nearly the same as the cloud. Compositionally, the two juxtaposed shots are breathtaking. A third reverse shot from up high looking down shows Philip in his own extreme long shot through another gaping rock portal, waiting for Kate. Soon we see her running across the beach towards

The Manxman (1929)

Philip, still shot from an extreme distance, dark rocks tightly framing and pressing in on them this time. The black smoke spewing from the ship carrying Pete home anticipates Uncle Charlie's train arrival in *Shadow of a Doubt* fourteen years later.

Body parts take on powerful energy when Hitchcock films Pete's hand closing a door behind Kate as their wedding guests depart, a trap door that she will never really escape from. And the lovemaking Pete shortly attempts to perpetrate on an unloving, all-too-cool Kate is cannily contrasted by the blazing hearth in the background (shades of the more hopeful hearth in both *The Lodger* and *The Farmer's Wife*). Hitchcock recapitulates the earlier distant shot of Kate from behind when she confesses her love to Philip, not Pete, with a medium long shot of Philip as seen over Pete's shoulder in the background, a door framing and confining him now. The hearth keeps burning, flickering its anxious light in the home much like the lighthouse beams infiltrated themselves into these three peoples' lives earlier.

There's a highly charged, touching moment enhanced by a rocking chair back when the baby doctor comes down the stairs to announce a birth. He can't spot Pete, only Philip (the real father, it will turn out), for Hitchcock has Pete hidden behind that rocking chair which looms large in the foreground as he kneels down to pray—again, shades of the empty rocker from *The Farmer's Wife* the previous year.

Shortly, rather than pan or dolly left with Pete as he heads up the stairs upon returning home, Hitchcock keeps his camera focused in medium distance on a blank and empty arched doorway. Looking for the wife who has just left him, he descends the staircase a sad twelve seconds later—a poignant moment. It's a similarly framed door to the one in Philip's office that Kate will hide behind when Pete goes to his best friend, asking about her.

Knowing she cannot retrieve her child from Pete, Kate walks the streets bereft to arrive at a port, lighthouse beams keeping the story still quite tense. Barr accurately calls these beams recurring "emblem[s] of hesitation" (1999, p. 70). Attempting suicide, she falls into the water, bubbles rising to the surface. The shot immediately segues into a pool of black ink into which Judge Philip Christian dips his pen as he presides over his first day of court. "The water/pen transition picks up the imagery of the very first scene, which associated Phil with angular intellectuality; the pen and ink stand for the rational calculation, the career ambition that has led to her suicide attempt. A woman's emotions become something to just dip a pen into. And here she now is, saved from the water and brought before him, as his first case, to be judged" (Barr, 1999, p. 75).

Ironically, arches echoing the repeatedly closed doors from earlier parts of the film now frame, and judge, the soon-to-be-tested Christian character of Judge Christian, from behind and above.

When Philip finally admits his guilt to everyone in the courtroom, he resolves to right his wrongs. Philip removes his wig and stands between Pete and Kate, Hitchcock shining his camera's light brightly on their pained faces. Their hands are also brilliantly lit, grasping at each other in an almost sculptural frieze of emotions. (See similarly treated disembodied hands in *Jamaica Inn* and *I Confess*, in particular.) And, as Phil, Kate and their baby leave Pete's house, Hitchcock shoots dozens of women, four in the foreground, berating them publicly. The masses have now gone wild as both chorus and executioners.

Pete has nothing left to him on land and so heads back out to sea, the great leveler. That sea will return many times in subsequent Hitchcock films as a character that thwarts others with its unstoppable force and depth.

Blackmail (1929)

> The staircase is thus already, in Hitchcock's first sound film, firmly established as a transitional space between the normal world downstairs and the seductive, mysterious, dangerous world above ... [Leitch, 1991, p. 273].

Early in *Blackmail*, Hitchcock shoots the scene of Frank Webber, the detective (John Longden in his first of five films for the director), and his girlfriend Alice White (Anny Ondra) fighting through crowds to get dinner seats. Masses of humanity are yet again a major blockage to a potentially happy relationship (which will only be hinted at by the end of the film). As they race from table to table in an effort to beat others to empty seats—patrons who shove and push and are themselves

Blackmail (1929)

shoved and pushed—the chaos feeds Alice's frustration with Frank, and vice versa. In their struggles, her innocent loss of a glove and its retrieval by Frank is very shortly a harbinger of a similar loss (of the same glove) that could convict her of the artist Crewe's death. Frank's second retrieval of it will literally save her life and lead to another's death, the initial blackmailer, Tracy.

Shortly, we see that first blackmailer (Donald Calthrop in the first of his five Hitchcock films) skulking about in front of the artist Crewe's (Australian actor Cyril Ritchard in his only film for Hitch) flat, then summoning him for a brief chat that's drowned out by a passing car's horn, typical Hitchcockian intrigue implanted through an object. After convincing Alice to come up and see his artwork, and upon entering the building, Crewe says to her, "I'm right up there, at the top." Hitchcock suddenly cuts to a quick, sharply angled low shot of a forebodingly lit stairway. The two full cutaway staircases that they walk up, artificially constructed so the camera can follow all the way in a floating, hypnotic manner, give us a sense of impending doom. "It is a dizzy height to which this couple ascends, and an emotional tone of helplessness and tension is introduced" via this stairway (Spoto, 1976, p. 20). More dark shadows press in as they reach the final upper landing.

Inside, Alice spots a painting of a laughing jester pointing and looking directly at her (and us) for the first of many times. Though startled, she laughs innocently along with its own mocking mouth and finger. Again, like the first missing glove, subsequent encounters with this painting will prove more and more ominous.

When Crewe finally decides to try to rape Alice, Hitchcock directs him to stand before a chandelier in such a way that its shadow places a dastardly moustache on his upper lip. Later, when Alice nervously considers confessing to the crime, a shadowy noose slips over her head as she makes her decision.

A harmless bread knife quickly becomes the murder weapon that prevents her rape. Stepping out from behind the curtain afterwards, Alice becomes eerily robot-like as she tries to snap out of her shock. After she pulls her clothes off the jester painting, it has the second of many last laughs, this time not *with* her but *at her* expense. In a powerful point of view shot, Hitchcock cuts to Alice looking directly at us, the camera, the jester, and the horror of what she has just done, as

Crewe's lighthearted piano playing and song that he sang in jest returns in a minor key on the soundtrack.

> The symbol with the most profound alteration of character is the painting of the clown in Crewe's studio. At first the clown is the full-bodied work of the artist, massively superior to the independent effort or even collaboration of the amateur, Alice, in her attempt at art.... The clown image itself is of various expression. Upon her arrival in the studio the clown's face promises gaiety. Then it leers at her, as the atmosphere takes an erotic turn. The same face seems to accuse her after she has killed Crewe.... The painting, like its dapper, elegant artist, works as a test of the people it meets [Yacowar, 1977, p. 111].

In an extreme overhead shot, *Vertigo*'s vertiginous staircase nearly thirty years on is prefigured here at the beginning of her descent from Crewe's loft. (We saw a similar shot in Mrs. Bunting's imagining of the lodger in his descent of a staircase in *The Lodger* three years earlier.) Dozens of bodies and the sound of more car horns rush past Alice as she haltingly makes her way home, the *Daily Telegraph* newspaper appearing superimposed for a moment behind her recounting a "Crossword Puzzle Every Day." She passes through another huge crowd and under a theater sign that reads "A New Comedy," harsh irony striking like daggers in her heart. Likewise, body parts, especially via her memory of the dead Crewe's forearm falling out from behind a curtain, lash out at her physically and emotionally.

> Both the outstretched arm and the knife images haunt Alice on her walk through London. She sees a traffic cop's arm, and then she "sees" the victim's arm. She looks at a Gordon's gin sign in moving neon lights. Not only does its slogan—"White for purity"—taunt her (her last name is White), but the moving display in lights of a cocktail being shaken turns into a knife in a hand that alternates between two positions, as if stabbing something. (Like the forearm and knife that protrude from behind the artist's curtain, dissociated from any body; this visual disembodiment is analogous to the aural dissociation of the word "knife" from its context in the knife sequence through the blurring or elimination of the other words.) [Weis, 1982, pp. 47–48].

Scotland Yard's Frank is on the scene the next day. His simultaneous recognition of Alice's lost glove and Crewe's dead face is painfully reinforced by Hitchcock's cut once again to that damnable laughing jester. Frank hides the glove and so dooms both himself and Alice.

More car horns blast their trumpeting accusations just a little too loudly on the soundtrack. And, in the morning, Alice's bird abrasively trills from its unseen cage as she feigns awakening to her mother's comments on the previous night's events. A photo of Frank's stupidly stern visage in uniform frowns down upon her from a wall.

Blackmail comes full circle as Frank sees a way to blame Tracy for everything, certainly his effort to get back at and blackmail Alice for her lack of love. Sought now by the police, Tracy is himself dwarfed (like Roddy in *Downhill*) by the columns and stairs and statues and halls and dozens of glass cases at the British Museum, all filmed in long shots. (See, also, Armstrong's efforts to lose Gromek in the huge Berlin Museum in *Torn Curtain* 37 years later.) "The museum has the primary character of culture" (1977, p. 289), Maurice Yacowar accurately notes. Its imposing size reminds us of the furniture of Roddy's home in *Downhill*, the towering Statue of Liberty in *Saboteur*, the United Nations and Mount Rushmore in *North by Northwest*, and so many other huge objects and high overhead shots that miniaturize—in other words, objectify—humans throughout Hitchcock's pictures. "[The Berlin Museum] is large, spacious, dwarfing the people who rush through it. The intrusion of the blackmailer and the detectives suggests something of a violation of the Museum, particularly as its massive godheads give it the austerity and dignity of a temple.... The museum expresses the eternal, sober purposes of Art, while the comic clown expresses its subversive undertow" (Yacowar, 1977, p. 113).

Objects in the museum, like the museum itself, disembodied forearms reaching out, and the jester painting, all press in on Alice (or in her mind) to confront her guilt at not confessing the murder immediately. Of course, all of these objects, in Hitchcock's hands, implicate us as well.

Juno and the Paycock (1930)

No objects or even subjects are in sight for the first fifteen seconds of this film, for Hitchcock literally keeps us in the dark as the Orator,

Hitchcock's Objects as Subjects

Irish actor Barry Fitzgerald, barks out the beginning of his speech in total blackness (see, also, the beginning of *Suspicion*): "Fellow countrymen. Continuously and courageously we have fought and struggled for the national salvation of Ireland...." At this point, the only objects or subjects in this movie are wholly in our imagination. Fade up finally on Fitzgerald continuing to recite from Sean O'Casey's heralded play. Shot from above in a medium but tightly peopled composition, we see he is in a place dressed down to look like a crowded tenement alleyway during Dublin's troubled Civil War period. Interestingly, Fitzgerald took the role of Captain Boyle in the 1924 Abbey Theater production of this play, but the original Juno, Irish actress Sara Allgood, returns as her same character.

On the Orator's final strains of "...bonds of unity and peace," a ratatat of loud gunfire (which recurs throughout the film at both opportune and inopportune moments) is heard. Cut immediately to another tightly packed shot of Hitchcock's classic hordes of cattle—uh, I mean crowd members—falling all over themselves onto the floor just inside the front door of Foley's bar in an effort to escape the gunfire. During an ensuing three-shot of "Joxer" Daly (English actor and director Sydney Morgan), Captain Jack Boyle (versatile English character actor Edward Chapman in his first of three Hitch films), and Maisie Madigan (Irish actress Maire O'Neill) bantering about the precarious nature of humanity, a huge pile of beer bottles are conspicuously and delicately stacked on the left side of the screen. These beer bottles stand in for the masses of humanity and the coming tragic scenario. Whether conscious of it or not, we the audience half expect this threesome's carousing to knock the beer bottles over, our anxiety certainly intentional on the director's part.

Again, missing subjects are treated as invisible objects when Juno cleverly hides behind her flat's entrance door for a solid thirty seconds, the camera rock solid on *her* features, as she mimes watching Joxer and Jack sneak in for a snort, unseen, between herself and the camera. But where are they? Why aren't they visible? Either behind the camera or, more likely, via an edit, Hitchcock made sure they were never there in the first place.

A downpour of rain just outside a "screen right" window (where Joxer himself is being soaked, hiding on the balcony) plays momentarily

Juno and the Paycock (1930)

humorous but, ultimately, sadly ironic as a stand-in for the real troubles to come when Jack quotes a typical Joxer-O'Casey aphorism: "Every cloud has a silver lining. I'll never doubt the goodness of God again." Oh yes he will, as his supposed inheritance will be much more trouble indeed than a real inheritance is for the Kendalls' three pictures hence in *Rich and Strange*. Money as an object is *never* the key to subjective happiness in any Hitchcock film. It always represents a struggle that must be overcome, one at least as difficult as any real relationship or person moving toward maturity and happiness. See, especially, *The Pleasure Garden, Downhill, Easy Virtue, Champagne, The Skin Game, Rebecca, Mr. and Mrs. Smith, Suspicion, Lifeboat, The Paradine Case, Dial M for Murder, To Catch a Thief, North by Northwest, Marnie,* and even *Family Plot*.

Hitchcock shows us exactly this point when the conspicuous consumption of the bored Boyles means little to all the characters. Mary is drunk on their purchases (on credit) of a new gramophone and armloads of rugs, and Jack flings Charles Bentham's (actor John Longden) expensive hat, gloves and cane away, subsequently knocking out the old tobacco from his new pipe on the seatback of an exquisitely cushioned divan he's been resting his dirty boots on.

O'Casey's sharp script highlights the power of religion's ethereality—itself a false object of investment?—when the captain philosophizes with Bentham by saying, "Aren't all religions curious? If they weren't, how would you get anyone to believe in them?" Likewise, the ghost of Tancred, whose son Johnny betrayed to the IRA, is more tangible than the many boisterous songs that fill the middle section of this film and fade away with everyone's drunken revelry. Every time Tancred's death is mentioned, or gunfire erupts off-screen, Hitchcock inexorably zooms into a close-up of actor John Laurie's horrified face, knowing that he too will soon be exterminated. Laurie, a typically strong Hitchcockian character actor, has the haunted good looks and fearful youthfulness of matinee idol Ivor Novello that the director favored in earlier silent films, and is hardly recognizable here as the mean-spirited crofter from *The 39 Steps* just five years hence.

As two IRA members drag Johnny off to his fate, an allusion to two Christs on the cross appears suddenly when furniture movers are seen in foregrounded silhouette holding their hands over their heads.

"What can God do against the stupidity of Man?" wails Juno at the end of the picture. We are left bereft as well, for no furnishings remain in their empty apartment home. Again, as in *Number Seventeen* and *The 39 Steps*, objects only fill a room up, and can only stand in ever so briefly for relationships that may, or may not, come to fruition.

Murder! (1930)

> When Hitchcock uses the scene of Sir John before his mirror, it is in the technically most accomplished scene in the film, the scene which Hitchcock is most fond of citing in his interviews, and the pivotal point in the film, both in plot and in thematic movement. In that scene the mirror does not represent Sir John's self-concern but the precise contrary: It depicts his decision to involve himself in Diana's case [Yacowar, 1977, p. 133].

Depending on their usefulness in Hitchcock's films, single lamps (like mirrors) illuminate or obfuscate, while pairs of lamps (or their stand-ins) can double the cinematic pleasure. In his early sound picture *Murder!* (1930), lamps and a brightly reflected clock perfectly frame an empty door leading out of the jurors' deliberation room (Diana Baring has been accused of murder), prefiguring a similar design of lamps outside Sir John Menier's apartment door in the next shot. (Actor Herbert Marshall, in his first of two Hitchcock films, impeccably played the role.) Cut to his living room with even more conspicuous lamps framing a darkened, empty hearth (the realm of night, within which Sir John must search for his love). Motifs of balance, and constriction, have been firmly established.

The next shot continues this troubling sense of doubling—two sides to every coin, conflicted internal characters—when we see Sir John's face in his bathroom mirror staring back at itself as he debates with (and berates) himself during the film's justly famous voice-over. It is no surprise that a full orchestra just out of camera sight is playing the Overture to Richard Wagner's *Tristan und Isolde* (1857–1859), a story of the epitome of love's fulfillment at nighttime.

The lamp-framed yawning, ominous hearth reappears back in the

The Skin Game (1931)

living room as *Tristan und Isolde* sounds ever louder in our ears, nearly preventing us from hearing Sir John's musings with his sidekick Ted Markham (Edward Chapman). Upon closer inspection, the lamps are actually set on the wall in two tight groups of three each, and they now frame Sir John and Markham as symmetrical counterpoints. Details of objects like these are no accident in any Hitchcock film: "Often for the furnishings [Hitchcock] would pick out a neighborhood where the characters might live, knock on doors, and do an inspection for ideas. Sometimes he'd negotiate a loan of the furniture, the lamps, the wall hangings. He was as meticulous about the interiors of his films as he was about every other element that went into the production" (Patrick McGilligan; 2008 *Lodger* DVD audio commentary).

After Markham leaves the room, Sir John moves "screen left" as Hitchcock's camera pans ever so slightly left with him. As he pivots to stare off to the right, directly past one of the three-lamp bundles, we again see the black hearth (of night, of purgatory) in the center of the screen beckoning to us and him. Suddenly we realize that Hitchcock has directed Marshall to stand so his head is perfectly centered by the camera's eye in front of another heretofore unseen lamp. In this extraordinary shot, a rectangular halo effect has been created above his head. In this, just Hitchcock's third sound picture, inanimate lamps have already asserted their presence by amplifying their human characters' quandaries.

Another expert British character actor employed by Hitchcock, Edward Chapman is unrecognizable in this film as Ted Markham, having played Captain Boyle in the director's previous film, *Juno and the Paycock*, and Dawker in his next, *The Skin Game*. Like Miles Mander as Levet in *The Pleasure Garden* and Gordon Druce in *Murder!*, or Leslie Banks as Lawrence in *The Man Who Knew Too Much* and Joss Merlyn in *Jamaica Inn*, Chapman's chameleon-like transformations are extraordinary.

———————————

The Skin Game (1931)

A very talky one-shot scene (1 minute 45 seconds) between Hillcrist daughter, Jill, and Hornblower son, Rolf, regretting their families' hostility, is followed by a sharp visual rendering of the division. Jill passes on horseback through an avenue of mature trees, Rolf motors between lines of saplings, up to their respective family seats; the two shots rhyme, past against future, each image tightly symmetrical, suggesting both wealth and intransigence [Barr, 1999, p. 105].

A skin game involves someone putting up just enough deal money that it's as if the person is bartering off some of his or her flesh. In *The Skin Game*, Hillcrist (C.V. France) and Hornblower (Edmund Gwenn in the first of four films for Hitch) bring so much of their personal baggage to the fight over property that, over the course of the film, they each lose quite a bit of skin and, truly, their souls.

Trees, nature, homes, the town itself, angry people yelling, and machinery noise dwarf the humans throughout this object-filled film. People are so often treated as meaningless characters that the objects around them feel all the more important, perhaps one of English novelist and playwright John Galsworthy's points in this film adaptation of his 1920 play on tragic economic and cultural battle of wills.

> We then witness Hornblower power disrupting the sleepy tempo of the village: a van displaying the sign of their pottery business, its way blocked by sheep, hoots angrily. Since there is no lip-synch dialogue, just a cacophony of noises, Hitchcock can cut freely, and does so to the extent of 20 shots in 42 seconds, many of them repeated, creating a truly oppressive effect [Barr, 1999, p. 105].

Several times conversations occur offscreen about people onscreen as if they are not there. Conversely, discussions onscreen are often about people offscreen. People sometimes become commodities in this film, not characters, a fascinating reversal of subjects as objects.

The first encounter between Hillcrist and Hornblower reveals three burnt-out candles in a foregrounded candelabrum, anticipating the dry and lifeless conversation between them. The candles stay there prominently for the whole scene.

Shortly, the camera as stand-in for the auctioneer can't keep up with the bidding in front of him, rapidly panning side to side and dollying forward and backward in a desperate attempt to focus on the latest offer for the Sentry countryside property.

***Rich and Strange* (1932)**

Bright lamps, finally, force Charlie (actor John Longden) and Dawker (Edward Chapman) to speak the truth to each other, the first time in the film that lights force an action. And both Jill (actress Jill Esmond, Laurence Olivier's first wife) and Chloe (Phyllis Konstam in her fourth of four films for the director) wear purgative white dresses and are made up to look nearly alike. In their final scene together, as they deliberately resemble sisters, Chloe begs the Hillcrists to help her convince Charles that she is worth his love in spite of her past life as a co-respondent in divorce cases. "[I]t's in this alertness to the superficial that Hitchcock can sometimes open our eyes to the life around and within us more sharply than many an arthouse artist, for whom the superficial is the 'merely' superficial..." (Durgnat, 1974, p. 114).

Harkening back to their first meeting, the hands of Rolf Hornblower (Frank Lawton) and Jill Hillcrist reach out at the end of the film in an effort to bridge the families' gaps. A tree is seen being cut down and felled in the last shot. "[T]he tree stands for both families, for family feelings, for the love that binds families and should bind families into larger communities" (Yacowar, 1977, p. 144).

Do Rolf and Jill represent progress? Hitchcock only allows us to see their disembodied hands holding out towards each other in/for hope.

Rich and Strange (1932)

The thriller author John Buchan [1875–1940] once had a character say, quote, "Civilization anywhere is a very thin crust." Hitchcock could not have said it better [Leonard Leff; "Mystery Train"; 2007 *Lady Vanishes* DVD bonus feature].

As the crowds of London leave work behind and rhythmically open their black umbrellas at the rainy beginning of this film, we see them pour out into the street and down into the drains that lead them to the underground, rolling waves of humanity flowing into stuffed trams. Playing and filming them like packed sardines swimming downstream, Hitchcock has once again turned his subjects into objects that think and act as just one subject. In that inimitably funny silent screen way he often starts his movies, the first four minutes reveal mankind bereft of subjectivity, passive and anonymous schools of fish following each other to who knows where.

> *Rich and Strange* opens with rows of accountants bent over their columns of figures like so many adding machines, or insects. When six o'clock arrives, the workers, mechanically obedient to mechanical time, pop two by two from the office building. In paired synchrony, they open their umbrellas and go to join the hordes in the underground [Brill, 1988, p. 166].

Fred Hill (Henry Kendall in his only film for Hitch) finally gets his own stuck umbrella unstuck, but the rain has stopped and he's home now, its protection from the elements ill-timed and unnecessary after all. And the home he enters and feels trapped in will, ironically, comfort him in ways unimagined by film's end, unlike the empty hull of a home which is the real subject of Hitch's next movie, the furniture-less house with the number seventeen. The subjects of *Rich and Strange*, however, are about the evils that riches *can't* buy, courtesy of a generous aunt, and they will drive the Hills, Fred and Emily (Joan Barry, who dubbed Anny Ondra's voice in *Blackmail*), back to the safety of their humble abode. The soon-ignored pot boiling over on their stove, which closes the first act, foreshadows the dangerous heat of passion ahead of them on their rich and strange journey.

Hitchcock films their take of Paris—the Eiffel Tower, Notre Dame, and especially their visit to the *Folies Bergères*—in the same manner as the earlier London crowds, all rushing by, little fish in an overwhelmingly big sea. The huge ship they soon take to the East similarly dwarfs their tiny lives. Objects have become the subjects now, while the human protagonists have become mere sea creatures.

Hitchcock films Fred's feverish seasickness in his stateroom by bringing all the menu's items to daring life, their rich and creamy titles jingling and jangling and jumping off the page in a close-up rush towards the camera—Pea Soup, Lobster Mayonnaise, Boiled Leg of Pork, Cream Sherry Trifle, Coffee (Turkish), and Gorgonzola Cheese. Looking like mad, surreal creatures themselves, the words attack his and our startled eyes and almost make us as sick as Fred.

The ship and its myriad passengers, floating in the vast Mediter-

Rich and Strange (1931): Emily Hill (Joan Barry) attempts to soothe her husband Fred's (Henry Kendall) feverish seasickness, exacerbated by the earlier floating menu items.

ranean Sea, oppressively loom over the proceedings for much of the film. Hitchcock shows us shots of the cruise ship's pistons pumping feverishly, the inner workings and sounds of the many clocks shown earlier echoing within the cacophony of this larger machine. The director almost seems to be saying that mankind, dwarfed by the immensity of everything around it, should not even bother trying to escape one's fate in the face of it all.

An audacious shot at the twenty-minute mark startles us out of the hypnotic rolling of the sea's waves. When Commander Gordon (Percy Marmont, soon to embody the suspected spy Caypor in *Secret Agent*) calls Emily "the quaintest person, really," she answers, "Why do you say that?" Hitchcock immediately cuts to a medium close-up of one of the lifeboats hanging alongside the hull, a literal beckoning calling for these two strangers to jump ship together. (The director will metaphorically put our entire species in just such a boat full of life in a film by the same name twelve years hence.)

Leading up to their first kiss, the incessant and vertiginous lapping of the water at the ship's sides casts its spell on Gordon and Em. Hitchcock miraculously transfers its dizzying allure into lumps in our throat, too. And when Fred goes in for his extreme close-up clinch with the *faux* princess (German-American actress Betty Amann), Hitch cuts to a daring overhead shot of whirling Carnival dancers on another deck. (Shades of the beginning of *The Ring*.)

Later, Emily "gazes at the waves breaking on the beach outside the hotel room window, recalling the waves that broke against the bow of the ship [and] reflecting the tumult of her feelings as she and Gordon stood at the rail just before their first kiss" (Brill, 1988, p. 170).

The director has the last word, however, for after Gordon and Em's *final* kiss, the two separate and the camera perceptibly shifts down to stare at her empty hands, a strangely cold feeling of loss slipping through the gulf between them. Em is literally *and* figuratively at sea when she tells Gordon that she's "as much at sea as ever." And, later, when they reach Singapore and speed along in a car together, Em looks out the window and down at the street as it rushes by, the sea recapitulated by her dizzying view of the road as shot through Hitch's speeding camera.

Throughout the film, all sorts of objects—anchor chains, cats (they even eat one), buckets, shirts, veils, and chairs—conspire to impede the progress of the loves and lives of our supposed protagonists. And when a Chinese man horribly drowns overboard with his leg caught in a dangling rope, the impassive faces of his countrymen invert the subjects of this film once again into fated, will-free objects, blankly staring. It's an eerie, even creepy moment.

Hitchcock may be telling the Hills that they must find a way to embrace their hills and vales—or earth and sea—if they hope to achieve happiness. As the Chinese junk sails away, the rich and strange hopes of this film sink with their ship in the distance. The Hills have only their humble home to return to and hearten them. Isn't that enough? Briefly, we feel they may have learned something from their travails and travels, but Hitchcock lets the laughter catch in our throats when they start to bicker again, just like at the beginning of the film.

Number Seventeen (1932)

> In later films, Hitchcock would refine and perfect these matters of a film's texture, until critics could suggest that there's no detail in a Hitchcock film that doesn't relate to another detail, each playing its part in the whole [Mogg, 1999, p. 27].

A windblown hat gathers no moss as Hitchcock's camera dollies left in fast pursuit. An unidentified man picks it up in front of the door to a house with the number 17 on it. Opening all by itself, the door seems to say, "Come on in, we've got a little ghost story waiting for you." The man walks into the house with the camera following, but this time it feels hand-held. The door slams shut behind us and the camera, locking us in.

Shadows in this film stand in for the people and act almost independently of their owners. "To [Hitchcock], the attention-getting effect of a giant shadow was much more important than the fact that no hand, no matter what the circumstances, could ever cast such a shadow" (William K. Everson, 1972; 2012 *The 39 Steps* DVD special feature, "The Illustrated Hitchcock"). It *is* a ghost house, for there is no furniture anywhere, save a bathtub in one room, and the way the shadows and rooms are shot—numerous extreme overheads alternating with long pans down staircases, funhouse scenes shot from up under, close-ups, and sharply oblique angles—this empty home is in fact the lead character for the first two-thirds of the movie. As Yacowar notes, the old bum Ben "is caught in a shadow-web that anticipated Cary Grant's in *Suspicion*, but in No. 17 every wall quivers with shadows" (1977, p. 156).

And there are MacGuffins galore—vacant handcuffs and ropes and tickets and necklaces—all empty and vacuous objects, just like the rooms. While Number Seventeen is the main character, it, too, turns out to be as meaningless as its inhabitants, human characters that we can never tell apart.

And the details keep coming at us, annoyingly, like Fred's menu items in the previous film. Hitchcock's film reverses all the usual associations, however. This house is so much more interesting *because* of its emptiness than any of the actors playing their parts. And when we get to the basement—straight out of a Phantom of the Opera story—its myriad catacombs triple our sense of homelessness.

The train and bus chase rightly becomes the most interesting "character-driven" narrative of the whole film, our cut-out, meaningless characters hopping on board for more funhouse hijinks. It reminds one of what P.T. Barnum did once his Dime Museums kept burning down and the Transcontinental Railroad finally was completed in 1869. If people couldn't come to the shows in his building, he would take the building's shows, as circuses, to them via train. The immobilized Number Seventeen home of no life becomes the mobile choo-choo in the world of this film.

That barreling train and bus, life-sized and with obvious miniatures, are where the true suspense of this picture is focused. Shot with the loud clacking of rails alternating with a careening bus, the chase is more than worth the price of admission. The wind rushes past so much faster than the one that blew the man's hat in the beginning, and smoke billowing out of the train's exhaust helps make this fifteen-minute scene dizzyingly thrilling. I counted some 200 edits from the moment the villains clamber aboard at the film's forty-seven–minute mark throughout the fever pitch build that leads to its crash.

Waltzes from Vienna **(1933)**

And only when our ersatz hero Brant (Donald Calthrop) saves Nora (Anne Grey) from drowning does Hitchcock finally allow a sense of humanity to settle in to this object-driven, funhouse rollercoaster of a film.

Waltzes from Vienna (1933)

> [Schani Strauss'] inner life is expressed in musical terms: going round the bakery where he is under pressure to work, he "hears" the rhythms of the making and packing of the bread translating themselves into music. The gradual elaboration of this into the performance of the completed [Blue Danube] waltz is rather like the way the music will operate in *Rear Window*, with the progressive composition of the piece "Lisa" by the songwriter across the courtyard [Barr, 1999, p. 129].

Where there is smoke at the start of this film, there is no fire, as the weak efforts of a brigade to pump water up a ladder sputter to a trickle. No worries, for the source of all their concern is merely someone smoking a huge pipe, oblivious to the hubbub.

All the set pieces of this film show us workers rushing about as if they were actual pieces of a chess set (shades of the start of *Rich and Strange*). Musicians march back and forth in front of a bakery, waiters move all the tables covered with food outdoors in an effort to save everything from the false alarm, and half-naked girls with layers of undergarments on display scurry without shame from room to room. They lose further articles of clothing as if they were dolls or mannequins; it is clear that the director's heart was not in this film for even the objects to come alive.

Music does play a part as if *it* were a character, however. Might Hitchcock have seen the previous year's film *Love Me Tonight*, with music by Richard Rodgers and Lorenz Hart, smartly directed by Rouben Mamoulian? It's quite possible, for Hitchcock's treatment of Schani Strauss composing "The Blue Danube" pays homage to one of its songs.

Hitchcock's Objects as Subjects

In the 1932 film, Rodgers and Hart's early popular classic "Isn't It Romantic?" evolves similarly by starting in a tailor shop with Maurice Chevalier's character beginning the song, which is then taken up by another patron who leaves the store and enters a taxi cab humming the tune. The cab driver picks it up and it develops its themes and verses via transfer to soldiers on a train, men marching in a field, gypsies at their camp, and ending with Chevalier's eventual love, Jeanette MacDonald, in a castle far, far away, completing the song in her operatic soprano. Not averse to shamelessly borrowing ideas, Hitchcock was always up on the latest cinematic innovations, and Rodgers and Hart's work on their Hollywood film predated even the Fred Astaire and Ginger Rogers 1930s pictures at RKO studios which themselves used songs—and, of course, dance—to seamlessly move the stories along.

The Man Who Knew Too Much (1934)

> But the point I was trying to make is that from the very outset the contrast between the snowy Alps and the congested streets of London was a decisive factor. That visual concept had to be embodied in the film [Hitchcock; cited in Truffaut, 1967, p. 61].

Hitchcock was often quoted as saying that the first *Man* was the work of a talented amateur and the second a true professional, but it is clear right from the start that he was, for once, underrating himself (or just fibbing). Compared to his boredom with and paltry inclusion of them in *Waltzes from Vienna*, this film is literally brimming with objects as subjects. For example, at the one minute thirty second spot and lasting exactly thirty seconds, a vertigo-inducing crowd scene, wholly without dialogue and comprised of fourteen expertly edited shots, is brilliant in its execution. As usual with his manipulation of crowds, it establishes the power onscreen of the mindless masses to control our sympathies, even thoughts.

1. In extreme long shot, a ski jumper races towards us;
2. In medium long shot, we see a crowd looking "screen left";

The Man Who Knew Too Much (1934)

3. Medium close-up of Nova Pilbeam's character, Betty, holding a dachshund close to her chest and looking off "screen right"; in the same shot, the dog squirms out of her hands and drops below the frame;

4. Cut to a medium long shot of her point of view of the dog walking away from the camera onto the snowy track as glimpsed past a sea of the onlookers' legs;

5. Cut to an audacious long shot from *behind* the skier taking off, the crowd far below;

6. Cut to a medium shot of Betty running straight *toward* the camera, the crowd now behind her;

7. Cut to a close-up of the face of the ski jumper, who we will soon learn is the first man who knows too much, Louis Bernard, and he will be killed for that knowledge;

8. Cut to an extreme long shot of the skier falling after his (assumed) landing;

9. Cut to an extraordinary zoom from the extreme long shot through a medium shot and then to a close-up of Betty snatching up the dog and turning to run "screen left";

10. Quick cut to a medium shot of the crowd jumping out of their seats in both fear and fascination as they look "screen left" to follow Betty's movements;

11. Quick cut to a closer shot of the skier tumbling toward the camera with Betty crossing right-to-left in front of his image (which we suddenly realize was a rear-projection);

12. Quick, disorienting cut to the camera's effort to follow Betty's movement as it pans from left to right in a close-up blur of the crowd;

13. Cut to the skier sliding from right to left in a cloud of snow, finally coming to a halt;

14. Cut to a medium shot of Betty gratefully safe back in the crowd.

Almost immediately, at exactly the two-minute mark, we are privy to a thirty-eight–second scene still immersed in the crowd, but it is now full of humorous dialogue, not silent, and the camera remains still. First, as he seems to magically pop up from below the frame, we see the crowd part just enough to *reveal* the often sinister Hungarian actor Peter Lorre as Abbott, the terrorist. At the end of this scene's narrative, the crowd will conceal him again as he becomes reabsorbed into anonymity, exactly as the killer, Ramon (Frank Vosper), near the end of the film, is similarly lost in the crowd when he gives Jill Betty's skier pin to keep her mum.

Fun banter accompanies the narrative's next eight minutes, right up until Louis (French stage and screen actor Pierre Fresnay) is shot, deliberately at odds with the film's very light touch. (*Psycho* was a light comedy, too, until Marion is murdered a half hour in; that film's early murder was beaten to the punch by twenty minutes a quarter-century earlier in this film.)

Objects, or body parts alone—trees, skis, hat and mittens, teeth, hair—carry grave consequences in this short scene. The vertical shafts of tree trunks act as a foreboding barrier to communication (and death) to "Uncle" Louis (and, famously and poignantly, in the late film idyll between Cary Grant and Eva Marie Saint in *North by Northwest* 25 years later). As Bob Lawrence (Leslie Banks in his first of two films for Hitchcock), his daughter Betty (Nova Pilbeam in her first of two) and Louis meanderingly walk left to right, Hitchcock slowly pans with the three of them. Louis becomes separated, having to walk around two trees in his way. And, with skis placed by Hitchcock on Louis' back sticking horizontally out, Betty's hat and wrist mittens likewise show horizontal patterns, bringing them together in close identification via objects. Here, too, is when Betty's comments about Ramon foreshadow his villainy through reference to him having too many teeth and greasy hair. The name G. Barbor, on the dentist's grotesque three-dimensional sign, shocks with its oversized teeth, too, and when Ramon is secretly hidden in a late crowd scene, if we look fast, we can still identify him by his hair alone.

The next crowd sequence occurs during the full dress ballroom dance, extending the humorous tone of the film. But, opposite to Hitchcock's way of leavening seriousness with humor, as in *Sabotage*'s oyster discussion in the aquarium, the director injects murder in the subtlest possible way here, audacious in its almost matter-of-fact eruption. Bob has attached Betty's knitting string to Louis' jacket button as the latter dances around the room with Jill, slowly unraveling to create a labyrinthine knot that runs through the hoi polloi. Suddenly, but in a way that hardly registers as we giggle along with everyone as they notice

The Man Who Knew Too Much (1934)

the trick, an almost drowned-out-by-the-orchestra gunshot can be heard, followed by a split-second shot of a nearly indiscernible bullet hole in a window. At first, even Jill and Louis ("Oh, look," he says matter-of-factly as he stares down at the spreading blood) act as if nothing has happened. Cut to a long shot of a crowd milling about, nothing visible until Hitchcock finally cuts to a close-up of the window's bullet hole with seven successive pointing fingers circling it. The composition looks like a star, prefiguring the Tabernacle of the Sun iconography to come. Just ten minutes have passed in this highly compressed 75-minute picture.

In close-up, Ramon orders Bob in a hallway to hand over the secret

The Man Who Knew Too Much (1934): As Louis Bernard (Pierre Fresnay) dances with Jill Lawrence (Edna Best) among other dancers on the floor, a thread humorously coiled around his jacket button distracts us from the soon-to-be-heard gunshot that will kill him.

message, and Hitch ever-so-slowly pans back to allow more and more people to crowd the frame. He even has a waiter walk right through the middle of the masses carrying not just a food tray but a whole table, it's that absurd. And when Betty's kidnapping via sleigh ride through the woods is seen screen left to screen right, the earlier foreboding scene with the few trees surrounding her is multiplied tenfold, for she is now stuck with that horrid man with too many teeth and slicked-back hair.

City signs saying "Black and White Scotch Whiskey," "Guinness is good for you," "Sandeman's Port" and "Schweppes Tonic" lead into Bob and Inspector Gibson's (Royal Navy commander and actor George Curzon) discussion back at the Lawrence home, their drinking and smoking (apparently encouraged by the signs!) belying the tension of their wait for the kidnapper's call. The inspector even stops Bob from putting too much soda in his whiskey. And when Gibson and Lawrence discuss the fate of the world, Hitchcock shoots the scene with a portrait of a little girl visible directly between them on the wall, a stand-in for Betty. A phone call transferred to the room shows Bob and his wife also perfectly framing that picture behind them. Hitchcock slowly zooms in but his focus goes blurry as it sharpens on the picture—Betty's stand-in.

When the real uncle, Clive (Hugh Wakefield), and Bob head off to Wapping, Hitchcock cuts to an extreme close-up of an enormous casting of the earlier mentioned sign of oversized teeth—G. Barbor, Dentist. As Bob turns the tables on the dentist with knockout gas, Barbor's struggling hands humorously prefigure the horrific groping of Gromek as he is killed at a real gas oven in *Torn Curtain* thirty-two years later.

Shortly, we see Ramon walk up a darkened stairway to the dentist's office, recapitulation of the lodger's similar ascent in *The Lodger*. The stairs here are no less foreboding. And why is the door to the dentist's office padded, like an insane asylum's room? It takes us a minute to realize that it is meant to muffle any sound of screaming.

Bob's joke in response to Clive's question about the Tabernacle of the Sun followers—"They've probably got nothing on"—is as incongruous as the inside of the building itself: brick walls and rattling chains on gates with tall, pointy spikes. The place looks just like a torture dun-

The Man Who Knew Too Much (1934)

geon where one might expect to see Dr. Frankenstein, or at least Pugsley's rack and electrocution chair from *The Addams Family*.

In a swift cross-cutting telephone scene predating a greatly embellished version in *Dial M for Murder* twenty years later, Hitchcock shoots both Clive and Nurse Agnes (Cicely Oates) separately dialing phones to contact Jill about Albert Hall. Both have distinctly different purposes but are no less suspenseful.

At exactly the fifty-three–minute mark, Hitchcock clouds our vision (and Jill's) yet again with masses of people milling about, this time as patrons enter Albert Hall for the concert. As we (and she) peer through the tangle of bodies around her, shown via several point of view shots from all sides of the crowd, she begins to realize that an important official is in danger.

In a highly charged five-second shot, we first see her from the front in medium distance as she makes up her mind to approach the official, takes a deep breath to steady her nerves, and starts forward towards the camera. Hitchcock surprises us by directing the killer Ramon to walk in front of Jill at the precise moment before this five-second shot is complete, an instant that only allows us to register that *someone* has stepped in front of her, not necessarily Ramon ... unless one rewinds and plays the scene back in slow motion. The next cut is a *reverse shot* of the backs of Jill and this man, further concealing his identity a bit longer (compare to Devlin's introduction in *Notorious*), so that it is a complete shock to see who he is when he turns around and silently hands her, in a quick cut close-up, the little skier pin that Betty wore. No dialogue is needed for our—and her—startled reaction to occur. Hitchcock's pure cinema reveals the power of the mob, as Ramon quickly becomes reabsorbed—just like Abbott in the beginning of the picture—into its anonymous protection. Hitchcock closes the whole Albert Hall entrance scene by cutting back to his patented overhead shot as Jill herself now gets lost in the sea of bodies. (See, also, John and Constance's and Thornhill's escapes, both in Grand Central Station, from *Spellbound* and *North by Northwest*, respectively.)

The attempted murder scene in Albert Hall is a beauty. Medium long shots of Jill with unidentifiable crowd members pressing in all around her alternate with extreme close-up shots of the skier pin in her hand. This montage helps us feel her utter isolation (like Thornhill in the cornfield) in a way that simultaneously lets us experience her sense of impotence, need to act, and feeling of anonymity. The official is shot with an image of a dragon on a banner below him, recalling a similar one above the mantle over Jill's shoulder earlier in the picture, but this one's got sun rays or wings hanging out of its back, reminiscent of the Tabernacle of the Sun diagram.

During the siege scene, Hitchcock's fascination with small details shows a policeman being handed a cup of tea during a crucial moment:

> I did this because I have always found that, in a moment of crisis, a person invariably does something trivial, like making a cup of tea or lighting up a cigarette. A small detail of this sort adds considerably to the dramatic tension of the situation. Experience has taught me that if one detail is inaccurate, one gesture or one line of dialogue illogical, a situation loses its sting [Hitchcock, 1938; cited in Gottlieb, 1995, p. 199].

And, of course, Abbott is found out by his infernal hand watch that always tolled at the wrong time, done in by yet another object as protagonist. "[Abbott] is so identified by his musical Swiss watch that, when Lawrence is searching for him in the hideout-church, his presence can be revealed by the sound of the watch chiming while he is still offscreen" (Weis; cited in Deutelbaum and Poague, 1986, p. 105). Hitchcock once again conveyed essential elements of narrative through strictly visual, and often non-human, means.

The 39 Steps (1935)

> The husband ... is clearly a fanatic, a man who is possessive, jealous, and excessively puritanical. And this trait of his character has a specific bearing on a subsequent development: The wife gives Donat the farmer's coat, and when he is shot at, his life will be saved because the bullet hits the Bible the farmer carried in one of the coat pockets [Hitchcock; quoted in Truffaut, 1967, pp. 66–67].

In *The 39 Steps*, as Hitchcock fans know, there are no thirty-nine steps, for the title and, say, a staircase (or secret treaty) made up of any number of steps, are MacGuffins, that essential yet finally meaningless "character" that drives so many of the director's stories forward. It is

The 39 Steps (1935)

ironic, of course, for while the MacGuffin is "the motor of the plot," says Charles Barr ("Hitchcock: The Early Years," 2000; 2012 *39 Steps* DVD audio commentary), any object that causes the story to move must surely also be a protagonist of sorts, just like any other character with drive who aspires to accomplish a goal. In the context of this book's subject, the MacGuffin itself, then, has a great deal of import. "A code name for a network of spies, a gobbledygook secret formula—the mysterious MacGuffin box is empty" (David Cairns; "Thirty-Nine Steps to Happiness"; 2012 *39 Steps* DVD Criterion booklet essay).

The Music Hall fight sequence at the beginning of the film confirms Hitchcock's treatment of crowds as single mad characters that quickly disrupt any sense of decorum that may have been established. Conversely, the "sheet-covered and strangely barren apartment" (Marian Keane, 1999; 2012 *39 Steps* DVD audio commentary), like the empty house in *Number Seventeen*, reeks of ghosts and lacks any sense of hominess—bereft characters in need of filling. "Misplaced trust in the apparent values of public places (political meeting, music hall, fete) is played off against, this time, more intimate mistrust (between hero and heroine); while the commercial travelers and the crofter's home typify the smaller furtiveness, hypocrisies and ignominies of settled private lives" (Durgnat, 1974, p. 128).

Eyeglasses make an important early appearance as metaphorical characters in this director's oeuvre, Leonard Leff notes in "The Borders of the Possible" (2012 *39 Steps* DVD virtual essay). When Richard Hannay (English film and stage actor Robert Donat) attempts his first of numerous ruses to escape the police by suddenly kissing Pamela (Madeleine Carroll in her first of two Hitchcock films), a total stranger, in the train compartment, "[she] loses her poise [for a moment]. Her glasses convey her intelligence as glasses do for Ingrid Bergman in *Spellbound*, Pat Hitchcock, the director's daughter, in *Strangers on a Train*, and Barbara Bel Geddes in *Vertigo*. The glasses also hint at her vulnerability."

Of course, the most important "objective" character in all of Hitchcock's films, second only to the audience itself, is the camera, stand-in *for* the audience. Marian Keane (from the audio commentary noted above) discusses its value during the lingerie salesmen scene, especially when one of them looks straight into our, and Hannay's, eyes: "In Hitchcock's work, the camera is capable of the kind of vision we impute to the salesmen in that shot. The camera can know who people are, reveal them, unmask them, and expose them. This is another subject of Hitchcock's films from the beginning to the end of his career and, indeed, one of the reasons Hitchcock's films are masterpieces of cinema ... because they reflect on the nature of the camera and what a camera's gaze is."

The characterless (and characteristic) emptiness of Hannay's apartment is recapitulated in the many shots of wide-open Scottish landscapes. No one is truly home in either. Keane again:

> When we fade in on the landscape, the frame's feeling of vacancy is sustained. This is one of the shots in Hitchcock's works where film's capacity to present an inhuman aspect of the world is visible. It's visible not just because no human beings were in that first landscape but the world's inhuman face is visible in the starkness of that landscape, the impenetrability of the earth and the sky. The Mount Rushmore sequence in *North by Northwest* is [also] about this aspect of the world.

Framings in film, like the frames around a painting or the wings of a theater, are also potent forces impacting what lies within. Leff noted their power in the earlier train scenes, particularly when Hannay could not, finally, escape the police, with their "curious combination of liberty and entrapment" (Leff, 2012). Keane, too, identifies a similarly stunning moment right at the end of the Crofter's sequence: "The shot in this sequence that is absolutely critical is a long shot framing of Hannay, Margaret and the Crofter through the up and down bars of the back of the chair. Ironically, this framing hits the screen the moment Margaret tells Hannay it's your chance for liberty. The bars in the frame tell us that there is no freedom" (1999/2012).

Likewise, not only does the Crofter's Bible literally save Hannay's life, by catching a bullet we assume has killed him, but his jacket is metaphorical stand-in for Margaret (Peggy Ashcroft), the Crofter's wife:

> In a final gesture Margaret gives Hannay her husband's overcoat because Hannay's jacket is "so terrible light." [The coat, of course, holds the Bible, which has the most ironic of inscriptions within it: "To John from Margaret: The Lord bless thee and keep thee, Easter 1928."] The coat provides an image of her protectiveness, her desperate need to care for someone [Silet; cited in Deutelbaum and Poague, 1986, p. 113].

Secret Agent (1936)

***The 39 Steps* (1935):** The foregrounded chair stands in for the emptiness of the crofter (John Laurie) and his wife Margaret's (Peggy Ashcroft) marriage, as well as a possible entrapment for Richard Hannay (Robert Donat).

The 39 steps lead nowhere, for they are inconsequential and, frankly, non-existent. But they do bring Hannay and Pamela together by the end of this film, so they must have done something right.

Secret Agent (1936)

The howling dog rhymes off the long, single note that the dead organist projects. Ashenden's and Elsa's guilt at Caypor's death will be expressed by the whirling music of the coin, growing into a shrill metallic scream. Beside these pure expressions by noise, man's mere civilized vocabulary seems feeble indeed [Yacowar, 1977, p. 200].

The empty coffin that opens *Secret Agent* recalls the vacant homes that housed not even furniture in *Number Seventeen,* and nothing but ghosts in Hannay's *39 Steps* flat. As R (precursor to 007's Q) tells Ashenden about whom he's got to kill and why, Hitchcock fills the foreground with oversized piles of papers, subliminally imprinting upon us a sense of the inhuman(e) determination (translation: politics) behind such acts. Actor Sir John Gielgud's Edgar Brodie/Richard Ashenden walks left to right, crossing behind a blinding lamp that first hides, then highlights, his response. (See, also, Devlin's and Scottie's similar walks in *Notorious* and *Vertigo,* respectively.)

Speaking of lamps, dual ones frame Ashenden's failed attempt to shake hands with R (Charles Carson) after their meeting on a stairway landing, as well as his anticipated introduction to his "wife" as he hurries down a Swiss hotel hall—objective symmetry first thwarting, then prefiguring relationships. The next inanimate object to "talk" to characters in this film—first in German and then, translated via a wash, in English—is a bar of chocolate unwrapped by a long-bearded, pipe-smoking old gentleman, who subsequently throws the sweet and inner wrapping away to reveal a warning note about spies.

Once in the casino, Hitchcock shoots the massive hall filled with people in such long shots that he makes it difficult for us to spot anyone easily—his signature use of crowds, but this time in a wider context. The distance of the masses from the camera in this shot keeps us from getting close to our lead couple, Ashenden and Elsa (Madeleine Carroll, in her second of two Hitchcock films), and also imparts a sense of emotional and psychical distance between them. Pushing the intimacy of interloper Robert Marvin (Robert Young playing against type, we will find out) with her instead, Hitchcock shoots Marvin and Elsa in close-up, whether they're standing still or in motion. Again, it is the camera's proximity, through both placement and zoom-in, which helps determine our feelings. Note, too, the direction of movement of Marvin and Elsa—screen left to right—which will be reversed in a later scene.

In order to incriminate Caypor (Percy Marmont in his second of three pictures for Hitchcock), Marvin assertively associates a lost but-

Secret Agent (1936)

ton with Caypor's jacket which, from the distance of our view—and also Marvin's, for Hitchcock has worked assiduously to get us to subjectively identify with him up to this point—must have been nearly impossible to identify. Caypor's dog rushes in with its ubiquitous warning bark.

Implicating not only Ashenden and Elsa but ourselves, the plot to finagle Caypor into guiding the general (a brilliantly eccentric Peter Lorre, in his second of two films for Hitch) up a mountain (to be murdered) is punctuated by Hitchcock's filming of Ashenden's hand snuffing out a cigarette in extreme close-up. Elsa's thrilled response to Caypor being taken in by the false bet between Ashenden and the general is likewise squelched by the taut comment Ashenden makes to Elsa as they waltz: "Oh, I know it's war and it's our job to do it but it doesn't prevent it from being murder, does it? Simple murder. And all you can see in it is fun." The sickeningly vertiginous pull of the music and dancers swirl about them. In other words, we can literally feel all the whirling bodies turn Elsa's good humor into genuine shame, a powerful turn of events.

After Caypor's death, mercifully done offscreen—but no, worse, in our minds, as the director wanted—and with his howling dog's prescient cry still echoing in our ears, Hitchcock cranks up the annoying music of the Oktoberfest-style, accordion-and-bell calliope tune on the soundtrack in order to grate on our nerves further. The next yodeling song, accompanied by the increasingly louder sound of a coin circling in a ceramic bowl, physically makes Elsa sick, and it works on us, too.

Yet another translated note tells us what we dare not hope to hear: "You are after wrong man—look elsewhere." Now we *are* sick, as Hitchcock cuts to the button that Marvin identified earlier swirling in close-up via double exposure with the coin in the bowl. "In the director's world, people often live and die by using objects as extensions of their ... identities" (1982, p. 65), says Elizabeth Weis, in her estimable *Silent Scream*.

Just as a third increasingly annoying song begins, Hitchcock doesn't back off on his pressure by showing Elsa leave the crowd in a dolly of extraordinary energy. The scene starts in an extreme long shot from high above to a pull back and pan left. Our sentiments are so attuned to her vertigo that Hitchcock can keep the camera at a distance now, another typically effective cinematic trick of his, and this tracking shot movement from right to left is a bitter-tasting, complete reversal of her earlier lighthearted extreme long shot entrance left to right with Marvin in the casino.

The burgeoning love story between Elsa and Ashenden is perhaps the most complicated Hitchcock has ever put on camera. Her confession of love from the start of their meeting is sorrowfully leavened with her obviously ironic account of "love" for the Swiss and hatred of murder and murderers, a real change of her feelings about war. Anticipating Devlin's struggle between love and patriotic honor during the post–World War II *Notorious* ten years hence, Hitchcock's prescience of that pending war, here in 1936 by looking back to a World War I story, is as unnerving and uncanny as Caypor's wailing dog. Sealed with a kiss, the lovers' smiles and laughter the next morning still catch in our throat, their jokey banter not able to break free from the gallows mood built up so inexorably before this scene.

And, of course, the jokes can't last. After the general pulls Ashenden away one last time to the secret German spy building, a chocolate factory, Elsa cuts up their resignation note with her scissors into a spiral shape, foreshadowing the spiral staircase the general must climb at the factory in order to retrieve yet another secret note. Saved by a crowd, Ashenden and the general escape in successively distant long shots of the huge building. "The crowd of assembly-line workers is suddenly turned into a panicking stampede, and this temporarily prevents the would-be arresters of Ashenden and the general from entering the building. Thus the transformation of order to chaos has been used to their advantage" (Weis, 1982, p. 66).

Their accomplice, punched by the general as he tries to reveal the real spy's name, hands them one final note that needs no translation this time, its last word telling us what we need to know, and may have guessed already: Marvin. Of course, Hitchcock will share yet another of his black humors as Marvin hands Elsa a photo of himself with a dastardly moustache drawn on his upper lip and signed, "To the Heroine from the Villain." Truer words were never written.

On an escaping train, the incessant crowds of passengers and soldiers all push in on our heroes, while the frames of the cabins and passageways increase their claustrophobic pressure. Like the earlier coin in the bowl, louder and louder military songs on the soundtrack grate on our nerves. And, in a brilliant bit of anthropomorphizing of the train, if we listen closely as Elsa walks ahead of Marvin "through the train where Ashenden and the general are hiding, [we and she] seem to hear the wheels saying, 'Save Ashenden!'" (Leitch, 1991, p. 98).

Through even tighter hordes of soldiers and smoke, Marvin shortly takes her from Ashenden and the general in their 1A-numbered cabin to move screen right to screen left; again, this movement shot reverses the direction of their intimate moments back in the casino. In much the same way we feel at the end of *Blackmail*, when Alice goes free and the jester laughingly points at her, the *deus ex machina* of R's strafing planes saves us from ever finding out if Elsa could actually pull a gun's trigger. Both objects, planes and painting, sustain their respective ambivalent endings in our minds.

Hitchcock shows Gielgud's hands in extreme close-up profile going for Marvin's throat. The next shot jumps to a close-up of Marvin staring straight into our eyes, Robert Young's handsome face never before or since in this film placed in such a hand-made noose. And the only murder we ever see is by Marvin immediately after we start to feel sorry for him, Hitchcock ever ambiguous with our sentiments (precursor to our feelings for Willie in *Lifeboat*), as he shoots the general in cold blood, then dies himself. An often maligned film due to its complexity, *Secret Agent* remains one of my favorites for that very reason, rewarding multiple viewings.

Sabotage (1936)

[Joseph] Conrad [1857–1924] called the London of the novel, quote "a cruel devourer of the world's light," as it certainly becomes in Sabotage.... Hitchcock sets much of [the film] in narrow corridors, dusty back rooms, and darkened surroundings. This dark, transitional area separates the public from the private lives of the Verlocs. Spatially, it reminds us of Winnie, who, in various ways, will soon find herself betwixt and between [Leonard Leff; 2007 *Sabotage* DVD audio commentary].

Hitchcock's Objects as Subjects

The source for this film *Sabotage*, Joseph Conrad's *The Secret Agent*, should not be confused with Somerset Maugham's 1928 novel *Ashenden; Or, the British Agent*, upon which Hitchcock's previous year's film, *Secret Agent*—without the word "The"—was based. I trust that explanation clears things up.

Sabotage opens with a close-up and then a long shot of a single light bulb, and a long shot of London's lights, all meant to illuminate. But sabotage, we soon realize, will make all of the lights in this film flicker and blink out. When the city does goes dark, we see a man in close-up demand his money back from the Bijou theater. He is wearing glasses so thick that he rapidly blinks his eyes in an effort to make himself heard. Like both light and sight, even sound fails to work in these circumstances, the director seems to be telling us. We are shown, in typical Hitchcock fashion, the sheep that make up London crowds as they blindly press in around this bespectacled man, his near-sightedness embodying the mob's senseless quality. Hitchcock unrelentingly pounds home that meaninglessness by having our current hero, sergeant-in-disguise Ted Spencer (admirably played by John Loder in his only Hitchcock picture), double-talk the heck out of the crowd via screenwriter Charles Bennett's clever dialogue: "[A]n act is defined as any activity activated by actual action.... You didn't know that, did you? You're all ignorant." And blind. And in the dark.

Even though Hitchcock tips us off that Viennese actor Oscar Homolka's Mr. Verloc is feigning sleep and alarm when his wife, Winnie (American actress Sylvia Sidney), shines her flashlight on him, our sensibilities are curiously heightened by the director's close-up of his face in "fright," eyes ablaze and wide. This stunning stare-back at us, as if he were already caught red-handed as the saboteur, highlights the fact that he *is* the saboteur. An authoritative subjectivity is bestowed upon Winnie's flashlight as Hitchcock suddenly cuts to Verloc's point of view, the flashlight's rays now blinding *us*.

Withholding views, lack of illumination, and the inability to see via actual blindness or idiocy suffuse this dark, pre-noir, and strongly Expressionist film. Hitchcock scholar Leonard Leff's quote at the top of this chapter properly characterizes the narrative by quoting author Joseph Conrad from his original source book, *The Secret Agent* (1907). In other words, the city's dark surroundings and interiors become pal-

Sabotage (1936)

pable protagonists that insistently bear down on the film's characters. Hitchcock himself, in the famous February 12, 1963, interview by fellow film director Peter Bogdanovich, stated that "when I get a locale—and this is a very important thing in my mind—it must be used dramatically" (2007 *Sabotage* DVD interview excerpts).

Elsewhere, Hitch deliberately hinders our vision of the movie screen in the Verloc Theater throughout all the actions in Disney's "Who Killed Cock Robin?" scene, affording at best glimpses of its corners, sections, or behind-the-screen shots. (Recall similar obfuscation of our view via crowds in, especially, *The Ring* and first *Man Who Knew Too Much*.) Outside, in the ticket booth, frames and framing devices not confined to the theater's movie screen include two burning candles on the counter like an altar, lighting Sidney's glowing face. Perhaps they are a symbolic portent of her innocent younger brother Stevie's coming murder. Similarly, the zoo's two fish aquariums are starkly visible in a scene shortly, split down the middle by the dark line of the tanks' shared wall. In medium distance as filmed from behind the conspirators, the aquariums brightly backlight them. "Because it is a source of destruction, the sea (or here, its miniature, the aquarium) is an image of the chaotic in life. It recurs in almost every Hitchcock film" (Spoto, 1976, p. 60).

Leavening the seriousness of the proceedings, as Hitchcock often does during high intensity moments, another man with thick glasses (prototype for the 1980s nerd?) appears in the same scene explaining the sex life of oysters to his sweetie. Screenwriter Bennett's funny banter continues: "This bivalve's rate of fertility is extremely high. After laying a million eggs, the female oyster changes her sex." The girl harrumphs, "I don't blame her."

As with all of Hitchcock's villains, Homolka's Verloc remains an ambiguous, torn, and ever contradictory individual never wholly certain of his dark calling. Hitchcock, however, will not let him escape his fate. At one point, he directs the actor to try to walk through a revolving door the wrong way—replete with bars on its windows looking not unlike a jail cell. The image recalls the ignorant sheep he only recently put in the dark.

I've never seen a cowering cow before, and I never hope to see one, but we soon are privy to two small ceramic table figurines of a boy

Sabotage (1936): Two burning candles on the altar-like ticket booth counter frame Winnie Verloc's (Sylvia Sidney) glowing face.

and a girl standing next to two bovines. Are shepherds watching their fields of flock? As Verloc moves into the frame from screen left, the cows and children seem to stare at him wonderingly to ask: "What will you do now? How will you carry out your next act of sabotage?" Their sense of guilelessness, and young Stevie's, become doubly insinuating at the one instant Verloc loses his composure. Jumping up from the (false) security of his ubiquitous comfy chair, he screams at Stevie while a cherub's face within a circular portrait on the wall blankly gazes back at us over the older man's shoulder. Shortly, when Ted learns of the explosion that kills Stevie, that same little cherub is seen in the background perfectly centered between Verloc and Winnie, its inscrutably inexpressive, dare one say *objective* face blamelessly looking back at us and them.

Blowing Stevie up had to be done in accordance with the story, Hitchcock admitted, but the inanimate-until-detonated bomb holds

Sabotage (1936)

within it all of the screen characters' and audience's emotions. The lead-up to its explosion is done via typically visceral Hitchcockian editing.

> Among the bits and pieces [of the exploding bus montage] are the close-ups of the bomb, which Hitchcock composed and shot from different angles [via a total of ten different shots]. He did so, he said, to "animate the bomb. If I'd shown it constantly from the same angle, the public would have become used to the package. Oh well, it's only a package, after all. But what I was saying was, 'Be careful. Watch out!'" [Leonard Leff; 2007 DVD *Sabotage* audio commentary].

As with the lamp bulbs and city lights and cow figurines and city streets, the bomb had become, in Hitchcock's hands, an animate and powerful protagonist, a character in its own right.

When Verloc tries to argue his way out of his eventual murder at the hands of his wife, Hitchcock shoots him in medium close-up directly between and behind two powerfully symbolic objects—a delicate glass pitcher and Stevie's model sailboat. They certainly represent, respectively, the breakable crystal that is Winnie's heart and the dreamer that was her baby brother. Homolka gets up and saunters over to the boat as Hitchcock slowly pans in to a tighter two-shot. "What's done can't be undone," he exclaims, quickly swinging his right hand sideward and jarring the craft nearly off its perch. Moving in front of the boat and blocking Winnie's view of it, its sails stand taller, nevertheless, and catch the camera's (and her) eye.

> Thanks to the camera, the public is now actually living the scene, and if that camera should suddenly become distant and objective, the tension that's been created would be destroyed. Verloc stands up and walks around the table, moving straight toward the camera, so that the spectator in the theater gets the feeling that he must recoil to make way for him. Instinctively, the viewer should be pushing back slightly in his seat to allow Verloc to pass by [Hitchcock; cited in Truffaut, 1967, p. 80].

Just when Verloc realizes he will, *must* be killed, Hitchcock directs him to open his eyes wide again, just like when he had feigned surprise early in the picture, the bright flashlight in his eyes. The shot is the same, but this time, his alarm is real. In this scene, like other body parts such as hands and legs, "the eyes do not so much watch in *Sabotage* as act. So they are in harmony with, rather than alternatives to, the hands. There are many close-ups of Verloc's hands, dirty, being cleaned, twisting in nervous anxiety.... In the climactic murder scene Hitchcock alternates shots of the eyes and shots of the hands, by whose action the mood and the mind are expressed" (Yacowar, 1977, p. 215).

And, as Verloc moves toward his missus and enters her frame, we can just make out those querulous cow and children figurines again splitting the screen in the background. The knife on the table, too, has a subjective potency unrivalled since *Blackmail*: "Sylvia is unable to control herself. At the dinner table her hand returns to the carving knife, to serve the cabbage, to serve the potatoes, as if the hand—or the knife—had her will under control" (Yacowar, 1977, p. 207).

Right after Winnie stabs her husband and he falls to the ground out of sight below screen, Hitchcock allows the little cherub's portrait on the wall in the distance to briefly supplant him. Two songbirds chirp in their cage on the dresser beneath the portrait, harking back to Alice's bedroom birds in *Blackmail* and prefiguring, of course, the two love birds in *The Birds*.

Is it a coincidence that in the one shot where Winnie leans her head on Ted, right at the end of the film, a sign against the wall behind them reads "Health"? Revealingly, we see that Winnie's "shiftings alternately change the message from 'health' to 'heal'" (1988, p. 55), Lesley Brill rightly notes. By the end of this emotionally packed thriller, we can only hope the sign will prove correct on both counts.

Young and Innocent (1937)

> Again, the sea and its atmosphere are ambiguous, multileveled in symbolism. The sea is an image of the unconscious, the source of forces that are life-giving and death-dealing. It is in Hitchcock's work the source of chaos—and at the same time an image of potential wholeness and reconstitution [Spoto, 1976, p. 70].

In addition to the sea as noted above by Spoto, the motif of crowds is aggressively forwarded in this film (as begun in *The Lodger* and continuing through *Murder!* and *Sabotage*), as are jail bars and eyeglasses. The latter will be treated in very funny ways this time, contrary to

Young and Innocent (1937)

Hitchcock's ironic use of them in *Sabotage* and their cruel reflective quality in the upcoming *Strangers on a Train* (1951).

Prior to these images, however, the first scene in *Young and Innocent* reveals a bright lamp separating an arguing husband (George Curzon in the second of three Hitchcock films, as the eye-twitching drummer Guy) and his wife (Pamela Carme), the short-lived Christine Clay. Almost immediately, a brightly lit wood beam centered behind them more forcefully "splits" them apart. This vertical separation device—objects radically breaking connections, either through the camera's action, suggesting a protagonist's movement, or their physical proximity—will be recapitulated in humorous ways throughout the film by, respectively, a bedpost, a water fountain gone berserk, and a sculpture of a woman holding the scales of justice, of all things.

After Christine slaps Guy, the final catalyst leading to her strangulation by his hands, a number of similarly violent, linear images of objects quickly appear on the screen, portents of many threats to come: vertical iron bars on their front door; the downpour of raindrops outside; metal guard rails that frame the front deck of their house (which overlooks a cliff high above crashing waves on sea rocks); and a spider web shadow on the windows. Lesley Brill rightly notes that the "thunder, lightning, and crashing waves outside echo the shouting of the enraged man and woman" (1988, p. 45).

At the six-minute mark, actor Derrick De Marney's character Robert Tisdall, already assumed guilty of the crime, is framed by high windows with bars on them, more dangerous vertical lines. When he passes out from excessive and ridiculous questioning (law enforcers in Hitchcock's world are *always* incompetent, impotent, or both), he is seen slumped in front of a chair with vertical wooden slats on its back. In fact, all the windows in this film have bars on them, and are often shot with Hitchcock's patented German Expressionist, pre-noir lighting. Such imagery will recur with tremendous force in, particularly, *The Paradine Case*.

Tisdall's barrister Mr. Briggs is played by a typically spot-on British character actor—another Hitchcock signature—J.H. Roberts. He spills coffee on his own Coke-bottle glasses (shades of *Sabotage*, and prefiguring their use in *Suspicion*, *Spellbound*, and *Strangers on a Train*, among others), confirming his inability to literally and figuratively see anything. (Later, the Grand Hotel front desk woman neatly bookends the picture by wearing similarly limiting frames.) Stealing Briggs' glasses, Robert humorously fakes everyone out as a nerd in disguise, adopting the stereotype of banging into things. "Eyeglasses also suggest [the fragility] of ordinary perception ... because they are so often broken or mislaid in Hitchcock's films and because disastrous actions usually accompany or are related to their breaking" (Spoto, 1976, p. 72).

Crowd Scene #1: Two cops, two "hysterical," falsely accusing women, and numerous onlookers mill about the murdered actress on the beach, establishing early on their subjective power to confuse. The director always shoots these shots in ways that make spotting the films' main protagonists next to impossible. Forced to contend with the confounding nature of masses pressing in like sardines, we are intentionally made to feel bewildered and adrift.

Even though Erica Burgoyne (Nova Pilbeam in her second of two Hitchcock films) is the only one in her family who knows how to start their hand-cranked classic car, she cannot get it to kick in until her sixth try, and only when our now handcuffed hero walks by and shoots her a sardonic but clever line. Later, it only starts up when he cranks it; even the car has a cranky attitude.

Just before the fifteen-minute mark, Crowd Scene #2 occurs over a swift twelve-second, six-cut montage. Tisdall escapes both his captors (and us) so quickly that Hitchcock barely allows us time to spot how it's done; only rewinds reveal the ruse. We are meant to feel as befuddled as Detective Inspector Kent (actor John Longden).

During both family dinners in the Burgoyne household, there is a clever use of two crossed swords displayed prominently and forebodingly over the mantle behind Erica. The second time, they accentuate her struggle to help Robert, for Hitchcock dollies back for a full twenty seconds in a way that keeps her head looking "pierced" by them! Also during the second dinner, the top of her father's empty chair looks like bars over which we see Erica, another powerfully restraining image.

When the escaping couple arrives at the Tom's Hat truck stop, that wacky water fountain mentioned earlier can be seen convulsively spurting up and down in the background for twenty seconds behind Erica's head, a rhythmic recapitulation, for the same amount of time, of the earlier swords-through-the-head scene.

Young and Innocent (1937)

And, at the film's thirty-six-minute mark, Crowd Scene #3 occurs, a very funny knock-down, drag-out fight. Robert pushes hard past the rabble to get into a café to save Erica, only to spy her suddenly at the same time we do, miraculously back outside. Again, the great unwashed have purposefully clouded our vision. We will feel equally lost in the ballet crowd during Michael and Sarah's attempted escape in *Torn Curtain* three decades on.

A frequently used mirror motif from *The Wrong Man* is prefigured briefly when Robert steals into Erica's bedroom. As she walks "screen left" toward her bed, one vertical bedpost visually separates them in medium shot as the new "married" couple in the film, supplanting in the positive the earlier bickering, murderous spouses.

And the justly famous crane shot, which pans in for a full 145 feet

Young and Innocent (1937): As a passerby looks on, Erica Burgoyne (Nova Pilbeam) comforts Robert Tisdall (Derrick de Marney) above a water fountain that had recently gone berserk.

over a 70-second period to stop in an extreme, almost uncomfortable close-up of Guy's twitching eyes, prefigures the fourth and final Crowd Scene in the Grand Hotel at the end of the film. With this extraordinary camera movement, Hitchcock "strips away the glamour and the joy by focusing in on an object of private concern and terrible tension ... the drummer's right eye" (Yacowar, 1977, p. 227). Immediately after that unnerving extreme close-up, Hitchcock pulls the camera back for *exactly half the time of the famous crane in*—thirty-five seconds—staying high above the dancing hordes in a similarly concealing way as his crowd close-ups, but now we must look ever more closely to maintain our connection to the heroes. With this pull-back, "the camera takes on an unpitying nature, as its own order remains untouched by the madness of the sufferer" (Yacowar, 1977, p. 229). The two Hitchcock scholars on the 2008 *Young and Innocent* DVD audio commentary, Stephen Rebello and Bill Krohn, properly remark upon this visual challenge the director sets up: "And so much less noticeably we have the pull back and still the question: 'They're all the way back here. Are they going to notice? Are they going to see his eyes? Are they going to realize who he is?'"

In fact, Old Will the tramp (played by scene-stealer Edward Rigby) hammers Rebello and Krohn's point home: "I can't see nothing with all these people crowding about." The shot is also "an important incident in Hitchcock's continuing obsession with the eye, with sight, with the ambivalence of watching.... It goes back to the unseeing, all-seeing eye of the gods in the British Museum in *Blackmail*, indeed back to the spying in *The Ring* and *The Lodger*, back to the monocle of *The Pleasure Garden*" (Yacowar, 1977, p. 230).

Body parts, once again, stand in for the entire person. Conversely, it is the swarm of bodies as one objective unit, noted above, that helps the camera corral, and befuddle, our attention.

The Lady Vanishes (1938)

> [I]t's memorable because of the speed and elegance with which Hitchcock tears through the strained machinations

The Lady Vanishes (1938)

of the plot, using the forward motion of the train—symbolized by those spinning wheels—to represent the barreling progress of his story [Mike Hale, "One Disappears, the Other Delves," Retrieved on August 16, 2013; http://tv.nytimes.com/2013/08/16/arts/television/the-lady-vanishes-on-pbs.html?ref=arts].

As inconsequential as it always is, the MacGuffin of this film turns out to be, uniquely, a musical tune, one that can be heard over the opening credits and then, straight through to the end. While not an object per se, the fanciful little song nevertheless drives the narrative forward faster than a speeding locomotive.

> [Music] is a centerpiece to the plot. Listen to the tune that we're hearing [over the credits]. That music is going to be important even though we don't know it yet and won't learn why it's worth killing two people over for almost 100 minutes [Bruce Eder; 2007 *Lady Vanishes* DVD audio commentary].

Hitch will have his little double entendres, both narrative and visual, for in the beginning of the film, sexual innuendos between Charters (thoroughly British Basil Radford) and Caldicott (Welsh-born Naunton Wayne) are visually punctuated by Iris Henderson (actress Margaret Lockwood at the top of her game) in her lingerie atop a table squatting and then jumping over a magnum bottle of champagne. Simultaneously toasting and bemoaning her pending nuptials directly to the camera while two half-naked female friends frame her, Hitchcock directs the hotel attendant to place piles of food before them on a foregrounded table. Large and looming metaphors, the food stands in for all the consumption that Iris has been spoiled by her whole life (as well as more than hinting at real sexual hunger). Masses of food will be similarly treated during Pengallan's orgiastic feast early in the next film, *Jamaica Inn*, and play in humorous counterpoint to Mr. and Mrs. Oxford as late as 1972's *Frenzy*. Likewise,

> along the way certain [other] things underscore the sense of danger and menace: things like staircases, handcuffs, keys, dizzying heights and, or so we assume, spiked brandies. Eyeglasses belong on that list, and so do birds, which in one movie could appear on the periphery of the frame or in passing, and in another movie assume center stage [Leonard Leff; "Mystery Train"; 2007 *Lady Vanishes* DVD audio commentary].

The Lady Vanishes (1938): Champagne and food brought by the hotel waiter (unknown actor) serve to distract Iris Henderson (Margaret Lockwood) and her friends Blanche (Googie Withers) and Julie (Sally Stewart) from thinking about real relationships.

Just like the songs and sounds of Switzerland that messed with our heads in *Secret Agent*, this film's train tracks and cars racing by, whistles, electric wires overhead, and staring strangers all conspire to make Iris (through her irises) dazedly mesmerized in a nightmare world that lasts a full six minutes of the film.

> In *Lady Vanishes*, [Hitchcock] uses the train setting to create a very naturalistic tension. The movements of the characters are dictated by the setting in which they're trapped. The noise of the train makes it hard to hear each other and makes the characters tired as they have to speak in louder voice and listen more attentively. They're always walking a bit awkwardly and bumping into each other as they move through cars [Bruce Eder; 2007 *Lady Vanishes* DVD audio commentary].

It is not until Gilbert (Sir Michael Redgrave in his only Hitchcock film) spots the Harriman's Tea label that Iris had sworn she had seen

The Lady Vanishes (1938)

stick briefly to a window does the director finally use a shot of the zooming train in a *positive way*, punctuating a turning point in their relationship through their teamwork search for Miss Froy. Shot in one of the few points of view during the film from its right side, the train now resounds with *our* right and proper, hopeful attitude as well.

> Fortunately, nature—or Fate—or accident—or God—or the physical world in all its healthy intransigence—conspires to lend a check to the nightmare of cold psychology. A signature in dust on a window and a flapping tea wrapper renew Iris's confidence in her own sanity and keep her from the vertiginous maelstrom of herself and her self-doubt [Yacowar, 1977, p. 244].

There is not much more to this film other than a rip-snorting train and car chase (*à la* the end of *Number Seventeen*), one that barrels along on the prolific screenwriting of Frank Launder and Sidney Gilliat's brilliantly crisp, witty script. Hitchcock does a neat play with extra-large, foreboding wine glasses at one point, highlighting the (supposed) narcotic placed in them that is meant for our protagonists.

> [The] scene where the hero and heroine are served drugged drinks is pure suspense. [Instead] of creating suspense in the usual way by having the hero half raise the glass to his lips and lower it again and never quite get down to drinking it, I did it by cinematic means. I had the glasses served and left on the table while the two go on with their conversation. But I still had to make the audience ask "When are those glasses going to be picked up?" So I photographed the whole dialogue through the two glasses in the foreground [Hitchcock, 1950; cited in Gottlieb, 1995, p. 127].

And we feel real fear for Gilbert as he dangerously makes his way outside the train, almost falling into the path of a (realistically backscreened) oncoming one. Uncle Charlie will tumble to his own ghastly death five years hence in a similar scene from *Shadow of a Doubt*. "The train itself can be taken as an emblem for a fantasy speeding uncontrollably through the mind" (Yacowar, 1977, p. 244).

Just after Gilbert shoots back at the Nazis for the first time with a gun, Hitchcock ironically shoots him in profile looking back towards the camera with an art deco poster of two happy people on it waving from the open deck of a steamer or train. The image echoes the better times imagined by some of the reluctant Brits just moments earlier, and could easily represent Ashenden and Elsa on their honeymoon two years after *Secret Agent*.

And notice actress Josephine Wilson's Madame Kummer, Dr. Hartz's evil sidekick. With her ever-present cigarette dangling dangerously out of her fiercely set mouth, Wilson is the spitting image in spades of actress Madame Konstantin's Mrs. Sebastian in *Notorious* eight years later.

Jamaica Inn (1939)

When the movie begins, the ocean as a punishing and impervious character lashes at a ravaged boat that has crashed upon a rocky shore. Masses of murderous pirates pillage the adrift ship, the waters violently washing away any remains of the looted dead.

Shortly, four runaway carriage horses are seen from behind in a medium close-up from the driver's perspective. At the mention of Jamaica Inn, their loud hoofbeats on the soundtrack strike an immediate echo in our minds of the earlier roiling sea, waters that will almost convince the new Mrs. De Winter in the very next Hitchcock film to jump from her window to certain death. Fortunately in this picture, our lovingly lit heroine Mary, played by the gorgeous Irish actress Maureen O'Hara, causes the carriage she is hurling along in to stop, portent of her power later in the film to escape calamity.

Our first shots of Sir Humphrey Pengallan, brilliantly portrayed by the ever eccentric and estimable actor Charles Laughton, are of his verbal trashing of King George IV at a dinner party. Ostentation and artifice are sickeningly on display in oversized foreground as a huge candelabra with four brightly lit candles looms above the proceedings. Toasting "Beauty" itself, Sir Humphrey gloats that a certain figurine on the huge table before them, among all his booty, "is more alive than half the people here." Jewels and portraits and gobs of food and the trappings of overstuffed wealth crowd out the humans in every frame of this scene. Of course, the *most* beautiful object of all, Pengallan notes, is his prized horse Nancy, literally brought into the dining room for all to see. These objects are clearly intended by both Hitchcock and

Jamaica Inn (1939)

Pengallan to be much richer "characters" than the rabble Pengallan has corralled for his amusement.

Wagering a guest that the newly arrived human Mary is uglier than his horse, Pengallan in a two-shot close-up asks the exquisitely lit O'Hara to take off her coat for a better view. Hitchcock cuts to a medium four-shot of Sir Humphrey, Mary, and Chadwick the butler all framing a huge marble bust set on a pedestal. The bust "stands" at exactly the same head height as our heroine, while Pengallan preens two steps lower, looking up at these two "treasures." Upon losing the wager, he flings a bag of coins across the room onto the dinner table, where all the pigs at a trough scurry to scoop up their winnings. The candelabra leers down at them. Rightly, even when we see Pengallan skulking about upstairs later at Jamaica Inn, Hitchcock shoots him surrounded by reams of booty, his only link, false as it is, to real life.

For once—unlike in *Blackmail, Torn Curtain*, and *Sabotage*—a knife saves rather than ends a life in a Hitchcock film. Mary grabs one from a dinner tray and cuts the noose that's nearly lynching our soon-to-be hero Jem Trehearne, played by the English actor Robert Newton. As in *Number Seventeen*, Hitchcock shoots Jamaica Inn as a labyrinth of claustrophobic rooms, all pressing in and nearly squeezing the lives out of the characters. Jem and Mary barely escape.

As if it were the doors of the inn itself, even the wide-open sea is tightly framed by Hitchcock. Foregrounded waves thrashing them about, Trehearne and Mary cling to some rocks in both medium and close-up shots, their pursuers' boat passing perilously close behind. Likewise, tall candles appear to buttress characters throughout this film, anticipating their ubiquitous presence in *Rope* nine years hence. Are they columns through which mere mortals must fight to pass?

Of all things, airborne particles play their part in this film, adding to the tension. "I shall come back when it's blown over," Pengallan promises, a huge gust of smoke from the hearth's fire billowing about the room as exclamation. As the climax approaches, mist from the sea, too, blows in across pounding waves. Hitchcock shoots this late scene from high above, his go-to point of view of impending doom. A gale is blowing again, perhaps even worse than when the picture opened. Even the sound of the wind seems to insinuate itself into the conscience of Aunt Patience (Marie Ney) as Hitchcock cuts to a two-shot of Trehearne tied up, Patience holding a gun on him. A large cask of brandy can be spotted between them, also helping her waver.

During this second storm, Hitchcock lets the waves wash over his camera for a moment at the 70-minute mark, startling the viewer as if we are being washed away. Hitchcock's close-up of hands, so highly charged in films such as *Blackmail* and *Torn Curtain* and *Marnie*, makes its appearance here as Pengallan ties Mary's. (Laughton's same pudgy paws reappear eight years later in his pawing of Gay Keane after dinner in *The Paradine Case*.) We can hear the wind blowing at gale force on the soundtrack as Hitchcock pans in ever so slowly and painfully to an extreme close-up of Laughton's hand on Mary's dark cloak.

The film ends with Pengallan's fall from a huge height. A watching crowd absorbs our couple, Jem and Mary, just as we sense they may be moving toward a relationship, a typical ending (and masses manipulation) for Hitchcock.

Rebecca (1940)

> Manderley is already a prison, as Hitchcock's visuals make clear.... The first shot of the newlyweds eating dinner together begins as a close-up on a napkin embroidered "R de W" before the camera cranes slowly around, up, and back along the length of the table to a point which dwarfs both living de Winters and emphasizes the space between them. The only bedroom the camera lingers on is Rebecca's own, which has the character of a museum or another public place [Leitch, 1991, pp. 113–114].

Hitchcock told many people, including François Truffaut and Peter Bogdanovich, that the house called Manderley was a living character just as important as the actors in *Rebecca*. "[I]n a sense the picture is the story of a house. The house was one of the three key characters of the picture" (Hitchcock; cited in Truffaut, 1967, p. 94). Hitchcock's treatment of houses in *Number Seventeen* and *Jamaica Inn*, and Hannay's apartment in *The 39 Steps*, are true precursors to Manderley in this film, and later to Mrs. Paradine's mansion in *The Paradine Case*.

Rebecca (1940)

Throughout *Rebecca*, extreme long shots of hallways, grand staircases, arches and columns fill the screen while smaller objects within this huge object also loom menacingly everywhere. When Joan Fontaine's character—the new Mrs. De Winter, who is without a first (or last) name of her own, and only referred to as "I" during early narration—enters the house for the first time, she is filmed deliberately dwarfed by its enormous size. Even in her own room, Hitchcock frames objects such as lamps and chairs and flowers crowding up the screen, trying to push her out.

If one looks closely, even the door handles are shot at shoulder height, like in an Alice in Wonderland story. (At one point, Maxim de Winter wonders aloud if his new wife will dress up for their ball as Alice in Wonderland.) As an actress, Fontaine runs with the pressure put on her by this house, giving us a palpable, sympathetic feel for her mousiness and being overwhelmed by it all. Yet, slowly and determinedly, she works to understand the malevolent world of both her husband and housekeeper Mrs. Danvers' (Australian-born actress Dame Judith Anderson) place in it all. A house does not make a home, it's the people who do, and while the film labors under the burden of a search for identity, a frequent theme of the director, the goal for both of the main protagonists is to work on their relationship as part of their growth and maturity. Fontaine's character does finally stand up to Mrs. Danvers once she figures out how the house itself functions in its oppressive way.

Conspicuous consumption is on display right from the start in the Monte Carlo hotel room, a clear allusion to the overkill of objects to come, or what objects *become* (shades of the meaninglessness of money in *Champagne*, or avarice in *Jamaica Inn*). The huge bouquet of flowers that Maxim (an uncharacteristically restrained Laurence Olivier) practically throws in Fontaine's face during his so-called wooing shows his contempt for things. Later, he flings cigarettes and other objects all over the place, shades of Miles Mander's dismissive character all the way back in *The Pleasure Garden*. Mrs. Van Hopper (Florence Bates) drags on a cigarette incessantly, the smoke conspicuously insinuating itself between Olivier's Maxim and Fontaine during their first formal introductory meeting (where there's smoke, there's fire). And, of course, the big reveal near the end of the picture is that Rebecca was not pregnant, as she had claimed, but cancer-ridden and soon to die, most certainly due to smoking, as an ashtray full of her cigarette butts tells us in the sea cottage.

As Mrs. Danvers wails lovingly over Rebecca's (supposedly) charmed life and preserved clothes, Hitchcock shoots Fontaine in front of wall mirrors shaped like fractured triangles or diamonds, shards of Rebecca's past pointedly aimed at her. As "Danny" (the nickname cousin Jack Favell gives Mrs. Danvers) continues on about Rebecca's lingerie on the bed, Fontaine is suddenly seen standing in front of patterned wallpaper covered with so many shadows that her image is nearly lost; the house is that powerful. Heightening the intensity of the housekeeper's jealousy, Hitchcock shoots Danvers like a ghost—a nonhuman object—rarely seen walking and, usually, suddenly materializing beside Fontaine from offscreen. Hanging straight down from her hips during the whole film, Danvers' black dress allows her to walk as if she hovers just above the ground (the model for Morticia in the *Addams Family* TV series?).

> Mrs. Danvers was almost never seen walking and was rarely shown in motion. If she entered a room in which the heroine was, what happened is that the girl suddenly heard a sound and there was the ever-present Mrs. Danvers, standing perfectly still by her side. In this way the whole situation was projected from the heroine's point of view; she never knew when Mrs. Danvers might turn up, and this, in itself, was terrifying. To have shown Mrs. Danvers walking about would have been to humanize her [Hitchcock; cited in Truffaut, 1967, p. 93].

At the climax of her harangue, when Fontaine is wearing the last dress Rebecca had worn, look quick as "I" is seen standing against the same patterned wall. This time, the shot is taken from just around the room's corner, and the wall's designs are even more perfectly aligned with Fontaine's body to absorb her contours.

"You can't fight her," Mrs. Danvers says. "No one got the better of her. Never. Never. She was beaten in the end, but it wasn't a man, it wasn't a woman. It was the sea." Like in *Jamaica Inn*, the first of Hitchcock's three du Maurier adaptations (including *Rebecca* and *The Birds*), here it is also the sea that possesses a powerful, protagonistic character that moves others. (See also *The Manxman, Young and Innocent*, and, of course, *Lifeboat*.) "Listen to the sea. So soothing. Listen to it. Listen.

Rebecca (1940)

Listen to the sea," Mrs. Danvers hypnotically cants, urging Fontaine to jump out of a window. "[The] sea has been a leading motif of the film. But the sea is no home for Rebecca living or dead, since it is eternally in motion and keeps bringing everything to the surface" (Leitch, 1991, p. 115).

Even Maxim wrongly admits to Fontaine that "Rebecca has won. Her shadow has been between us all the time, keeping us from one another." His lament occurs in the little sea cottage where Rebecca died, which is full of real shadows in a film with that word in its title just three years away. As he speaks, a brightly lit lamp hovers over them, centered in the background, spider webs all over it. His confession about Rebecca's unfaithfulness reaches a peak as he sits in front of a huge, empty, and darkened bird cage—this bird had flown. Dead flowers, too, are strewn all around the place, stand-ins for a love that never existed. At one point, the camera slowly moves right to left as if it's the ghost of Rebecca herself, briefly pausing at two vases full of empty branches and a painting of the roiling sea centered behind them on the wall.

Another element from that very sea had actually killed her, Maxim surprisingly reveals: "She'd struck her head on a heavy piece of ship's tackle." "The final solution to the mystery of the wicked and doomed Rebecca is connected with the sea where she was buried, that element of chaos in Hitchcock which finally yields terrible truth" (Spoto, 1976, p. 93).

With Fontaine's loving help, the turning point in this film occurs with a gorgeously shot kiss between Maxim and her framed before a blazing hearth. This kiss seals a more mature love that is, finally, just beginning. It was a long time coming; we were never sure it would actually arrive ... but Hitchcock finally delivers.

Animals, stuffed or alive, curiously play their parts well in this film, too. During Jack Favell's murderous and blackmailing accusations—played to the hilt in full villain form by the estimable George Sanders, who soon would be ingratiatingly charming as another man with a last name beginning with "f," ffolliott—Maxim is frequently shot foregrounding an elk's head on a wall behind him, as if he is a trophy Favell is trying to shoot, stuff and mount. By the end of the film, however, even Jasper the dog has finally accepted Fontaine, patiently sitting in her lap waiting for Maxim to return to Manderley. The house had to burn down to the ground for them to begin to build a home together in their hearts ... the place where any home must start.

Foreign Correspondent (1940)

> When I am given a locale—and this is very important in my mind—it's got to be used, and used dramatically. We're in Holland. What have they got in Holland? Windmills? Tulips? [Alfred Hitchcock; cited in Bogdanovich, 1963, p. 22].

"Clothes do not make the man," sayeth the proverb, although Mark Twain noted, contrarily, "naked people have little or no influence on society." Clothes do not indeed make the man in *Foreign Correspondent*, for our intrepid foreign correspondent Huntley Haverstock (née Johnny Jones, acted by American everyman Joel McCrea in his only Hitchcock film) proceeds to lose hats several times in the film and almost has a hand horribly crushed when his overlong trenchcoat gets caught in windmill machinery. Played mostly for laughs, hats especially wear out their welcome and become real portents of doom.

In yet one more typically choreographed crowd scene, we see the gentle diplomat Van Meer (played by the illustrious, rhythmically vocal Albert Bassermann, justly nominated for an Academy Award), one of two signers of the Dutch Treaty with Belgium, disappear from view in a more startling way than when the lady vanished two years earlier. Hitchcock's edit is so seamlessly discreet that we scarcely notice he's gone from the crowd. Shot first from behind in a medium distance two-shot alongside Haverstock, Van Meer enters a check room filled with other men milling about wearing similar hats and coats. Fixated (deliberately) on the jokiness of the visuals, we humorously watch in a quickly edited close-up as Haverstock reaches to take his own hat off, but it and Van Meer have suddenly vanished. Distracted by recurring jokes like this one about clothing, Van Meer is truly nowhere to be seen in the scene—lost, like a misplaced hat (or umbrella).

Foreign Correspondent (1940)

Cleverly, Hitchcock shows us windmills several times as they flutter their sails in the breeze in a counter-clockwise direction. However, the *clockwise*-moving sails on one of the windmills is hidden in plain sight on screen, and can easily be noticed but only if we really look for it, for once again we are so caught up in the humorously shot car chase that the director knows we won't spot the discrepancy. In Hitchcock's hands, of course, everyday Dutch objects such as these have multiple meanings, for they "contrast between all that a windmill implies of the rustic and the idyllic and the torture-chamber associations of its internal gearing" (Durgnat, 1974, p. 175). Hitch always exploited locations in his stories in ways that gave them as much subjective characteristics as the human characters.

> The windmills, images of Holland's identity and tradition, represent a past of serenity and security. But we discover that they are to be sabotaged by the Nazis because they serve as signals for approaching airplanes. The loud interlocking of cogs and wheels when we go inside them suggest not only the inexorable wheels of fate but also the horrifying destruction of a vulnerable, small country from within [Spoto, 1976, p. 104].

Among a myriad of similar examples, one easily thinks of the extended chocolate factory scene in *Secret Agent*, Mount Rushmore in *North by Northwest*, the Statue of Liberty in *Saboteur*, and in this picture the windmills of Holland and rain and umbrellas of London. Critic Charles Barr rightly observed that the machinery inside *Foreign Correspondent*'s set-piece windmill is truly frightening, creaking with grinding wood sounds and stark shadows straight out of the 1931 film *Frankenstein* (1999, p. 67). As a dangerous protagonist, that machinery almost crushes a body part of our hero, as earlier noted.

Tongue firmly in cheek, Hitchcock himself addressed the protagonistic qualities of such objects in his 1965 "After-Dinner Speech at the Screen Producers Guild Dinner":

> I will admit that I have, from time to time, hoped that technology would devise a machine to replace the actor. And I have made some progress of my own in that direction. In *Foreign Correspondent* Joel McCrea played a scene with a windmill and in *North by Northwest* Cary Grant's *vis-à-vis* was a crop-dusting airplane. I believe the airplane had real star quality, for it drew an amazing amount of fan mail. However, when I

attempted to sign it up for my next picture, it was already asking too much money [cited in Gottlieb, 1995, p. 56].

The versatile British character actor Edmund Gwenn reappears in *Foreign Correspondent* as the Cockney assassin Rowley, his third and most nefarious of four acting jobs for the director (see also *The Skin Game, Waltzes from Vienna* and *The Trouble with Harry*). He lures Haverstock to the top of a London cathedral; our blood runs cold as Hitchcock shows him gently picking up a young boy in medium shot and perilously holding him way out of an unprotected area for a better view of the city. Cut to an extreme long shot overhead of the boy's hat floating down, the director's inimitable mix of humor—a piece of clothing again—and the grotesque never failing to pack a punch to our solar plexus.

"Don't you think you've been talking through your hat?" exclaims Scott ffolliott, actor George Sanders again, but this time in a wholly sympathetic role, unlike his dastardly, leering, and blackmailing cousin from *Rebecca* earlier in the year. (The two small "ff's" at the beginning of his last name had been humorously explained during the earlier car chase.) Haverstock says much the same thing a bit later—"I'm talking through my hat"—when he and Carol Fisher (American actress Laraine Day) seal the deal on their love for each other. Spoto rightly notes that the "hat is also the film's symbol of a facile sense of respectability, which is no real defense in such a time of gathering chaos" (1976, p. 102). Its narrative use in this film recalls the opening of *Number Seventeen* eight years earlier.

Normally, impeccably placed objects in Hitchcock's frames reveal their foreboding nature in a straightforward way, like the lamps in *The Paradine Case* and *Rope* or the staircases in any number of movies. In this film, the director treats lamps in yet one more unique way in order to increase the tension in two specific scenes: Cruel Mr. Krug (Italian baritone and character actor Eduardo Cianelli) and debonair villain Stephen Fisher's (Herbert Marshall in his second of two Hitchcock films) plot to kill Haverstock halfway through the picture and ffolliott's later revelation to Fisher that he kidnapped his daughter.

For both scenes, Hitchcock foregrounds a stack of five books screen left with a screen right 1940s-era black phone and receiver in a way that frames a small porcelain figure on a table raising a cup to

Foreign Correspondent (1940)

toast life—domestic civility personified. But in the first scene, Krug and Fisher are brightly lit by large, obtrusive lamps while the tone of their dialogue is lightly played, their talk all the more sinister because of that contrast. Fisher happily feeds his huge mastiff biscuits out of a tin as Krug delicately reminds him of the existence of the recently retired Rowley, who could easily be hired for Haverstock's murder. (One suspects that Hitchcock had seen the previous year's Basil Rathbone-Nigel Bruce Sherlock Holmes film *The Hound of the Baskervilles*, for Fisher's dog, the same breed, could have been as easily hired as Rowley for *Foreign Correspondent*.) The ironic gentility of the scene turns black comedy when Fisher tells Krug he has a particularly clever grasp of the English language. Krug graciously thanks him for the compliment.

Conversely, ffolliott's attempted blackmail of Fisher in this same room is framed by the same books and phone and figurine, but this time the scene is shot full of shadows and from all sorts of noirish angles. The trio of desk objects are lit by the same earlier lamps much more darkly, prolific Hollywood composer Alfred Newman's apt music swelling on the soundtrack as Fisher moves menacingly closer to ffolliott.

Of course, just as we think that through subterfuge ffolliott will receive the address of the kidnapped Van Meer's whereabouts—the camera alternates on a close-up of Herbert Marshall's inscrutable face and his hand appearing to write the address on the top page of a pad—our expectations are crushed by an out-of-sight object that only Fisher can rightly interpret. Had we been attentive, like Fisher, we might have just made out a muffled sound on the soundtrack and heard their mastiff bark. When Carol suddenly bursts into the room, not kidnapped after all, and the startled ffolliott still manages to take the folded sheet from Fisher, we along with him surprisingly discover the following as he reads the note: "I'm sorry but I hear Carol's car arriving." With a shrug, ffolliott briefly smiles over his failed ruse.

Cut to the apartment where the Nazis, never named, are holding Van Meer. Always pining for birds to be fed in the city (one of the few if only times birds represent peace in Hitchcock's films), Van Meer's work in this scene culminates in a revelation of the follies (the word ffolliott actually stands for folly) of mankind. As he speaks the final lines of screenwriter Bennett's despairing monologue—"There is no help for the whole poor suffering world"—Hitchcock cuts away to all six characters in the apartment: the Nazis, the recently arrived ffolliott, and the innocent but blackmailed Germans, who own the building. Shooting from up under in an immobilized and silhouetted darkness, Hitchcock makes them look like inhuman pawns in a giant chess game. Stark and backlit in a medium shot, they stare off to the right while framing a large painting the camera has picked out several times in the scene, two golden retrievers sitting happily side by side. Hitchcock may in fact be saying that, while clothes do not make the man, perhaps man's best friend does. A similar pastoral portrait of canines hangs over Mark and Marnie's head in Mrs. Edgar's home twenty-four years later.

Haverstock's first big scoop finally gets sent back to his newspaper from *The Mohican*, the ship that rescues all the major protagonists but Fisher, who had redeemed himself via suicide earlier. When he surreptitiously hides a phone receiver, a call from his newspaper boss "uncle" Powers (Harry Davenport, who had played Dr. Meade in the previous year's *Gone with the Wind*) is viewed in a three-shot close-up over his shoulder next to a bookend of what appears to be a mold of a Mohican Indian head holding up its end of a pile of books. Hitchcock pulls out all the references at every opportune time, tongue firmly in cheek.

Haverstock's second scoop (written by another longtime collaborator, active Zionist Ben Hecht, as a tag scene right after World War II had been officially declared) ends the picture as his radio broadcast, started as a script, turns off-the-cuff—or, perhaps, out of his hat—as bombs crash all around him. "The Star Spangled Banner" rises on the soundtrack as the film fades to darkness, but his last words call for one of Hitchcock's favorite objects to help freedom's cause: "Hello, America. Hang on to your lights. They're the only lights left in the world."

Mr. and Mrs. Smith (1941)

Mr. and Mrs. David Smith certainly love each other, however many troubles their marriage will pass through in this RKO film that David

Mr. and Mrs. Smith (1941)

O. Selznick lent Hitchcock out to do. Problems brewing are implied early on when David trustingly allows his wife Ann to shave him, the razor safely but dangerously close to his throat. If we did not know this to be Hitchcock's only screwball comedy with one of the original queens of screwball, the energetic Carole Lombard, we might think twice about her use of neurotic rules in their marriage such as "always tell the truth, no matter what the consequences," as the blade hovers above David's neck. The uncertain dangers represented by a razor will make an even sharper appearance in *Spellbound* several films later.

To highlight the lightness of the story, though, the Smith home is designed and hung with art director Van Nest Polglase's classic art deco portraits of women. (David's office is ringed with men.) Polglase did all the sets for the Astaire-Rogers pictures in the thirties, also at RKO. David and his friend Jefferson Custer's (Gene Raymond) apartments have that typically impeccable fantasy vibe about them that is perfect for this funny little film.

In answer to his wife's question about whether he would still marry her if they had to do it all over again, David, at the insistence of Ann's never-lie rule, really puts his foot in it (which sets up the entire rest of the film) by saying no, he'd prefer being single. After he is kicked out of house and home and returns to his office, a small sculpted figure on his desk—a golfer at the end of his swing—punctuates that point. And, as Mr. Harry Deever (character actor Charles Halton), David's lawyer, shares with him the strange news that their marriage was inadvertently illegal due to zoning laws, the golfer sculpture and a huge law book also on the desk loom large in front of Deever as seen in a medium distance shot from behind David. Hitchcock films David in such a way that the law book looks like it is resting heavily on his left shoulder! Hammering *that* point home, at the split-second Deever says their marriage "isn't legal," Hitchcock cuts to startling close-ups of alternating shots of Deever and David, each perfectly wedged in between the golfer and the law book. And when Deever gets up to leave, the two humorously banter over this strange turn of events while they frame a deliberately oversized photo of a rather stern-looking Lombard chastising them, a portent of things to come.

It's really a very funny film at times. At Momma Lucy's, their favorite restaurant from earlier days, Ann says, "Eat your soup, dear."

HITCHCOCK'S OBJECTS AS SUBJECTS

David: "There's something wrong with the soup. [*Pause*] Why doesn't the cat eat the soup?" Ann: "It's your imagination." David: "That cat knows something." Said cat sits stone-faced, asleep on their table.

Hitchcock plays his champagne-bottle-that-looks-like-a-male-body-part joke from *The Lady Vanishes* again as David ices one up in a large round bowl that resembles another male body part. This time the director ups the ribaldry by adding two champagne glasses that are held in both of Lombard's hands directly in front of her breasts. Keeping David and Ann in a close two-shot for a solid, sexually teasing fifteen seconds, Hitchcock dollies back as they walk towards the camera from the kitchen to the bedroom door, David all the while stirring the champagne bottle's head. Upon entering the bedroom, he tells her to "keep twirling it, honey," and she grabs the neck and does just that, then disgustedly walks across the room to stew in front of a double door with another Polglase design that cannot be described here because Hitchcock is just too naughty. Cut to a half-naked David inside the next room pulling on a new set of pajamas. The justly famous sexualized shot of the crossed skis at the end of *Mr. and Mrs. Smith* has nothing on this scene.

Swirling smoke and gravelly dust play their parts in both *Shadow of a Doubt* and *The Birds*, from Uncle Charlie's locomotive and Mrs. Brenner's pick-up truck respectively, but here in *Mr. and Mrs. Smith*, the uniquely intangible object as protagonist is steam. When Ann goes into Momma Lucy's kitchen to answer the phone, she is surrounded by steam from the food cooking all around. Ten minutes later, in the Beefeater's club steam room, David, too, is almost completely hidden by the steam he is stewing in, having been kicked out of the house again, this time for good, after his clothes had been flung outside by Ann (shades of clothes not making the man, from the previous film). And, when he realizes back at his home that his supposedly good friend Jefferson is trying to cozy up to Ann, David flings his hat across the room with such violence that it just misses whacking Ann in the face. Look fast for her amazed double-take as the hat goes streaking by.

Crowds keep forming around this couple, acting in their typically upsetting fashion. First, at Momma Lucy's, David and Ann ask to have an outdoor table, but all the local kids congregate to gawk, humorously filling Hitchcock's frame. Second, their argument about garters outside

Hall's department store brings more people. A policeman sends David and Ann in opposite directions with the help of a crowd that had pressed in so close they were forced to separate. Third, David's hot blind date at the Florida Club with Gertrude is humorously stymied by a crowd for a solid forty seconds. The two must outmaneuver waiters carrying tables aloft by zigzagging their way around and through hordes of dancing couples. To be fair, perhaps a portent of the inevitable happy ending necessary for screwball comedy, Hitchcock has dancers repeatedly jar *Jeffery's* hand as he holds a lit match (he is trying to light Ann's cigarette). He, too, keeps getting shoved from behind by the masses.

Suspicion (1941)

> As Joan Fontaine's fingers arrange those letters into the word "Murder," the camera places us in her position: They are our hands [Robin Wood, 1965, p. 25].

True, the glass of milk Johnnie carries up the stairs near the end of the film is an excellent and rightly noted example of an object projecting menace in *Suspicion*. But it is actually letters and, more specifically, the use of eyeglasses to read them are more important objects as subjects in this quirky, almost surrealistic little film. And, considering four out of five of the bright-magnitude actors in the movie are wasted and constrained by their inconsistent and unbelievable line readings—Cary Grant, Joan Fontaine, Dame May Witty, and Sir Cedric Hardwick—my perspective on this film runs contrary to many other critics. The Academy even gave Fontaine a Best Actress award here, which should have gone for her work in *Rebecca* the previous year, as her part in *Suspicion* is really the weaker one. In other words, it is easier to look for and find objects in this film that are empowered to play more interesting parts than many of the leads themselves. (Nigel Bruce, the fifth, briefly free from his bumbling but ever-lovable Dr. Watson in the Sherlock Holmes series, literally steals the film with his bumbling but endearingly charming Beaky Thwaite.)

Similar to how *Juno and the Paycock* begins and *Foreign Corre-*

spondent ends, *Suspicion* starts in total darkness, so we do not know where we or even the two main protagonists are located. We do hear a disembodied voice say, "Oh, excuse me, I didn't know anyone was here," and it will turn out that knowing who each person really is will be a major theme of the film.

Interestingly, our first sequence with Fontaine's Lina McLaidlaw makes us immediately wonder if we're not back at *Rebecca*'s Manderley. Hitchcock gives us an extreme long shot of what could easily be the new Mrs. De Winter sitting and reading in a window seat dwarfed on the far side of a huge living room full of furnishings. Her character, as I stated, is very much the same as her earlier one the previous year—spinsterish, shy, and delicate.

In response to overhearing her father exclaim that he doesn't think she will marry ("Lina has intellect and a fine solid character"), she impulsively kisses Cary Grant (as Johnnie Aysgarth) and runs into the house, giant cross-hatched shadows on its high walls hovering above her. In fact, spider web shadows in the great hall provide menace in a great many scenes throughout the picture, so much so that they are intended, I think, to take on a creepy, surreal life of their own.

In Lina's favorite room, Johnnie speaks the truth to the words he puts in the mouth of a huge portrait of General McLaidlaw, a portrait that appears as often as the spider webs (or the jester in *Blackmail*). Speaking about himself and Lina, he says: "He can only bring her unhappiness. Warn her. Speak up, man, it is your last chance.... [*To Lina:*] He's not exaggerating a thing, dear. It's all true, every word he isn't saying." The portrait, "which dominates the newlyweds' home" (Spoto, 1976, p. 119), will play a much larger part than the actor who actually plays the general, Sir Cedric Hardwicke, even while he's alive through just the first part of the picture.

> [Her father's] influence is felt even after his death—his portrait is constantly emphasized in their home. This is not the first or the last time we see Hitchcock's fascination for the theme of the power of the dead to affect the living.... It occurs most clearly in *Rebecca, The Paradine Case, Vertigo* and *The Birds*, in each of which (as here) a portrait manifests the deceased's presence [Spoto, 1976, p. 122].

As if the general's visage and Johnnie's words don't augur badly enough for them, rain pours down and gloominess rules when the two

Suspicion (1941)

quietly wed at a local Register. The short scene is shot objectively from a distance outside the window. Later, after Johnnie admits he's completely broke, we know immediately what he will do with the two gorgeous heirloom chairs that arrive as the general's gift. With his best mischievous, mock-innocent grin, which doesn't look quite right on a still young (37) Grant, Johnnie flops himself down in one and props his feet up on the upholstery of the other. A younger version of both Captain Boyle and Pengallan, from *Juno and the Paycock* and *Jamaica Inn*, respectively?

As they walk up their home's huge staircase together, more spider web shadows reach down at them when Johnnie yells at Lina for interfering in his phony money-making scheme, ostensibly at their friend

Suspicion (1941): General McLaidlaw's wedding present of expensive heirloom chairs reflects the conspicuous consumption that Johnnie Aysgarth (Cary Grant) embodies throughout the film.

HITCHCOCK'S OBJECTS AS SUBJECTS

Beaky's expense. Lina's faint from imagining Johnnie's murder of Beaky in a waking hallucination (more portents of surrealism, which was to be given its own dream sequence in *Spellbound* four years later) drops her from the chair she had been playing anagrams from (she spelled out "murder," of course), her gorgeous velvet dress spreading out upon the floor in all directions like a pool of blood. Hitch would brilliantly recreate and far surpass this shot in full color from a camera set on a high crane twenty-eight years later in *Topaz*, with the shooting death of Juanita de Cordoba.

Lina's premonition over Beaky's death still fresh in her mind the next morning, she drives out to the cliff she had pictured in the dream and spots tire tracks going over the edge, but nothing else. Upon her return home, she pulls the car up to the front door, brightly lit with the morning light. As she gets out and looks up, a passing cloud almost turns the door dark gray with dread. Reinforcing the tone of impending doom, Hitchcock zooms in on her black coat shrouded in shadow after she enters.

Mr. Benson (Vernon Downing), one of two inspectors who call looking for Aysgarth, cannot help but stare at a small, cubist-looking painting of a still life on the wall, a microcosm image for this strange film. Upon learning of Beaky's death from drinking a full beaker of brandy on a bet in Paris, Lina has another conversation with her father's huge portrait, which by now merely rests on the floor against a wall, for some reason. Perhaps it is trying to stand up on its own. Right before the inspectors exit, Benson still can't figure out what the little still life means.

It is clear that Lina can see fine at a distance—she spies Johnnie putting mysterious envelopes in his coat pocket from afar in a mirror—but for some reason she is always looking for her glasses. Upon finding them, she laboriously places them on her nose each time. The use of eyeglasses to read letters and books and newspaper articles is so insistent in this picture that Hitchcock seems to be telling us how difficult it is to really see the truth about people and objects in all situations. Benson's consternation over the cubist painting makes sense now. One must take the time to put one's eyeglasses on and let them do their job properly before one is able to fully see, and understand, anything.

Saboteur (1942)

> [T]hat concept of a man being more isolated in the middle of a crowd than in a deserted spot recurs in many of your films; your hero is often trapped in a movie house, in a music hall, at a political rally, at an auction sale, in a ballroom, or at a fund-raising event. It sets up a contrast within the scenario, especially when the hero starts out more or less on his own, or in isolated surroundings [Truffaut, 1967, p. 108].

Until *North by Northwest* bested it seventeen years later, *Saboteur* had often been called the American *39 Steps*. It's a valid statement, for the film nicely borrows the "innocent accused of something he hasn't done and must prove it himself while eluding the police" trope. The first twenty minutes, in fact, gives us rapid expository along this trajectory. With only the reality of World War II impacting these early proceedings, no objects stand still long enough to identify as subjects.

Shortly, however, when Barry Kane (everyman Robert Cummings in the first of two Hitchcock appearances) stops by the home of Mrs. Mason's (Dorothy Peterson) in a failed effort to comfort her over the loss of her son in a sabotaged factory, she is seen bent over a table perfectly framed between four candles, two on each side, like an altar. At another point, she stands near a "lampshade that is decorated with an eagle-and-star design, a rather vulgar expression of the family's virtue and patriotism in contrast to the 'class' of the villains" (Yacowar, 1977, p. 287). And when Barry stops at a blind man's house ten minutes later, they are seen eating at a table with just three candles set in a candelabra. Because none of the seven is lit, both scenes have a somber tone.

Objects telegraph Patricia (Pat) Martin (Priscilla Lane), a model at one point in her life, to us. She is seen three times on billboards, humorously "commenting" on the narrative. The last two are especially pertinent: "She'll never let you down if he keeps a case of Cocarilla on ice," reads the caption for a luscious blond, the sentiment ironically true as Pat drives Barry to the police, not to safety. No Cocarilla is visible in the car as she tries, in fact, to let him down. And, as he is later driven to another appointment with death, the billboard's narrative is black humor indeed: "The final tribute.... Beautiful funeral $49.50 and up."

Hitchcock's Objects as Subjects

Shortly, a large lamp cleverly frustrates our view of Mrs. Van Sutton (Alma Kruger) as she paces back and forth behind it four times, foreshadowing a similarly concealing lamp in *The Paradine Case* five years hence. And later, the fifth columnist ringleader Charles Tobin (Otto Kruger, no relation to Alma) hides behind an even larger lamp which briefly blinds us as he passes on his way to "screen left." As Tobin sits to talk of his move to Havana, Hitchcock shows us a sculpture of a dancing woman on the side table by his arm, a small reminder of the better life he has carved out at the expense of democracy.

Awaiting their doom, Barry surreptitiously points to a book in Tobin's library for Pat's eyes: The title is *Escape*. It's lodged between others that read *Methods of Criminal Investigation*, *Sketch of a Sinner*, *Conquerors of Time* and *Bad Company*. Tobin puts an exclamation point on Barry's little ploy by finding his own title: *The Death of a Nobody*. Silent film effects with objects having "speaking parts" such as these abound in Hitch's art.

The director fills us with vertigo in the crowded ballroom scene noted at the top of this chapter, much like a similar love duet during a dance between Elsa and Ashenden in *Secret Agent* seven years earlier. Alternately encircling our heroes in intimate close-up for a full two minutes of screen time, the camera spokes out in 360 degrees from them all around the hall, chandeliers and dancers pressing in. Near the end of the scene, Barry kisses Pat and says, "This moment belongs to me. No matter what happens, they can never take it away from me"— clear reference to Fred Astaire's song of the same name by the Gershwins in RKO's *Shall We Dance* (1937)—but that is just what happens. In a quickly edited, longer shot, a fifth columnist breaks in on Barry out of the hypnotically moving crowd and asks Pat to dance. Gone in an instant, she is in fact taken away from him.

The showdown with Tobin occurs with the ringleader perfectly framed between two more imposing lamps, themselves bookending the large oval-shaped couch he sits in. Two huge portraits of women hang on the wall above him, a third bright lamp foregrounding them screen left. It's shot in middle distance. Hitchcock makes him up to look like a miniature Caesar speaking to his minions—an apt, ironic image.

The Statue of Liberty scene, justly famous, stands tall as the tallest "character" Hitchcock ever directed prior to Mount Rushmore. But, as discussed, it's the touches made by smaller objects in this film that help propel its plot in a quiet but no less powerful way.

Shadow of a Doubt (1943)

> Thus Uncle Charlie's city isn't just a city from the (industrial and sophisticated) East. It contains within itself the compromise between two extremes: the snobbery and irresponsibility of the "gilded age" upper class (now modified, except in dream) and the apathetic poverty of the Depression (which ended only four or five years before this film's date) [Durgnat, 1974, p. 185].

Hitchcock called *Shadow of a Doubt* his favorite film, but I find it quite nasty and misogynistic. It is certainly tightly scripted, thanks largely to *Our Town* writer Thornton Wilder, in much the same way the previous film, *Saboteur*, had some uniquely sharp and succinct dialogue by Dorothy Parker. Regardless, the hypnotic, vertigo-inducing strains of an endlessly repeating three-count waltz dominate the film from the start, while an extremely decrepit, broken-down wreck of an automobile, in the third shot (after we watch superimposed dancing couples over the credits), warns us that the end of civilization is near. Uncle Charlie, evilly played to the hilt by the estimable Joseph Cotten (in the first of two Hitchcock films), will speak frequently about it.

At the end of the landlady's discussion with him about two men who call, she pulls down a window's blinds to help him nap. Hitchcock cuts to a close-up of our villain lying in bed, head screen left to toes screen right. For all intents and purposes, as the blinds' shadow falls over him, he looks dead. And when he gets up to go out, we see nothing but darkened lamps in his room, reinforcing the dread. There is no light in this man's life. An extreme high angle overhead shot of the men chasing Charles through the beat-up streets of the city leaves them empty-handed, mice after cheese, and this entire scene feels as cold and bereft of life as the abandoned car we saw earlier.

Cut to a young Charlie, Uncle Charlie's niece, endearingly played by Teresa Wright, lying in *her* bed same as her uncle had been, head screen left to toes screen right. Above *her* head on the wall, however, are two paintings of what appear to be happy couples together. We see Charlie's little sister Ann (Edna May Wonacott) chatting with her father about not wanting to read *Unsolved Crimes*, the book under his arm, saying she's still "practically a child," perhaps a reference to the power of the book titles pointed at in *Saboteur* the year before.

As Uncle Charlie's train comes into Santa Rosa station, a doctor at a table leans toward one of the men playing cards with him and says, "Well, you don't look very well either." Cut to the man's hand holding all the aces, figuratively and literally—13 spades, two through ace—and we can just make out from behind that he is Hitchcock himself.

After such a light joke, the bright daylight of the train station is suddenly blotted out by the train's smoke, much as the window shade "embalmed" Uncle Charlie earlier. Beyond even a shadow of a doubt, trouble is clearly on the way.

> HITCHCOCK: I asked for lots of black smoke for [that] scene. It's one of those ideas for which you go to a lot of trouble, although it's seldom noticed. But here, we were lucky. The position of the sun created a beautiful shadow over the whole station.
> TRUFFAUT: The black smoke implies that the devil was coming to town.
> HITCHCOCK: Exactly [Truffaut, 1967, p. 111].

Critic James McLaughlin grants the smoke an even greater subjective purpose: "Those vapors of Uncle Charlie, the billowing clouds of smoke and gas—obscure, opaque, shadowy—permeate this film so insidiously and resemble, with their elusiveness and their delicacy, the singular strength of their progenitor" (cited in Deutelbaum and Poague, 1986, p. 145).

Young Charlie intuitively starts humming the Merry Widow waltz immediately after Hitchcock double-exposes a troubled-looking Cotten with those dancers again. And when the two "reporters" (translation: police) spot Charles returning from the bank, the same waltz plays like a dirge on the soundtrack. Charlie finally discovers at the library that her uncle really is the murderer, and Hitchcock dollies his camera up very high, long shadows further darkening the shadow-filled after-hours building. Her ant-like figure insignificant below, the waltz plays on.

Actress Teresa Wright and art director Robert Boyle, interviewed for the special 2000 *Shadow of a Doubt* DVD bonus feature "Beyond

Shadow of a Doubt (1943)

Doubt: The Making of Hitchcock's Favorite Film," rightly point out the importance of the camera as protagonist, particularly in this scene.

> BOYLE: The way Hitchcock described it to me, where she finds the newspaper piece—he said, "When she sees it, and she recognizes that indeed Uncle Charlie is not all he pretends to be, I want the camera to go [Boyle inhales sharply] like an intake of breath." Which I thought was terrific.
>
> WRIGHT: I think you can't work in a film with Hitchcock without realizing how important the camera is and how the camera becomes either you or the other character or another character. So it's very much something that is part of the story.

Just after her uncle thinks he's safe and Cotten in close-up gloats that he could eat a good dinner, Hitchcock cuts to another high angle shot of young Charlie's figure and shadow in the hall, just out of sight. Cotten gleefully jogs up the stairs as Hitchcock's camera just as quickly follows him through the door and upwards in an extraordinarily powerful shot ... until, near the top step, he senses young Charlie, the camera and us looking up at him. As we see Charles suddenly stop, turn and gaze back down at all three of us, Hitchcock immediately cuts to his point of view. Backlit by the setting sun, young Charlie stands silently just inside the doorway, her lengthening shadow on the floor (darkly "connected" to her feet) and her actual body staring quietly back. In this palpably unnerving shot, we know that Charles will not long escape his fate.

Just like the repeating figures waltzing throughout the picture, the vertigo-inducing train tracks at the end are shot in rapid motion just before Uncle Charlie attempts to murder his niece. The rushing tracks prefigure a similar use in *Strangers on a Train* eight years on, while reminiscent of dizzying shots seen from a speeding car in *Rich and Strange* eleven years earlier. During the powerfully hypnotic montage of his murder attempt, body parts once again are objectively filmed in close-up but stand in for the whole persons (see, especially, *Marnie*).

> The camera tilts down to the couple's legs, intertwined and violently locked.... From their intertwined legs, Hitchcock cuts to a shot of her gloved hand grasping the door latch: She is struggling desperately to keep from being pushed to her death. Then he cuts to the two framed by the landscape hurtling by, to her hand losing its grip on the latch, and again to the two struggling [Rothman, 1982, p. 238].

Hitchcock's Objects as Subjects

It is no surprise that Uncle Charlie dies at the hands of a revengeful, oncoming train, similar to the one that first brought him to Santa Rosa.

Lifeboat (1944)

> And, of course, [Gus'] boot is the detail ... that beats the Nazi to death. And look how these details are related.... Who dislodged the boot? The Nazi, in taking off his leg [Drew Casper; 2005 *Lifeboat* DVD audio commentary].

At first glance, due to the technical challenges Hitchcock gave himself with *Lifeboat*—a forty-foot boat in a huge tank of water, wind machines, rear projections, and multiple backdrops—there appear to be no objects that can be treated as subjects except the lifeboat itself. Not true, we will see.

> The spaces may or may not be literalized (a room literally exists for the characters; a frame does not), but ultimately they are psychological; the interior space represents subjective perception, which is threatened by reality from outside. The aural-intrusion technique is prominent in the single-set films (*Lifeboat, Rope, Dial M for Murder, Rear Window*), which, with their deliberate visual restriction, depend greatly on the tension between inside and outside space [Weis, 1982, p. 125].

Of course, a lifeboat *is* both an actual life-saving device and a metaphor for one. "The technical challenge in *Lifeboat* is analogous to its political theme, the fatal isolation of the Allies and their need for a selfless unity" (Deutelbaum and Poague, 1986, p. 21). Upon closer inspection, however, there are dozens of objects in the movie that take on a particular character, especially all eight of Connie Porter's (played to the hilt by actress Tallulah Bankhead) most prized possessions.

One of the biggest problems with *Lifeboat* is not really in the film but in many of its critics' assertions—the claim that the movie argues that the German Nazis were stronger than the Allies—when in fact Hitchcock and John Steinbeck (the original story's author) and Jo Swerling (the screenwriter) were warning the free world that they'd better smarten up and work together if they hoped to win the war. Hitchcock

Lifeboat (1944)

rightly films the stereotypical characters of Communist (Kovak), snooty businessman (C.J. Rittenhouse), upper-class reporter (Connie Porter), radio operator (Stanley "Sparks" Garrett), and cook (George "Joe" Spencer) as the stick figures the writers warned them about. Mute as bedposts, they dumbly stare back at the camera—Willy (Walter Slezak in perhaps his greatest role) as he tells them about Gus (William Bendix in perhaps his greatest role, too) falling overboard. This is a lie, for Willy has just pushed him to his death. He also admits to hiding a water flask and food pellets so he could remain strong, and they should be grateful to him. Stunned by the gall of this man and his cold-hearted, efficient rationale—which would have saved everyone to be interred in a concentration camp, no doubt—the Allies finally begin to work together by mindlessly gang-murdering him (all but Joe, the praying cook). Hitchcock's treatment of crowds as sheep is here taken to the nth degree: "They're like a pack of dogs," the director told Truffaut (1967, p. 113). Fellow film directors Eric Rohmer and Claude Chabrol also got the sense of this mob's madness exactly right: "Hitchcock has caught a whiff of the unpleasantness of collective halitosis, and he makes one of his usual rapier thrusts" (1957, p. 75).

All eight of Connie's prized possessions are slowly taken from her by the most powerful "subject" in the whole film, "the sea ... so big and terrible," says the nurse, Alice (Mary Anderson). Those objects are a stocking, which is ripped; her first cigarette, which she throws away; her camera, which gets flung overboard; her mink coat and typewriter, both also lost to the ocean; her last cigarette, which she gives to Gus; her suitcase; and finally, a bracelet that got her from the South Side of Chicago to the North Side. "Little by little, I'm being stripped of all my earthly possessions," Connie says, and we believe her as she breaks out into insane crying laughter. She could very well be an older version of Betty from *Champagne*, overcome by the loss of her character's objects. "Her uncontrollable laughter, we are made to feel, manifests not so much hysteria as a sense of release: she has lost all the external trappings that seemed to compose her identity..." (Wood, 1965, p. 31).

Elsewhere, cigars, boots, rope, playing cards, a chess board, money, chairs ... in fact, *all* earthly possessions of all these people that they've somehow saved in the lifeboat are given subjective value in the film, embodied by Connie's own comment, "Oh, ye gods and little fishes." As important as objects appear to be in life, Steinbeck and Swerling and Hitchcock seem to be telling us, they mean nothing compared to how we treat our fellow human beings. And it is finally Connie, growing up from a bitchy snob into a real person, who helps bring the varied Allies together in this microcosm of the world.

> The mannequin becomes a human being. She has abandoned earthly possessions—they've been stripped from her—in order to possess her soul. It is actually because of her development that she can unite the passel of survivors into a unifying force against Nazism [Drew Casper; 2005 *Lifeboat* DVD audio commentary].

Spellbound (1945)

> Shortly after the film begins, as its opening credits unfold, the movie's principal and highly romantic theme music begins playing underneath an image of a twisting and quite fragile tree. The boughs of the tree somehow suggest the stark lines of a fragmented mind. The leaves fluttering off the branches and floating through the frame suggest loss. And, on some level, that the life of the mind, the struggle of the unconscious to get free, come into the light, is a lonely and perhaps all but abandoned experience [Marian Keane; 2002 *Spellbound* DVD audio commentary].

Sometimes, a tree is just a tree (or a lifeboat just a lifeboat), but if we trust Hitchcock scholar Marian Keane's description of this early image of a fragile tree, what it reveals about John Ballantine's heart and mind is honest and true. So, too, might we interpret the white tracks a car makes, right after the tree imagery, on a dirt-covered street in front of Green Manors, a key locale in the story, as not really an accidental shot but a deliberate harbinger of the motif that hides Ballantine's memory from himself: constricting parallel lines. "The vertical lines are one of Hitchcock's characteristic charged images. They signal internal imprisonment, a confinement of knowledge, emotion and desire" (Marian Keane; 2002 *Spellbound* DVD audio commentary).

Gregory Peck, in the first of two films for Hitchcock, poses temporarily (but mistakenly, due to amnesia) as a Dr. Edwardes, the new

Spellbound (1945)

head psychiatrist of Green Manor. Upon his introduction, we see a library full of soft, cushy chairs, circular lampshades, and rounded double lamps on the walls. His bedroom is made up likewise, all dreamy and narcotic-like, keeping him and us under a spell. Conversely, the lamp, radio, calendar, and other desk objects of his soon-to-be love interest Dr. Constance Petersen are conspicuously large, square, and clunky, the perfect embodiment of her early cool-as-ice, linear demeanor. In her first of three Hitchcock films, Ingrid Bergman still carries the blush of youthful naïveté she shared so heartbreakingly in 1942's *Casablanca*, with Humphrey Bogart.

> How many compositions in the course of this film have a lamp in the foreground…? [T]here are invariably layers of action that are being played out and it is often a telephone, a lamp … domestic objects in the foreground [that] frame the action [Thomas Schatz and Charles Ramirez Berg; 2007 *Spellbound* DVD audio commentary].

Reinforcing her distanced character is the cigarette she smokes early on, held at a remove on the end of a cigarette holder. Near the end of the picture she will have traded in the holder for her own hand, directly gripping a smoldering cigarette.

When she walks into Peck's room (his real name, we find out eventually, is John Ballantine), Hitchcock films the scene in such a way that we can clearly spy two brightly lit round lamp bulbs on the wall over his shoulder, and a third one on beneath them, scrotum-like. Heightened by the *frisson* of this genital trio of subliminal brilliance, lightning strikes through the charged doubts that light up Bergman's gorgeous face as she enters. When she returns to her own bedroom, we see that it, too, is full of soft, rounded shades on the lamps, plus two bulbous ones flanking the French provincial vanity at which she sits for a moment. The film is, after all, often concerned with psychoanalysis and the importance of sex and dreams, but one wonders how Hitchcock got these objects past the censors.

Other objects intrude as if of their own volition. Four doors open by themselves in rapid succession as their love blooms, but Hitchcock slyly dampens the ardor of sexual awakening by having a prison jail cell door creak itself open and close later in the film.

After Ballantine takes it on the lam from Green Manors, Constance tracks him to the Empire State Hotel. Hitchcock films her mov-

HITCHCOCK'S OBJECTS AS SUBJECTS

ing through the lobby crowd in a long shot from screen left to screen right in a way that renders her wholly unrecognizable, until the camera finally picks her out and slowly zooms in. (This reveal prefigures a similar camera movement at the beginning of *Psycho*, when it sweeps across the city of Phoenix, hesitates, and then moves in toward one hotel window.) Constance will merge back into that crowd in a precisely reversed screen right to screen left shot at the end of this ten-minute scene. In his hotel room, a dark lamp hovers in the background between their forms, a real harbinger of doom when she starts to ask him questions. Shortly, her blockish desk lamp recapitulates its earlier rigidity, a reminder of her cool demeanor near the top of the picture.

They escape the hotel and purchase train tickets at Grand Central Station to visit her mentor Dr. Alex Brulov (actor Michael Chekhov, a nephew of the famed playwright Anton Chekhov). "In this tense scene, as they approach the ticket window, the Hitchcockian vertical bars loom larger and larger in the frame, signaling Ballantine's sexual and psychological tension, the barrier between him and his memory, him and his identity, him and his desires" (Marian Keane; 2002 *Spellbound* DVD audio commentary).

Shortly, Hitchcock shoots them descending the station's diagonally angled staircase, placed in the frame upper screen right to lower screen left—a precipitously dangerous image. We see them pause in a two-shot at the bottom of the stairs, the asymmetric stair rail in the background, and the scene fades out and then up on an extreme long shot of the train terminal, three of the sun's rays prominent at that same angle flashing ominously through a distant window. This diagonal embodiment of foreboding was anticipated back at Green Manors, when Constance first walked up a staircase to clinch her love for Ballantine and, again, when she confronts Murchison at the end of the film. It will be recapitulated several times in Dr. Brulov's home (as well as via a ski slope). The wholly cinematic montage of Ballantine holding a razor blade in his hand as he descends Brulov's sharply angled staircase is particularly harrowing. Of course, the "horrific accident that left [Ballantine] with crippling guilt occurs at the end of a slide down a stone banister" (Lesley Brill; "Love and Psychoanalysis"; 2002 *Spellbound* DVD booklet) is also set at that angle.

Only at the end of Constance and John's stay does Hitchcock sub-

Notorious (1946)

stitute the hopeful Brulov in place of Peck on his own staircase, working in opposition to all the earlier dangers. "[Look] how effectively we have been introduced to the geography of this house, which is going to be important.... We spend a lot of time in this house in the film. Look what's going on with diagonals, with depth, with space, with lighting, and orientation" (Thomas Schatz and Charles Ramirez Berg; 2007 *Spellbound* DVD audio commentary).

After Ballantine is imprisoned and Constance returns to her office, Hitchcock seems to taunt her with two sharply pointed, Freudian-tinged pens that frame her body (they were there at the start of the film, a rewind attests). The final castration is self-inflicted by Dr. Murchison, played by consummate character actor Leo G. Carroll, the performer used most by Hitchcock (six films). "The gun, seen from the subjective point of view of Murchison, corresponds to the glass of milk [in *Suspicion*] as the externalization of apparent danger" (Deutelbaum and Poague, 1986, p. 160).

Built oversized like a huge sculpture, the gun was held by an equally large fake hand, both of which pivot to directly face the camera. When the trigger is pulled, the only splash of color in the entire film—a blood-red wash—suffuses the screen for a split second (prelude to similar imagery in *Marnie*), no doubt the last thing Murchison would have seen before his death.

Notorious (1946)

> The atmosphere of extreme sensuality that reigns in Notorious does not in any way clash with the abstraction of the style. In this film of close-ups, "matter"—admirably emphasized by Ted Tetzlaff's lighting (faces, metal, glass, jewels, rugs, floor tiles)—shines with a light that is alternately glacial or burning [Rohmer and Chabrol, 1957, p. 84].

As alluded to above as early as 1957 by Eric Rohmer and Claude Chabrol, home furnishings do in fact play important parts in one of Hitchcock's greatest films. During her bantering scene with Devlin (the suave and uber-handsome Cary Grant in the second of four pictures

Hitchcock's Objects as Subjects

for the director) at the post-trial trying-to-forget party in Miami after her father's sentencing as a Nazi, the conspicuous wall lamp directly behind Alicia Huberman (the never more gorgeous Ingrid Bergman in the second of her three pictures) looks much too much like a chastising crucifix. And, back in her bungalow after a run-in with a cop, the combination of Alicia's tiger-striped dress, spider-webbed design of a figurine-filled cabinet, and similar pattern on the back of Devlin's chair gives us the same sense of entrapment she is starting to feel after his proposition to her to help in the spy game. These objects are easily overlooked at such an early point in the film, though, because we are more than happily distracted by Bergman and Grant's sensual and sexual chemistry.

After their flight to Rio, Dev and Alicia fall in love while awaiting instructions. As with similar scenes of transcendence in *Rebecca*, *The Birds*, *Torn Curtain*, and others, "Hitchcock dissolves to a hillside, the iconic place for lovers in his films, and appropriately so. After all, Hitchcock knows that a hill separates lovers from the pedestrian world below. A hill also is the closest [place] people can get to heaven" [Drew Casper; 2005 *Notorious* DVD audio commentary].

When told by his superiors in their office that he must go back to Alicia and explain that she is to seduce her way into Alex Sebastian's home and hearth, we see in medium shot Grant's Devlin struggling with his few options, a small brass figurine of the god Mercury—or, worse, Ares, the god of war—egging him on from the top of a chest just beyond his right arm. After he returns to Alicia's hotel room, Hitchcock fades out from a close-up of the forgotten champagne bottle he had promised to bring back for dinner onto a close-up of a pitch-black lampshade he momentarily crosses behind. Such temporary obfuscation by darkened or even lit lamps frequently occurs in Hitchcock's films. As he is blocked from his own insight by this lamp, he is almost completely blocked from our view at that precise moment, too. "It is typical of Hitchcock's strategies to attach multiple layers of meaning to inanimate items: [lamps and] the wine bottle here [in *Notorious*], the tie in *Frenzy*, the diamond in *Family Plot*" (Sharff, 1991, p. 31).

In fact, all the lamps and sculptures and corners of Alicia's hotel room hold foreboding shadows, and we can see storm clouds in the distance (on a rear projection screen of Rio's harbor) beyond the bal-

Notorious (1946)

cony that Dev steps out onto ... such a happy loving place not two minutes before. Hitchcock cuts to a long shot now, from far back in the living room, and we see Devlin as a small figure move further away from the camera and drop his head in sadness, small shafts of light flashing his way from a lighthouse miles across the (projected) bay. For another split second, when Alicia brings the chicken dinner she had attempted to cook into the frame and crosses in front of the lighthouse, she blocks our view. As she turns to kiss Dev, another shaft of light flashes ever so briefly, then blinks out.

Their love for each other remains strong, though, for Hitchcock deliberately pulls back on a close-up of them in an almost reluctant way, ever so slowly, the camera movement here encouraging us to feel both Alicia and Devlin's difficulty over her upcoming job. The alternating shadows and beams from the distant lighthouse rhythmically ebb and flow with their struggles, and we can just see in the bottom left corner of the screen the flickering light of a candle Alicia has lit on the outdoor table where she had prepared their pre-lovemaking meal. When Devlin tells Alicia that he is "waiting for [an] answer" to his prostitution proposition, dark shadows hover over his mouth. "Oh darling, what you didn't tell them, tell me ... that you believe I'm nice and that I love you and that I'll never change back," she says. Before their long trials are to take place during the rest of this deeply poignant film, Hitchcock lovingly lingers a final seven seconds on a close-up of Bergman's inimitable face and breathless whispers to him.

In spite of how well Grant tries to hide it on his face, if we look carefully, we can see that it is really killing him to have to act so coldly. He puffs on his cigarette just a little too hard, his stiff upper lip is just a little too tightly held. Cutting to and keeping Alicia in a medium close-up now, Hitchcock's camera simultaneously dollies *and* pans with her as she moves from the deck outdoors to inside, the shot veiled by a curtain and filmed through a window. In this same shot, Devlin enters the room and stands screen left while Alicia leans against the balcony door framing screen right, bookends. At this precise moment, we see a bust of Queen Nefertiti—aka the Sun Goddess, Lady of Two Lands, Sweet of Love, and Lady of All Women—staring Devlin down over his left shoulder from the top of a cabinet beyond.

Back in her room after visiting with the political hacks who thought up this crazy idea, Paul Prescott, the government agent cold-heartedly played by Louis Calhern, helps Alicia on with a borrowed necklace he had brought for the occasion of her first dinner date with Alex Sebastian. (One of Hitchcock's most sympathetic villains, Sebastian was played by the ever-understated Claude Rains, the cynical but ultimately redeemed Captain Renault in 1942's *Casablanca*, also with Ingrid Bergman.) As Prescott hooks the necklace around her neck, Hitchcock artfully shoots Bergman's face in left profile directly in front of Queen Nefertiti's left profile, effectively replacing her.

> Here once more, the jewelry carries emotional and thematic significance. Whether it is real, whether it belongs to the wearer, and whether the hero is able to fasten or unfasten it—these elements capture the

Notorious (1946): Jewelry in Hitchcock films—here a necklace being put on Alicia Huberman (Ingrid Bergman) by Paul Prescott (Louis Calhern), as Devlin (Cary Grant) looks on helplessly—is merely the veneer of character that must be rejected if people are to become real human beings.

Notorious (1946)

entire tone and quality of a relationship.... There are similar moments in *Shadow of a Doubt, Lifeboat, To Catch a Thief, Vertigo* and *Frenzy*. More than just suggesting the stage of a relationship, jewelry also externalizes Hitchcock's theme of the disparity between appearance and reality, for in all cases the jewels are either actually or emotionally worthless ... [Spoto, 1976, pp. 171–172].

The director holds his camera *outside* Sebastian's house as Alicia makes her entrance there for the first time, so that when the front door closes, we can feel it shut us and Devlin out. Conversely, at the end of the picture, this same door will close on *Sebastian* as he reluctantly returns for his comeuppance, happily shutting us and Devlin and Alicia out of his fate. The scenes with these emotionally laden doors are variants of similar ones from the previous film, *Spellbound*, as is the huge building itself, much as similar architecture was treated in *Rebecca* and *Suspicion*. "This set, this mansion, has been raised to the level of character.... [It is] remote, it is wide, it is deep, it is complex, it has many levels and many rooms, it is oversized and, excepting for the foyer, it is overstuffed and labyrinthine" (Drew Casper; 2005 *Notorious* DVD audio commentary).

In the library, Hitchcock shoots Alicia's entrance in a medium shot so that her body, all dolled up with furs and jewels, is made to look like just one more rich bauble alongside the room's ornate furniture and works of art. (Shades of Fontaine at Manderley and in her house from *Suspicion*.) A large bust on a screen left piano, a large portrait behind her on the wall, and a huge, looming lamp in screen right foreground are just three of the many objects Alicia is placed in proximity with for this eight-second shot. Shortly, when Alex's mother (Leopoldine Konstantin) first meets her in facing profiles, Hitchcock shoots them in a close-up with three small but brightly lit lamps between and behind them on a wall across the room. The composition highlights the two perverse and troubling love triangles in this film: Alex, Alicia, and Mrs. Sebastian and Alex, Alicia, and Devlin.

At the race track, Alicia's efforts to extract another "I love you" from Dev again fail miserably, and it pains us to watch Bergman's real tears well up in her eyes. Superimposed racing horses rush by in a "reflection" on her binoculars, the animals seeming to speak for her as she tells him, "I see, some kind of love test."

Hitchcock's Objects as Subjects

Just before the party that Dev has talked Alicia into talking Alex into throwing, all sorts of objects insinuate themselves into our consciousness, forebodings every single one: "We fade in on a charged framing of a grandfather's clock (a phallic shape), flowers (a representation of female sexuality), curtains (indicating theater), and the top banister of the main stairway (suggestive of Madame Sebastian's domain and secrets)" (Marian Keane; 2001 *Notorious* DVD audio commentary).

Alicia must find a way to get the Unica key to the wine cellar from Alex. That one object finally becomes the most important character out of all the others in this picture:

> In the dressing for the party scene and the party scene itself, we see Hitchcock's technique of investing a prop, a piece of this set's architecture, an object if you want, [with extraordinary import]. And that object is visual, palpable and tangible with enormous stature, point and meaning. While in this passage Hitchcock makes the object—the key to the wine cellar—the very stuff of one of the most suspenseful and thrilling passages in all of *Notorious*. And in the next passage Hitchcock will *star* that object ... in the most bravura passage [of the film—the crane shot] [Drew Casper; 2005 *Notorious* DVD audio commentary].

The furniture that objectified Alicia earlier turns the tables on Alex when he first spots Dev and Alicia at the party, for Hitchcock brilliantly shoots *him* now in close-up crowded out by his many home furnishings. A large, foregrounded screen left lamp completely obliterates his right side while an upholstered chair back hides his left. Cutting to his point of view, an extreme long shot of the two lovers are barely visible to his and our eyes far in the distance between all the partygoers milling about. Crowds continually cloud.

Devlin had better hurry if he is going to learn the secrets of this house, and of his own heart, in order to save both himself and Alicia: "As Devlin bends to have his cigarette lit, Hitchcock inserts the sound of a cork popping. This sound is both a reminder that time is running out and it might also suggest that Devlin's desire is coming to the fore [Marian Keane; 2001 *Notorious* DVD audio commentary].

The discovery of the MacGuffin object of uranium ore in the wine bottles and the stolen key to the wine cellar tip Alex off to Alicia's spying, leading to his mother's decision to slowly poison her. The famed

Notorious (1946)

crane shot highlights the power of that Unica key. "There again we've substituted the language of the camera for dialogue. In *Notorious* that sweeping movement of the camera is making a statement. What it's saying is: 'There's a large reception being held in this house, but there is a drama here which no one is aware of, and at the core of that drama is this tiny object, this key'" [Hitchcock; cited in Truffaut, 1967, p. 83].

Cut to a sleepless Alex and then a grandfather clock in close-up chiming six in the morning. One may be reminded of *For Whom the Bell Tolls*, also starring Ingrid Bergman, released three years earlier. (Hitchcock loved to exploit associations in his audience's mind between not only his own films but others, especially with famous actors.) In the morning, Alex checks his key chain on the bedroom table to find that the Unica key has been returned. Realizing he has been made a complete fool, he sits in his mother's bedroom and awakens her. Our sympathy for Rains' Renault from *Casablanca* finally expires as we see his duplicitous visage reflected across the room in a full-body mirror. Past and present push in on him from both sides, and a photograph of a younger version of himself on her bedroom table gazes pathetically up at him.

We have shuddered over Konstantin's role as Alex's mother since we first met her; there are few characters more cruel in Hitchcock's oeuvre. Right after Alex confesses that he is married to an American agent, Hitchcock cuts to a close-up of her lighting a cigarette with wholly savage calm. "She must be allowed to move about freely, but she will be on a leash," the real Mrs. Sebastian proclaims, literally referring to Alicia like a dog or other pet. Similarly, in a hotel room, the lack of concern for Alicia by Prescott is reinforced by his lying about in bed smearing cheese on crackers and chugging beer.

Realizing that it's possible that Alicia is being poisoned, Devlin has to cool his heels and stew in his own bitter juices when he goes back to Sebastian's house, forced to wait on a small and uncomfortable high-backed seat in the foyer. We hear the grandfather clock ticking, tolling quietly. With a mere five minutes left in the film, Devlin's love for Alicia belatedly but finally spurs him to action, and he scampers up a huge curving stairway to search. He finds her sick in bed from slow arsenic poisoning; Hitchcock directs him to rest his head on her pillow in a close-up that makes it appear that they are lying together.

"I was getting out because I love you," he whispers. "I couldn't bear to see you and him together." No music now, just the sounds of their breathing and slight rustling of her nightgown on the soundtrack, the camera lovingly, erotically, achingly circles them in palpable extreme close-up for the first and only time. With all subjective objects obliterated, their final clinch comes with Alicia whispering, "Oh, you love me. Why didn't you tell me before?"

The Paradine Case (1947)

> *The Paradine Case* carries forward the director's progressively refined sense of light and shadow, his idea of balancing pairs of characters, and his insistence on the potentially symbolic value of quite ordinary objects—eyeglasses, statues, portraits, swords, cut-glass lamps [Spoto, 1976, p. 175].

"Quite ordinary objects" do, in fact, make a statement almost immediately in this underrated film. Right after the credits roll, Hitchcock shows us a butler in long shot walk screen right to screen left with a tray in his hand. Shot in a huge hallway, he is framed by two towering candelabras nearly two body-lengths taller than he is, set atop two three-legged and six-foot high tables. Coiled snakes carved out of wood wind their way up the legs, punctuated by three glaring gargoyles at the top of each table. The foreboding shot embodies the effects of frustrated lust.

Humorously, in his second and final Hitchcock film, Charles Laughton's Judge Lord Thomas ("Tommy") Horfield is introduced to us almost exactly the same way he appeared in his first film years earlier, *Jamaica Inn*: surrounded by the excesses of drink, food, and dining table clutter. Another huge candelabra with four lit candles looms over the proceedings, all objects in the frame lending their ostentatious, even gluttonous character, to his. And, when Laughton grabs Gay Keane's (Ann Todd) lovely and delicate hand in his puffy and coarse one and places it atop his knee, Hitchcock films them in a medium two-shot sitting behind more liquor bottles, the neck of one rising up directly in front of his lap! When Gay disgustedly tears herself away

The Paradine Case (1947)

from his lusting actions, Hitchcock cuts to a medium long shot of the two of them from another angle, but the liquor bottles are now conspicuously gone.

As in, especially, *Rebecca*, *Foreign Correspondent*, *Suspicion* and *Marnie*, paintings assert their back-from-the-dead character in very strong ways. The Horfields have one over their mantelpiece, as do the Keanes, and the portrait of Maddalena Anna Paradine (Alida Valli), just like Laura's in director Otto Preminger's *Laura* three years earlier, hovers menacingly throughout much of the picture. "Portraits are always sinister in Hitchcock. They're images, specters in a way, and they usually do bad things to people. They judge and look down on us" (Stephen Rebello and Bill Krohn; 2005 *Paradine Case* DVD audio commentary).

And, without any lying about in it, a bed does a lot of Gay's accusing as she holds the mirror up to her husband's philandering desires. "I love that she is confronting him about his sort of emotional infidelity already with a bed being so present" (Stephen Rebello and Bill Krohn, 2005 *Paradine Case* audio commentary).

Gregory Peck's second and final film for Hitchcock, *The Paradine Case* includes one scene in particular that stands out in terms of subjectively acting objects. Barrister Anthony Keane has been falling hard for Mrs. Paradine during his defense of her accused murder of her husband. In an effort to win the case (and the girl, in spite of the mutual if rocky love still simmering between himself and his wife Gay), Tony hopes a conversation with Mrs. Paradine's butler Andre Latour (Louis Jourdan) will provide illumination. Contributing to his increasing frustrations, however, Latour cannot be found, for Hitchcock keeps them from each other (and us) via extended tracking shots of his search throughout the huge Paradine mansion (again, shades of Manderley). Latour, like Mrs. Danvers, is almost invisible or barely glimpsed among the shadows of this home. Adding to our annoyance, there are several tilted, sharply angled camera shots of Latour's back and head, never his face; shades of Hitchcock's German Expressionist training.

After nearly ten minutes of real and screen time, just when Hitchcock has successfully made us give up on ever seeing Latour, there he is suddenly in a held close-up behind a window pane. The shock of actor Jourdan's handsome features rocks us, so long withheld from Keane's and our desire, for the montage leading up to this reveal had been done through increasingly longer tracking shots. Hitch is clearly practicing here the vertiginous languor of Scottie's drives through the streets of San Francisco eleven years later in *Vertigo*.

With that feeling of exasperation freely flowing in our minds and hearts—remember, Tony's personal life has been integrally twisted up with his professional all along, and our identification with him is strong—Hitchcock's startling use of a simple but imposing lamp as a confounding character coming between Latour and Keane and us (*ménage à trois*? *ménage à quatre*?) is primed for action. "As Latour and Keane talk at a country inn, a low-hanging lampshade with daggerlike glass drops hangs between them. This kind of lamp, whether suspended from a ceiling or placed on a table or mantle, runs like a motif through the film" (Spoto, 1976, p. 179).

During a full eight minutes of verbal jousting, there are no fewer than twenty-five cuts, close-ups, two-shots, and sharply angled camera movements on and around and above this bedeviling lamp. Set squarely above the table and centered between the two men, the intrusive object completely disrupts their argument as if it *is* a third wheel—a stand-in for Tony's love for Gay, perhaps, his misplaced infatuation for Mrs. Paradine, or even Latour's mysterious past—roiling their banter. With every verbal prod and parry, Hitchcock's camera keeps the lamp "moving" in such a way that it pushes and pokes at each of them, too—annoyingly, insistently, and cloyingly—like a dinner guest who just will not leave.

During the denouement, Horfield and his wife Lady Sophie (an Oscar-nominated performance by Ethel Barrymore) argue over the need for love between two married people; he is against it, she for. As when we were first introduced to Laughton, they sit at an enormous table eating dinner and dwarfed by huge, threatening candelabras, wine glasses, and excesses of food. (It is interesting to note that, while Laughton has a fully cooked meal before him, Barrymore is given only one apple, two walnuts, and a conspicuously placed nutcracker.) "Emotional distance [is] telegraphed by length of table," Rebello and Krohn note (2005 *Paradine Case* DVD audio commentary).

After Horfield throws his wife's broken wine glass into the fire,

Hitchcock shoots him in an imposing close-up with a ridiculous-looking mass of unlit candles bunched together (at least eight, perhaps a dozen) on a wall behind him. As he begins to pace back and forth in that background space, we see a candelabra with four lit candles foreground Laughton in juxtaposition with the deeply shadowed, unlit candles behind him, love vs. lack of love respectively embodied. No such hope for the Horfields; the film properly ends with a hint of a loving future for Tony and Gay.

Rope (1948)

> Hitchcock's style is narrative. His camera chooses, relates [and] takes sides.... When employed with skill, the frame is, to use [André] Bazin's expression, a veritable "keyhole"—but an ideal, a mobile, keyhole, the infinitely malleable contours of which are not noticeable [Rohmer and Chabrol, 1957, pp. 95, 96].

Obfuscating lamps as insistent subjects abound in Hitchcock's films. In *Rope*, the three lamps spread around the apartment where Brandon Shaw (John Dall) and Phillip Morgan (Farley Granger in his first of two Hitchcock films) have just strangled David Kentley (Dick Hogan) smartly play their part. For example, when we watch Anita Atwater (Constance Collier) in a medium shot mistake Kenneth Lawrence (Douglas Dick) for her nephew David, Hitchcock's camera quickly pans right to follow her gaze across the room. The first pan in a long while, it alerts us that something important is about to happen, and the blurring movements of the camera's focus zip past the brightly reflected white surfaces of two lampshades, warning flashes nestled among the dark blues of everyone's suit colors. During this rush of movement, and exactly when she squints and asks if that is David, we can just make out the sound of breaking glass on the soundtrack, even though we're not quite sure what we've heard. The camera tells us immediately what it was, however, as it settles in on a startling close-up shot of Phillip's bloodied hands, foregrounding his own dark suit and caused by his shocked response upon hearing the dead man's name

HITCHCOCK'S OBJECTS AS SUBJECTS

called out. A third bright lampshade within our view helps us focus on his frightened response.

How do we know no one else on the screen hears or sees this shot? Because Hitchcock's sudden pan had forced our identification with Mrs. Atwater and her near-sightedness. In retrospect, we begin to realize that from the moment we laid eyes on her entering the apartment, we could see that her mock smile was actually an effort to disguise poor eyesight. In other words, our view had been deliberately shifted from a medium shot of her to a close-up of Phillip's hands as hidden behind Kenneth, literally out of everyone's sight except our (and the camera's) view. Here are the dialogue and object descriptions that helped blur our vision:

> MRS. ATWATER [*happily surprised*]: "David!" [Her face is in medium close-up, squinting across the room; camera pans quickly right to follow the direction of her voice.]
>
> BRANDON [*off-camera*]: "Oh, no, no, uh ... this is, uh ... you've *made a mistake*. This is Kenneth Lawrence." [Camera continues panning right with blurred bodies and lamps hurtling by, then slows for a moment until quickly zooming in to Phillip's red-stained hands wrapped around a now-crushed martini glass.]
>
> MRS. ATWATER [*still off-camera*]: "Oh, I'm sorry." [The camera pans with Phillip's hands as he moves left behind Kenneth, ostensibly to further hide his injury and find a cloth.]
>
> MR. KENTLEY [*soothingly*]: "Oh, that's all right, Anita. Kenneth is often *mistaken* for David, even by people who aren't *near-sighted*. We haven't had much opportunity to *observe* the *resemblance* lately, my boy. You haven't been *studying*, have you?"
>
> KENNETH: "I've been *trying to*, sir."
>
> MR. KENTLEY: "Oh dear, the *resemblance* is only *visual*." [All italics added.]

The above italicized words directly or indirectly refer to correct or incorrect illuminations of the scene, and reinforce the mixed signals that lamps signify—one turned on, the other two shut off. Through both visual and aural means, Hitchcock reminds us that, once again, all is not as it appears. And, as people can choose to reveal or conceal things, lights and lamps as protagonists in Hitchcock's films can take on similar roles.

The film's story is drawn from the infamous Nathan Leopold and Richard Loeb murder case of 1924, a thrill-seeking experiment

Rope (1948)

based on the theory that murder should be the privilege of an elite few. Interestingly, the way Hitchcock filmed it, the murdered young man named David plays a larger part as a dead "object" than if he were actually alive. "David is the center of the film, the person on whom all the others base their identity. David's central position ... is reinforced by Hitchcock's constant reference to a third home, the chest in which his body is hidden and which serves, as Brandon remarks, as his burial ground.... [Instead] of wandering around offscreen, he has actually been present, in this visual and ceremonial home, all along" (Leitch, 1991, p. 141).

Hitchcock would treat the dead "object" of Harry Worp seven years later in *The Trouble with Harry* with an even greater boldness, for he would hardly ever be hidden. "That wooden chest in which John Dall and Farley Granger, as the two young intellectual murderers, placed the body, practically played second lead in the picture. This chest with the body inside of it was always in the center of the living room—so far as the audience is aware" (Hitchcock, 1948; cited in Gottlieb, 1995, p. 281).

In the case of candles, which unlike lamps reveal only so much when lit, Hitchcock directed these characters along similar lines. Two three-pronged candelabra play prominent roles in mirroring the ultimate sterility of Brandon and Phillip in their murderous, faux-philosophical embrace. "The candles, lit for the meal and placed atop the chest, are also for a funeral. Once again, then, Hitchcock interrelates the themes of play, sex, food, murder and ritual" (Spoto, 1976, p. 188).

We see Brandon fruitlessly work for several minutes at one point trying to right a tilted and flaccid, half-melted candle in its holder. Thinking it fixed, he turns away only to miss it drooping again at the end of his effort. The six now-spent, unlit (translation: impotent) candles are then moved from the top of the buffet table to the top of the crypt, the large chest within which their victim has been placed. Those candles remain unlit for quite some time, as do the lamps, which Phillip urges Brandon *not* to turn on immediately after the murder, in order to (perversely) savor the moment—as, perhaps, in post-coital bliss. But during the meal, their weak flickering "support[s the] funereal atmosphere" (1976, p. 170) of the entire scenario, Spoto rightly notes.

Hitchcock's Objects as Subjects

Under Capricorn (1949)

> [On] a low chest beneath [a] portrait rests a small statue of a mounted knight slaying a dragon. The gallant knight Charles has come to the rescue [Brill, 1988, p. 264].

Recalling the name of Mrs. De Winter, who lived in a huge home named Manderley, there is something unnerving in the fact that the last name of one of the servants in the large Australian manor of this film is also Winter. The house in *Under Capricorn* has a name, too—Minyago Yugilla, meaning "Why Weepest Thou." It plays a similar part in our narrative, closing characters off from each other as they move from room to room and conversation to conversation. References to another earlier film, *Notorious*, occur twice in one scene: Sam Flusky (Joseph Cotten, in his second of two Hitchcock films) demands that Milly (Margaret Leighton) give him the keys to the house, as Alex had of his butler. He then gives them to Ingrid Bergman, as Hattie here, the same actress in both films..

Regardless, the story of *Under Capricorn* (as in Tropic of, south of the equator) takes place in the year 1831, decades before the invention of electricity. Hitchcock's use of burning and unlit candles, therefore, in tandem and triplicate, must carry all the illumination meanings. Most often, though not always, Hitchcock firmly plants two candles side by side on a wall or in a single candle holder and, usually but not always, has them lit and representing all three sets of competing couples for each other's attentions: Sam and Hattie, Charles Adare (a very good Michael Wilding in his first of two Hitchcock films) and Hattie, and Sam and Milly. The doubled candles insistently compel us to wonder who will end up with whom, while the occasional trio of candles reminds us of the competing love triangles so often at work throughout this drama.

For example, as Charles and Hattie's love for each other flickers on (just a bit), Sam is shot between two burning candles, uncertain of his fate. Later, Charles stands between two looming pillars, the person now caught between and torn by the real love Sam and Hattie have for each other. Adare will ultimately act properly to save their marriage and love.

Under Capricorn (1949)

Under Capricorn (1949): Charles Adare (Michael Wilding) chases Lady Henrietta Flusky (Ingrid Bergman) through a large crowd within another huge home, like *Rebecca*'s Manderley, that closes them off from each other.

Still later, as Charles becomes aware that he really does not have a chance with Hattie, Hitchcock shows us two lit candles side by side again, but the one closest to Hattie in the frame has burned lower than the one next to Charles, her possible love for him literally burning out. After Hitchcock lovingly follows Hattie and Wilding in a circle all around the room during her justly famous ten-minute monologue, Adare (who had "dared" to insinuate himself into this loving marriage) finally accepts his supportive, not primary, role for the true loving couple. As Rohmer and Chabrol rightly note, the "camera moves with an extreme ease and audacity [and] hugs the characters more and more closely" (1957, p. 102), particularly in this scene, and finally comes to rest in a gorgeous, tight close-up of Bergman's ravishing face. Now, and only now, two equally burning candles directly behind her balance out the truth of her story.

Charles is accidentally shot by Sam. As he recuperates in bed, a final trio of candles remains unlit behind him on the wall. The love triangle in this costume drama no longer burns with intermingling desire.

Stage Fright (1950)

> One example to me in *Stage Fright* is the moment when Alastair Sim wants to bring this blood-stained doll up to Marlene Dietrich while she's singing the song in the tent. So now you see this little boy carrying this doll with this big blood stain on it and it suddenly becomes something quite other than this doll [Guillermo del Toro].

At the beginning of *Stage Fright*, we see a safety curtain, normally representing the start (or finish) of an onstage production, rise to reveal a long shot of the city of London. Is Hitchcock warning us that the story about to be told by Jonathan to Eve is also a fiction? The murderer will be horribly killed himself, full circle irony, by that very same safety curtain. "As befits [Jonathan's] unharmonized dichotomy, he is chopped in half by [it] on the theater stage" (Yacowar, 1977, p. 267). Nevertheless, numerous critics felt so deceived by Jonathan's bald-faced lie that they blamed the director for misleading them, and he apologized. Ha! How prescient Hitchcock turned out to be with all the false leads we relish today in so many films and TV detective series.

The hand-held camera that follows Barton into the house at the beginning of *Number Seventeen* nineteen years earlier is recapitulated here when Jonathan Cooper (Irish-born actor Richard Todd) regales Eve Gill (American actress Jane Wyman) with his false story of murder at the beginning of the film. Honky Tonk music composed by the British-born Leighton Lucas plays on the soundtrack as Hitchcock's famed moving camera physically follows Jonathan as he enters Charlotte Inwood's (Marlene Dietrich) house, the door (on rollers) silently closing behind him and us. In a brilliant single take exactly one minute long, it climbs the stairs with him, too. (Hitch will silently, horribly reverse this climb in *Frenzy* twenty-two years later.)

Stage Fright (1950)

Still viewed within Jonathan's lying account of the murder, images of the two muses Terpsichore and Polyhymna on a door above the dead husband laugh down at Jonathan's difficulty in opening it to retrieve a fresh dress for Charlotte. As we watch him first imagining the police figure out who the guilty party might be (and really is, ultimately), then actually calling him on the phone as a suspect, we see and hear his phone ring, Hitchcock deliberately hammering home the feel of reality in our minds to this extraordinarily detailed lie.

We see Jonathan stand by that phone for a couple of minutes ruminating, a painting over the mantle showing a Dali-like surrealistic corkscrew building and a staring woman's face looming over him. Upon stealing Eve away from her acting rehearsal at the Royal Academy of Dramatic Arts—more realism about fictions, for all the film's a stage in this one—Hitchcock shoots them both backstage foregrounded by three large curtain ropes, harbingers of his doom. A full thirteen minutes of screen time after his lie began, Hitchcock finally fades back out to the "present" at the film's fifteen-minute point.

Commodore Gill, Eve's father (played to the hilt by the marvelously eccentric Alastair Sim), figures out that someone smeared blood on Charlotte's dress, our first hint that Jonathan's story may not ultimately hold water (or any other liquid). But we're now so caught up in Eve's love for him, also working its way into her father's sympathies, that we still do not question his innocence. Cleverly, Jonathan flings the damning garment into the fire.

As they plot in a bar to substitute Eve in her place, the maid Nellie Goode's (Kay Walsh) two-timing reflection stares back from a mirror behind them at not only herself but Eve and us, too. Nellie grabs her bribe before Eve can cover it with her hand, and Hitchcock shows us the back of everyone's heads in the mirror now; deceptions multiplied. Thinking it's her reflection, more mirror-based (and eyeglass) humor ensues as Eve peers through her too-thick bifocals prop at her shadow on a door. A small portrait of a laughing fiddler playing a tune hangs on the wall behind her while pizzicato violin strings pluck out a jaunty tune by Lucas on the soundtrack.

Smoking like a steam engine, Dietrich's Charlotte is shot by Hitchcock in a glorious, gauzy haze, the smoke enveloping her both in front of and through the mirror's image as an extraordinary double veil.

Hitchcock's Objects as Subjects

Shades of the disruptive character of steam from *Mr. and Mrs. Smith* and *Shadow of a Doubt* spring to mind.

> Charlotte is usually photographed regarding herself at a vanity table or in a hand-mirror. She is thus not usually looking at her interlocutor but gazing directly out at us (or at least gazing to one side of the camera). This naturally draws the viewer more deeply into Charlotte's character and makes our response to her the most complex in the film. (The important mirror imagery reoccurs in *Psycho*, where all the characters are components of one another and, finally, of *one* character—the viewer of the film.) [Spoto, 1976, p. 206].

As Jonathan puts the moves on Eve yet again in an effort to get her to hide him from the police, her face turns not toward his chest but toward the piano where the detective Ordinary Smith had played a lovely romantic tune the day before. The piano, not a person, motivated her decision to face that direction. Michael Wilding's detective is a much more sympathetic character here in black and white than in his work in the previous Hitchcock color film, as Charles Adare, and reminds us of Macdonald Carey's kindly police character Jack Graham from *Shadow of a Doubt*.

During the climactic scene in the theater, the echoing of Charlotte's disembodied voice and Hitchcock's extreme high overhead shot make it remarkably powerful. More smoke running across her gorgeous face is the last shot we have of the delicious Dietrich, and Hitch holds his camera on her for a glorious five seconds in a stunning extreme close-up.

Eve and Jonathan try to hide in the prop room beneath the stage, but the camera itself seeks them out mercilessly via dolly shots, eventually finding them in a horse's carriage not unlike the one Maureen O'Hara's Mary took to Jamaica Inn eleven years earlier. When they reach their lair, all Hitchcock allows us to see for five painfully tense minutes are their disembodied eyes in alternating close-ups. Right at the end of those five minutes, Hitchcock cuts to a viscerally powerful ten-second hold on Jonathan's hands and fingers as they open, foreshadowing the frequent close-ups on Bruno's hands in the next film, *Strangers on a Train*. Here we see Eve's fingers suddenly clasp his in hopeful, prayer-like supplication, a poignant juxtaposition.

The film abruptly ends (reminiscent of a dying Mr. Memory, also backstage, in *The 39 Steps* fifteen years earlier) as the heavy iron curtain of the theater drops down to crush the pathetic Jonathan. Lucas' romantic music swells with deep irony.

Strangers on a Train (1951)

> The imposing, insistent background imagery of Washington's public edifices underscores Guy's rather distant, austere mien. Like the buildings, he has notable stature and solidity but little warmth. In the last sequence, when Guy and Ann leave the Capitol, we have the sense that the stony Guy may be softening into flesh [Brill, 1988, pp. 74–75].

As in so many Hitchcock films, disembodied body parts speak loudly in this picture. Introducing us to Bruno Anthony (Robert Walker in his second to last film before an untimely death) and Guy Haines (Farley Granger, in his second of two Hitchcock films), shoes and the lower half of their bodies stand in for our lead protagonists for a full seventy-five seconds, until the legs accidentally crisscross and bump into each other on a train to Metcalf. (Two pairs of shoes of two other total strangers will recapitulate this seemingly harmless meeting in the latter part of the picture as Guy rushes to stop Bruno from placing damning evidence on the Magic Isle at the amusement park.) "That accidental collision of the two men's feet is the point of departure for their whole relationship, and the concept is sustained by deliberately refraining from showing their faces up to that point" (Truffaut, 1967, p. 144). Close-ups of their twisted legs grotesquely recall young Charlie's struggles during her fight with Uncle Charlie in *Shadow of a Doubt*, as legs representing people will be used in similar fashion in the future, during several of Marnie's inner demon battles.

A sign that reads "On sale here" in Miller's Music Store, where Guy's wife Miriam (Kasey Rogers) works, proves all too true as she tries to blackmail him into keeping her as a kept woman in Washington, D.C., and bringing up the baby that was fathered by someone else. When Guy has to yell into the phone to his real love, Anne Morton (Ruth Roman), "I said I could strangle her," over the loud background train sounds, Hitchcock audaciously cuts to a close-up of Bruno's hands, another body extremity standing in for the entire person. Hands as the "spokesperson" of a character's thoughts and emotions, the reader will recall, were seen in the previous year's *Stage Fright* and most notably with Uncle Charlie, and from *Blackmail* all the way through *Frenzy*. Later in *Strangers*, "[the] contrast between fingertips straining for a lighter and tennis-champions smashing volleys at one another has a beautifully orchestrated physicality about it, as empathy alternately provokes and represses energy in the spectator" (Durgnat, 1974, p. 229).

Upping the ante, Hitchcock continues to use objects in this film to deliberately block our vision. When Bruno is alerted at his home to a call he has placed to Guy in Southampton, the camera follows his striding walk in a medium long shot from one room to the other at a slightly increasing speed with a zooming pan screen right to screen left. Set to foreboding music by the Russian-born stylist Dimitri Tiomkin, Bruno successively passes behind one large darkened lamp, a huge pile of flowers in half darkness, and a second huge unlit lamp. As he forcefully moves past all these obstacles on his way towards murdering Miriam, the many objects blocking our view but bypassed by Bruno encourage us to feel this man's sense of rage and omnipotence.

Miriam's near-silent murder as reflected in the famous convex-lens shot of her broken eyeglasses takes a harrowing twenty-two seconds, ending with a close-up of Bruno's hands in grotesquely perverse elongation (there is a palpable sexual tension to the montage). Later, when Bruno calls Guy from across the street to tell him what he has done, Hitchcock shoots the scene with them *both* barely visible behind the "prison bars" of that home's privacy gate.

Flowers, books, and lamps in Senator Morton's home—all the trappings of wealth—crowd in on all four of the people in the scene (Leo G. Carroll as the Senator, Ruth Roman as Anne, Farley Granger as Guy, and Patricia Hitchcock in the second of three films for her father, as Barbara "Babs" Morton) as they discuss the murder. And when Guy and Anne amorously kiss, a bright lamp in the background is their only support. Contrastingly, a similarly bright lamp between two people will act as darkly ironic commentary during an argument between Guy and Bruno in Mr. Anthony's bedroom.

Strangers on a Train (1951)

Guy looks at a clock while switching sides in his tennis match, immediately followed by Bruno seen in front of a large sundial outside his home. There's more irony as Guy rushes to beat Bruno back to Magic Isle, hoping to retrieve the damning evidence of his lighter. Just as he leaves the tennis stadium, we can see the words of a quote etched in the Wimbledon overhang above him: "And treat those imposters just the same." Hitchcock may be asking us if this is how we would want ourselves to be treated.

An extreme close-up of Bruno's deadly yet perfectly manicured fingers straining to reach the fallen lighter is also sexual in its potency, a typically erotic juxtaposition for Hitchcock. Ironically, Bruno admits shortly that he doesn't even know what "schmoochers" are, proving his asexuality, if anything. Robin Wood equated the lost lighter with an even more intimate quality, saying that the "leaving of the lighter is one of the visual equivalents Hitchcock finds for the interior, psychological analysis of the Patricia Highsmith novel that was his source" (1965, p. 45). And the extreme long shots of Grand Central Station are reminiscent of *Blackmail*'s British Museum, *North by Northwest*'s high overhead of the United Nations, and *Torn Curtain*'s Berlin Museum. People, meaningless ants far below, fall under the power of these buildings' sway.

As Bruno returns to the amusement park, he passes two boys this time, each with balloons, a reminder of the one boy's balloon he had earlier burst with a cigarette. Children will not let him get away with it a second time, Hitchcock seems to say. And then he walks beneath the park's arch with the numbers and words "20 BIG" centered above him. Could it mean "plenty big," as in this story is plenty big even for him, or "too big," a play on the number two? Either makes sense. As he waits in line for the boat to Magic Isle and moves from shadow into light, the scene is a clear reversal of the fearsome shot of his boat's shadow gaining on Miriam's in the earlier Tunnel of Love sequence. The shadows this time tell us it is his time for comeuppance.

Hitchcock shoots the justly famous finale of the runaway carousel horses from various angles and in extreme close-ups, making them alternately stampede around and impede Bruno's attempted murder of Guy. Their visages are frighteningly real, the shots of this merry-go-round reminiscent of the swing carousels standing in for the chaos of humanity in *The Ring* three decades earlier. Certainly their hooves in close-up are nightmarish recapitulations of the two men's own legs and shoes that introduced us to them, quite harmlessly, at the beginning of the picture.

I Confess (1952)

> If you love Hitchcock you have to love this [one]. It's one of his most visually stunning films. The way that he turns real marble and clouds and concrete into shot after shot that express states of the soul, nobody can do today [Bill Krohn, "Hitchcock's Confession: A Look at *I Confess*," 2004 *I Confess* DVD special feature].

Because it is still only seven years since the end of World War II, painful associations about Germans are still part of the zeitgeist, and clearly recalled in this underappreciated film. Any sympathies, therefore, which we might have for Otto Keller—played by actor-director O.E. Hasse with a scary, bug-eyed delirium—are hard to sustain.

This is a difficult but deeply rewarding film. The only relief from its seriousness is provided by Brian Aherne's Crown Prosecutor Willy Robertson who, at least until his schnauzer-like relentlessness during the trial, is all about fun and games with glasses—the drinking kind, not the kind for eyes. First, he balances a coin and two forks on a glass and then, at a party, he balances one filled with water on his head as he tries to limbo down to the floor! Later, of course, Hitchcock insists that Aherne is the one to bring a glass of water to Anne Baxter's Ruth Grandfort prior to her confession of love for Michael Logan.

> Brian Aherne's characterization as the prosecutor was quite interesting. The first time we see him, he's playfully balancing a knife and fork on a glass; the next time he's lying on the floor, balancing a glass of water on his forehead. I had the feeling that both incidents were related to the idea of equilibrium, that they were put there to suggest that in his scale of values, justice was merely a parlor game [Truffaut, 1967, p. 152].

Objects obfuscate yet again in a Hitchcock picture when Pierre

I Confess (1952)

Grandfort (French actor Roger Dann) confronts Ruth, his wife (Anne Baxter), over her love for Father Michael Logan (an excellent Montgomery Clift). Our view of them during this confrontation is nearly impossible with a host of darkly silhouetted *objets d'art* strewn about their living room. When Pierre storms out in anger, saying, "I hope he's in trouble, terrible trouble," Hitchcock shoots Ruth in a medium long shot looking trapped among all the accouterments. As in *Rebecca*, *Suspicion* and *Notorious*, lamps, a sofa, wall candles, vases, and party glasses hover menacingly all about. Running into her den, Ruth is all but obliterated by the oversized lamps, phone, and chair back foregrounding the screen. In a medium shot, Hitchcock only allows us see to her jewel-covered wrist dialing Michael's number, and from behind only. Likewise, the silhouette of Inspector Larrue observing the priest "suggests, as do silhouettes generally in Hitchcock's work, an incompleteness of vision" (Brill, 1988, p. 100). Like the black smoke pouring forth from the train that brought Uncle Charlie to Santa Rosa in *Shadow of a Doubt*, the ferry upon which Logan and Ruth meet also spews out its soot.

These are real human beings in this film—albeit actors playing real human beings—but the screenwriters, Hungarian-born George Tabori and Trinidad-born William Archibald, test the veracity of that phrase by having first Keller and then Ruth ask Logan and Inspector Larrue respectively whether they *are* human beings. Is the implication that they are objects, not people? No, the questions are asked to find out *how* human they really are. Of course, just prior to Ruth's confession of love for Logan to Larrue, she asks Willy to bring her that glass of water.

Hitchcock alternately shoots nearly everyone in this picture as if he or she is on a pedestal—or, more accurately, speaking at a confessional or to a savior. Logan is seen at length looking down on Keller as he stands on a ladder painting a wall; Ruth is viewed by Logan in slow motion during a flashback scene looking up at her as she descends a spiral staircase; Larrue stands above Logan during his interrogation; and Pierre looms above Ruth during her confession of love for Logan. Finally, in a brilliantly cruel reversal of all these God's-eye views, Keller is *looked up to* by Prosecutor Willy Robertson during the trial. This last shot—held the longest, too, for maximum effect—is the most bitterly ironic, of course, for Keller has been lying the whole time and *is* the evil one in the picture, not a godsend.

Quick and frequent cuts during the trial to Keller's wife, Alma, played by the estimable German actress Dolly Haas, reveal her deeply pained, intimate reactions to his lies, based on what we no doubt attribute to a long marriage of suffering from before the war in their homeland. Keller may very well have worked for the Nazis, although it's never revealed. As our hearts go out to this woman, her husband's non-stop duplicitous falsehoods on the witness stand in front of hundreds of onlookers is shot from such an extreme camera angle that it makes us palpably cringe at his hypocrisy. The camera has once again been placed in the perfect position for maximum effect.

During Ruth's flashback confession to Larrue, Hitchcock shoots her in the pouring rain from above and behind as she waits in vain outside her home for letters from Michael during the war. We can see several more spiral staircases cascade down from next-door tenements, harkening back to the dream-like vision of herself on a similar staircase when they were in love, but these images now painfully twist her vision out of shape. Cut to Larrue listening intently to her story in his office, a map of the Quebec streets on the wall behind him flaring out its avenues in chaos around his head like static electricity. Later, Ruth even says, "They'll twist what I've said. They'll turn it, they'll use it," which is meant to refer to the damning evidence she has supplied to the authorities but, on second thought, could certainly refer to any authoritarian regime's tactics.

As Michael walks the streets, trapped by his priestly vows over Keller's original confessional and uncertain of what to do, he passes a sign and photo in a movie theater for the recently released Humphrey Bogart drama *The Enforcer* (1951). The film is about a hunt for a murderer, and the photo is of a man's empty dress suit, reference to an imagined or earlier life of Michael's, perhaps, but also, certainly, his present circumstances as he struggles with what it means to be both a human being and a priest. Again, the suit is empty and so, it seems, is he.

Cigarette smoke swirls and conceals the briefly shown jury room deliberations in the same way as *Shadow of a Doubt*'s train smoke, this film's ferry, and Marlene Dietrich's clouded double veils in *Stage Fright*.

And the crowds of hateful people inside the court building who hang on and over the huge spiral stairs that go down to the first floor (twisted shades, once again, from Ruth's dream), and the larger masses outside taunting Father Logan, cause him to smash an elbow through a nearby car door window. These people are not human beings but mindless, heartless lemmings, clearly harkening back to the wartime Nazi collaborators. "The crowd will not accept the verdict. Walking in dignity through the hooting populace, the priest, who does not even have the recourse of washing his shame away, slowly leaves the courtroom. We see him surrounded by hostile faces, descending the great stairway all alone, like Christ carrying his cross" (Rohmer and Chabrol, 1957, p. 117).

When Alma runs to protect Logan, her husband raises his pistol—a German Luger, of course—and then aims and shoots at her (and us) directly at the camera in a close-up *à la* Murchison's suicide in *Spellbound* seven years earlier. Again, it is difficult not to associate this atrocity with the hatred behind the inhuman mass exterminations of World War II.

Dial M for Murder (1954)

> Each gesture, each thought, each material or moral being, is the depository of a secret capable of explaining everything: and this light dispenses as much fear as comfort [Rohmer and Chabrol, 1957, p. 112].

Dial M for Murder recapitulates *Rope*'s lamps five-fold. As with *Rope*'s restrictions to a single set and, even more confined, the one in *Lifeboat*, *Dial M* takes place almost entirely inside a two-room apartment. There are a few brief forays out into a hallway, the street, and a glimpse of a harbor, but the room itself is a powerful character that dictates much of the action of the original Frederick Knott play. "In *Dial M*, I made sure that I would go outside as little as possible. I had a real tile floor laid down, the crack under the door, the shadow of the feet, all part of the stage play, and I made sure I didn't lose that" (Hitchcock; Cited in Bogdanovich, 1963, p. 32).

Hitchcock's Objects as Subjects

Hitchcock publicly claimed he did not open out the film at all, but his direction of the film's five main characters—and the lamps, furniture, liquor bottles, handbag, and latch keys—allow us to experience a myriad of protagonists in these cramped rooms. (Hitchcock ostensibly treated the two early plays he filmed the same way—1931's *Juno and the Paycock* and 1932's *The Skin Game*—but my analysis of both of those often unheralded films in my 2006 book, *Hitchcock Nonetheless: The Master's Touch in His Least Celebrated Films*, demonstrates otherwise.)

Dial M for Murder, Hitchcock's lone foray into 3-D, is worth seeing in that format if for no other reason than to notice the director's restraint with the special effects. Close-ups of keys and other objects occur discreetly throughout the film, heightening their subjectivity. And at one particularly dramatic moment, like Marion Crane's hand reaching out for help directly towards us after her murder in *Psycho*'s shower scene seven years later, Margot's straining fingers literally grab backwards at our faces as Swann attempts to kill her. We palpably spring back.

Again, as with *The Paradine Case* and *Rope*, huge lamps simultaneously illuminate and obstruct the proceedings at key moments, in both obvious and subtle ways. Paralleling the five human protagonists, there are five other object characters, three of which appear to be all the same. Those three are conspicuously green, jade-like, square-ish ceramic table lamps with oversized, rounded tops framed by rectangular-patterned shades. The fact that they number three certainly reflects the tensions in the plot's tangled love triangle, and their green color hammers home the driving forces behind Tony's murder attempt on his wife Margot—jealousy and envy.

> The *instruments* of lighting receive visual emphasis.... The several lamps are used as props between actors and thus create admirable composed frames. One on a low table between Tony and Lesgate serves as a unifying and dividing element between them and is a focal point around which the murder is planned [Spoto, 1976, pp. 233–234].

There are two other lamps that insinuate themselves into this film's plot: a very large desk lamp, itself a cylindrically shaped ceramic in the Chinoiserie style, and a chandelier with eight small and round attached

Dial M for Murder (1954)

lights. Naturally, the little shades on the lights are colored envy-green, too. This chandelier is viewed just twice, shot once in close-up and then in middle distance, from the director's favored bird's-eye view perspective.

For a variety of reasons, the contrasting round and square shapes of the lamps—and the room architecture, furniture, tennis trophies, and murder weapon (scissors)—are keys to their affective character in the film. Tony Wendice's (the estimable British actor Ray Milland in his only film for Hitchcock) world and subsequent murder plot are meant to feel very deliberate, precise, and perfect, just like all the straight and sure lines in this room. Tony was, after all (this part of the plot is hard to believe, frankly), a tennis champion, and his line-up of numerous oval-shaped trophies on the mantle attests to the exactitude necessary to achieve such "perfection." In fact, the French name for the film was *Le Crime Était Presque Parfait,* "the crime was almost perfect." His wife, apparently, had been treated as one of those trophies, too, otherwise she might not have looked to the Bohemian life of an American mystery writer for freedom.

The apartment, then, is one of those prim, trim, proper, traditionally English, well-heeled but not flashy types with lots of clean, straight lines. Even the mass line-up of cylindrically shaped hard liquor bottles—foregrounded in close-up as Mark Halliday (an excellent Robert Cummings in his second and final Hitchcock film) and Margot Wendice (Grace Kelly in perhaps her finest role, in the first of three consecutive films for the director) discuss their surreptitious and dangerous love affair—imply an ordered and orderly existence (gone to pot) by their architectural verticality. Their shape, frequent reference and use via overlarge snifter glasses allude to the overturning of propriety. But the intended impression by this apartment's accouterments, certainly, is one of control, everything in its proper place.

> An art director must have a wide knowledge and understanding of architecture. On the other hand, he must be able to distinguish between what characterizes a type of dwelling and what individuates the inhabitant of that dwelling. The profession of a man may be characterized by what is on his walls.... Increasing awareness of the capacity of the camera to show reality, to set the action in real streets under real trees, created the demand for reality even in interior sets. Therefore the

woodwork and the lath and plaster of sets, no matter how manifestly artificial from behind, must face the camera with all the appearance of visible reality [Hitchcock, 1965; cited in Gottlieb, 1995, pp. 219–220].

Milland's measured delivery of a calculating murderer's thoughts is equally precise, cold and cruel. Even the block letters of the opening credits have that curt and crisp, no-nonsense look and feel. It is not far-fetched to imagine Cary Grant's Johnnie Aysgarth's redemption at the end of *Suspicion* (1941) overturned by Milland's Wendice here—an ending impressed upon Hitchcock by the studio twelve years earlier, and not the preferred one of the director, as he drove Grant to act against type in that picture. Milland clearly recalls the earlier actor in accent, poise, and posture.

As characters, the three green-jade lamps worm their way in and among the three main protagonists and, at several key moments, a fourth—Swann's hapless and sacrificial would-be murderer, perhaps Scottish-born actor Anthony Dawson's finest role. (Although his role as Dent in the opening film in the James Bond series, 1962's *Dr. No*, comes a close second.)

Early on, Hitchcock slowly dollies the camera left so that one of those green lamps wholly blocks our view of Margot as she crosses the room to sit next to Mark in the only soft, cushiony chair in the apartment. This camera movement deliberately foregrounds the lamp in a way that foreshadows coming conflicts. By now, Kelly's outfit has been changed, too—by costume designer Moss Mabry—from her pure white, lack-of-passion wife's blouse to a revealing fiery-red gown. (Mabry was most famous for designing James Dean's red jacket in 1955's *Rebel Without a Cause*.) The gown does an excellent job of exaggerating her small breasts into bright mounds of titillation. This is the only time Hitchcock dazzles us with her beauty in this film, as her outfits subsequently and progressively get darker and drabber (except during the attempted murder, when she again looks ravishing while being ravaged). Her lush look at the start contrasts brilliantly against the strict prison-like lines that stand at attention throughout her husband's apartment fortress of linearity and control.

Shortly, the same bright green-jade lamp is filmed in a way that *makes it seem to move* between Tony and Mark during their first con-

Dial M for Murder (1954)

frontation. All sweet and conversational on the surface, theirs is a raging battle over turf, and the *mise en scène* is exactly like the one between Keane and Latour in *The Paradine Case*. Of course, an inanimate lamp cannot physically travel, but Hitchcock's camera dolly as the men move to sit on the couch deliberately calls our attention to this oversized lamp in a way that feels like it is moving *itself* to a precise midpoint between them. In effect, the lamp stands in for Margot, or conflict personified; both together, if you like. Tony is also foregrounded in this scene by the prim, square shape of what appears to be a wood block cigarette case, while Mark is foregrounded by the soft, rounded top of Tony's cane. Famed Hitchcock researcher and punster Raymond Durgnat would most assuredly have made a clever *jeu de mot* on the uncanny similarities between "Anthony Keane" and "Tony's cane" from their respective two films.

Brilliantly lit single lamps repeatedly appear alongside Tony during the first half of the play, visually reinforcing our association with his single-minded control. Meanwhile, Swann stands framed between two lamps (translation: imprisoned) during the same period, as well as within the rectangular lines on the cold white front door of the apartment. If you look closely, these relationships are reversed as Chief Inspector Hubbard closes in on his prey. Hubbard is played by Hitchcock's oft-employed actor, fellow Brit John Williams.

Elsewhere, in two charged scenes, Hitchcock uses the curvaceous Chinoiserie lamp on the writing desk as a cruel spotlight of sorts. Shot from below and aimed upwards, its light looks like the eerie mood we have all created when holding a flashlight to our own faces in the dark. The first time this occurs is exactly when Tony has fully reeled Swann in. Dawson is directed to move slightly screen right so that he hesitates for a moment with his face directly above the lamp. Caught in its glare, the harried Swann already looks doomed.

> Hitchcock exaggerates deep space at moments of emotional intensity. He marks the stages in Tony's cat-and-mouse game with Swann by placing Swann behind a lamp that looms menacingly in the foreground.... Hitchcock favors compositions that place lamps, knickknacks, and pieces of furniture in the foreground, walls well in the background, and human subjects in a middle-ground clearly distinct from either, emphasizing the ways in which the *mise-en-scène* serves as a trap ... [Leitch, 1991, p. 164].

Hitchcock's Objects as Subjects

The second time is perpetrated on poor Margot at the precise moment she explodes in hysteria, a *tour de force* bit of acting. Inspector Hubbard asks her if she saw Swann's face during the death struggle, and she screams: "But I saw his eyes, inspector, his eyes!" Kelly's frightened features are exposed above that same desk lamp in a way that helps us relive her harrowing nightmare.

A unique Hitchcockian use of an earlier couch lamp that had come between Tony and Mark ensues upon Mark's return appearance the following night. As the men get set to go to Tony's stag party together, we see the couch from the front this time, not from behind when the lamp had been foregrounded on the table in a position of power between the men. Now, Mark and Margot are seen sitting on opposite sides of the couch while Tony looks squeezed out of the picture by that green-with-jealousy lamp. (Even their names flow easily together, Mark and Margot, versus the harsher juxtaposition of Tony and Margot.) The way Hitchcock frames the action, Tony barely has room behind them to hand the loving couple their drinks. Effectively, the director has made him an unwelcome fourth wheel in our eyes (again, shades of the similar scene in *The Paradine Case*).

The accidental murder weapon—scissors—embodies both the linear, sharp lines of the apartment's precise structure and the rounded curves in the handle needed to hold it. And by the time Wendice realizes his round-faced watch has stopped, the rectangular cell of the phone booth (and similar lines on the walls of his apartment) begin to frame and close in on him. The phone finally free, he has to spell out the second half of his last name for the operator to hear him— D-I-C-E—for by now, he really is rolling the dice in this losing game of cat-and-mouse. At the time of Tony's capture by the inspector, Hitchcock shows him, not Swann, ultimately framed between the two envy-green lamps ... but their lights have been extinguished by now.

At the end of the film, when Margot finally says she's about to have that breakdown, it's more than ironic that she sits on Tony's bachelor pad bed that had been set up in the living room. Its rectangular frame belatedly holds his last (and now lost) living trophy. Hitchcock's final image shows her sagging in sadness between two carved trophies on the end of the bedpost.

Rear Window (1954)

> A sealed world inside that other sealed world represented by the City, which can be seen through the gap of a narrow alley, it is made up of a given number of small sealed worlds ... and, because of this, exist not as things in themselves but as pure representations [of] strange silhouettes [that] are like so many shadows in a new version of Plato's cave [Rohmer and Chabrol, 1957, pp. 125–126].

Up go three window shades in the apartment of Jefferies (James Stewart, in his second of four films for the director) to reveal a wonderfully constructed and highly detailed Greenwich Village courtyard. Just like curtains for a play, we don't see anyone effect this movement, so they must have rolled up by themselves. At the end of our feature, only one will close, again, all by itself. "The apparently self-generating movement of the blinds ... anticipates and "triggers" the subsequent slow pan around the courtyard, a shot pointedly unauthorized by any character within the fiction" (Stam and Pearson; cited in Deutelbaum and Poague, 1986, p. 202).

Our introduction to Lisa Carol Fremont (the stunning Grace Kelly, in her second of three films for Hitch) is done via objects, too, the turning on of lamps. As if they could illuminate the person behind this fabulous name and body, we are asked by Hitchcock to see her here as more an object than subject.

> "Who are you?" Jefferies asks; and at once she moves back from him, then swirls round the room switching on lamps: "Reading from top to bottom: Lisa"—first lamp—"Carol"—second—"Fremont"—third. We watch a woman become a mannequin, or even a magazine illustration: it is all Jefferies can accept [Wood, 1965, p. 66].

A question comes to mind before long: Do curtains—and shadows, again, as in so many Hitchcock pictures—provide any safety in *Rear Window*? The answer is: not much, really.

The first shot we see outside Jeff's apartment is a dolly following a black cat crossing the yard, an obvious portent of trouble. Raymond Durgnat rightly notes that the city itself is another important character in this film, as the "apartment window looks into the secrets of the city.... These bright, translucent, open-plan cells are like a hen-battery for human beings, a teasing limbo which is the human condition" (1974, pp. 235–236).

Consistent with this microcosm view of the world, Jeff, then Lisa, Stella (comedic actress Thelma Ritter), and Detective Lieutenant Thomas Doyle (Wendell Corey), all begin to objectify and stereotype the people they see out back: Miss Lonely Hearts, Miss Torso, the composer-musician, the newlyweds, etc.—until the older couple with the (dead) dog pulls them up short, accusing everyone that they forgot what real neighbors should be, caring individuals. Similarly, after Jeff tells Lisa, "You've got this town in the palm of your hand," she retorts, "Not quite, it seems." People as objects, again, contrast with the primary theme of this book, and only the sculptor's sculpture in her backyard, titled "Hunger," reveals any genuine character.

When Jeff responds to Lisa by saying, "I'm not hiding anything," Hitchcock shows him in fact hiding beneath a lit lamp half in shadow. Jefferies moves back and forth in his wheelchair in and out of shadows all the time, to either get a better look out of his window or to not be seen. In *Shadow of a Doubt*, shadows proved deadly; same in *Strangers on a Train*. They almost do Jefferies in, too.

Jeff's friend Inspector Doyle comes around for a visit and, presumably, is a believer in Thorwald's guilt. We presume wrong. As they discuss new evidence, each gently warms the brandy that Lisa has given them in huge snifter glasses with their hands. The conspiracy literally heating up, it turns out that Doyle will rationally lay waste to all their theories. Sustaining the uncertainty of doubt in everyone's minds, however, they keep swirling and warming their drinks. In an extraordinary close-up shot, Hitchcock shoots Doyle's final offer of having "a nice friendly drink or two" with his oversized snifter directly foregrounding a brightly lit lamp, its light seeming to waft up from the brandy's odor. Rejected and rebuffed, Doyle gets up to leave and takes a final rushed snort, spilling brandy all over himself. His soon-to-be-disproven theories will themselves be similarly doused. And as he leaves, dampening their hopes for a good, juicy murder, we briefly see his *doppelgänger* double of a shadow accompany him out the door, more portents of doom.

Lisa's evening outfit, by the way, a white skirt and jade green form-

Rear Window (1954)

fitting top, plays off of the color and structure of the jade green lamp and its bright white lampshade that she stands next to. Kudos to costume designer Edith Head, who worked on eleven pictures with Hitchcock (from *Notorious* to *Family Plot*). Head does it again during the discussion about Thorwald's pet flower bed (an appropriate name), as Lisa's dress is covered with floral designs. "Why would Thorwald want to kill a little dog?" she asks. Did the dog know too much, like the two men in their respective films of a similar title from 1934 and 1956?

As she first closes hers, curtains falling almost prove curtains for Miss Lonely Hearts, for our confused heroes stay so focused on Thorwald's world that they (and we) forget about this sad spinster who may be about to kill herself. Talk about objectifying a human being.

Shortly, Hitchcock films Jefferies more and more from the outside in, making *him* the final object, ironically, out of all the objects that he has viewed throughout *Rear Window*. "The invaded room is thus central to the Hitchcockian attempt to penetrate our complacency, par-

Rear Window (1954): The light from the bright white lampshade in the foreground causes Lisa Fremont's (Grace Kelly) skin, hair, pearls, scarf, and fingers on her right hand to literally glow.

ticularly within domestic situations.... In each case the outside world that is at first the source of threat then becomes the source of salvation. The victim must communicate with the outside world to save his life" (Weis, 1982, p. 128).

And, of course, when Thorwald attacks him, objects associated with Jefferies' photography profession must be used to heighten the audience's identification with him.

> TRUFFAUT: He will defend himself by blinding the killer with his flashbulbs.
> HITCHCOCK: Those flashes take us back to the mechanics of *Secret Agent*. You remember, in Switzerland they have the Alps, lakes, and chocolate. Now, here we have a photographer who uses his camera equipment to pry into the backyard, and when he defends himself, he also uses his professional equipment, the flashbulbs. I make it a rule to exploit elements that are connected with a character or a location; I would feel that I'd been remiss if I hadn't made maximum us of those elements [Truffaut, 1967, pp. 162–163].

Rear Window has truly treated the city, a city's apartments, and all their accouterments front and center as characters wielding real force against their human protagonists. In a way, this film represents Hitchcock's most successful attempt to treat a city as a living, breathing person.

To Catch a Thief (1955)

> Get a closer look [at the opening credits] and you'll note that the titles are slightly skewed, creating a diagonal line. Now, the diagonal line is a line that suggests movement, energy that ultimately suggests tension, something unsettling, [and] something unfinished. You see, a diagonal line is neither vertically upright or horizontally at rest, but somewhere in between. And that is your clue that this film is not going to be totally happy and pleasant, serene and fun [Drew Casper, 2009 *To Catch a Thief* DVD audio commentary].

The theme of the dangerous doubles game from *Strangers on a Train* is recapitulated in a lighter way all through *To Catch a Thief*. For

To Catch a Thief (1955)

example, a high-backed chair in the upstairs room of John Robie's (Cary Grant, in his third of four films for Hitchcock) Riviera villa boasts large, circular head pads that quite humorously and obviously resemble Mickey Mouse's ears! Continuing the jokiness of this same doubles idea later—the film is packed with double entendres, too—the name of the getaway boat used by Danielle ("Dani") Foussard (French actress Brigitte Auber) and Robie is called the "Marquis Mouse."

Shortly, another piece of furniture, a double-sided table lamp with green glass, can be seen screen left forebodingly foregrounding Robie's charged discussion with restaurateur Bertani (French actor-director Charles Vernal). Likewise, a large foregrounded screen right telephone seems to crowd Robie out of the window-boxed room of the same restaurant. Shot like a claustrophobic jail cell, the scene clearly recalls Guy and Miriam's close encounter at the music shop where she worked in *Strangers on a Train*, Melanie's telephone booth entrapment in *The Birds*, and the silent film montage of the refrigerated flower shop scene in *Topaz*. The design on Robie's thinly striped shirt more than hints at a stereotypical outfit of someone already incarcerated.

Getting lost in this film's played-for-laughs flower scene is reminiscent of so many of Hitchcock's dizziness-inducing crowd shots, except in this case Robie actually gets caught (purposefully, it turns out). And later, just before the forty-five-minute point, Hitchcock goes for more disequilibrium after he fades out on a startling close-up overhead of Robie and fades in on a long shot of dozens of beach umbrellas blocking our (and Dani's) view of Robie and Frances "Francie" Stevens (Grace Kelly, in her third and final Hitchcock film). Hitchcock connoisseur and fellow director Peter Bogdanovich, on the 2007 DVD audio commentary for the film, concurred: "And then, when he goes to the high angle to go out on [Robie], it was typical of Hitchcock ... to give you a sense of the loss of equilibrium and to isolate the figure. He does that in countless movies."

More blockage by objects occurs when we see Dani foregrounding two water skis at precisely the moment she looks for the couple. This false love *ménage* is shortly and hysterically tested out at the beach float, where at one point Cary Grant cannot hold back what appears to be real laughter over being stuck in the middle of the two women's waterlogged catfight.

Hitchcock's Objects as Subjects

Quintessential Hitchcockian wordplay also makes its appearance during this scene. When Robie swims out to the float after Danielle, the large and looming letters HOTEL CARLTON are prominently displayed on its side. But the director cleverly places his actor in front of the letters EL in the first word, leaving the other three conspicuously visible directly below the gorgeous, lithe frame of the curvaceous actress Brigitte Auber as she enticingly stretches out for us in a one-piece swim suit. When the women go at their fight in the water, Auber's head is brilliantly shot in close-up prominently foregrounding the central letter O in HOT. One will recall that a similar use of a hotel sign was treated in *Foreign Correspondent* to represent World War II on the brink via HOT EUROPE.

The Hotel Carlton's room furniture humorously punctuates Francie and her mother's perfectly timed thirty-second, counter-clockwise argument and chase. Hitchcock directs them to maintain a precise equidistance from each other on their circumnavigations: half a circle times two takes exactly twenty of the thirty seconds, followed by one full circuit double-timed over ten seconds. The brief scene is perfectly choreographed, laughingly rhythmic.

Other object-as-subject touches occur when Francie continues to woo John at the Sanford villa. Near numerous erect, towering cypress trees and sculptured cherubs, one large Cupid draws his arrow and takes aim. But when Francie acts betrayed later in her room, she angrily swings a closed umbrella up and down dangerously close to Robie's pelvic region, a not-so-subtle image of castration in her hands. Robie himself (dressed up as a Blackamore!) will shortly hold a much larger umbrella over her head in mock protection during the dance finale.

Once again, body parts such as hands can take on all sorts of human characteristics:

> The apocalyptic finale contains another icon of Hitchcock: hands. In the adventure part of ... *To Catch a Thief*, hands can stand for murder [or they can] stand for robbing [by someone named Robie]. You see a lot of hands robbing jewels. They can also be used for the reaching of help in the adventure of his films, and sometimes be stifled by handcuffs. In the romance[s], hands are used to make love, as we've seen Francie grabbing John's hands and when he holds her necklace. At the end of the film, Robie will grab Francie's hands and bring her to him. But hands also embody an ambiguity. In the adventure, they can be a

source of strength, murder, robbing, or they could lose their strength, they could weaken [or] control another person, empower another person [Drew Casper, 2009 *To Catch a Thief* DVD audio commentary].

The film ends with yet another body part, one eye, looking out at the camera with ambiguous uncertainty. Recalling Larrue's one-eyed gaze at Logan across a street in *I Confess*, this querulous look embodies John Robie's response to Francie Stevens' remark that her mother will love it at his villa.

The Trouble with Harry (1955)

> It's that turning of everyday things into dark things. It strikes you at the core of the primordial gel in the middle of your brain ... [Joe Carnahan; "The Trouble with Harry Isn't Over," 2000 *Trouble with Harry* DVD documentary].

Objects rule the roost from the get-go of this idyll from the New England countryside. First and foremost, the trouble with Harry, of course, is that he's dead, i.e., not a living person; ergo, an object, like the murdered David from *Rope*. As a corpse, ironically, his character humorously drives much more of the narrative than if he were alive. "The dead Harry Warp harmonizes the entire community as each member assumes guilt for his death [as] they all combine to conceal him" (1977, p. 261), Yacowar rightly notes.

Likewise, the character of the beautiful Vermont fall scenery, in contrast to the overpowering Manderley from *Rebecca*, sets and keeps the tone of this film pastoral, languorous, and playful. "It was shot in autumn for the contrapuntal use of beauty against the sordidness and muddiness of death," said Hitchcock (cited in Bogdanovich, 1963, p. 34). And, once the hobo strips Harry of his shoes, the deceased's outsized socks loom in the foreground as stand-in—more accurately, lie-in—for said corpse, their bright blues and reds complementing the autumn foliage. Lesley Brill properly identifies the importance of the film's flora as subjective metaphor, "in which the gorgeous New England fall gives spectacular visual emphasis to vegetative death and rebirth" (1988, p. 66).

Shortly, Sam Marlowe, endearingly played by John Forsythe in a firm tongue-in-cheek style, almost trips over Harry before starting to paint the landscape, oblivious. Getting angry at the dead Harry for lying in his view, he thinks better of it and draws a close-up of his portrait instead. Harry is, perhaps, the best model an artist could hope for. Arnie's dead rabbit, too, accomplishes much in the film, getting him via trade not just one live frog but two yummy blueberry muffins. "It's a two-muffin rabbit," he logically argues. Born, bred and died in New England, screenwriter John Michael Hayes wrote clever dialogue that kept close to the alternating light and dark comedy of British novelist Jack Trevor Story's original story.

Not only dead creatures but furniture and doors play their part in this delightful film. During the last third of the picture, which takes place mostly in the home of Jennifer Rogers (Shirley MacLaine in her screen debut), Hitchcock conspicuously places an empty rocking chair in the foreground of many shots, stand-in for the dead Harry and, presumably, his ghost. Like a closet door that we see repeatedly opening by itself, Harry's chair literally "moves around" too, maintaining its foregrounded position for much of the proceedings. Two examples:

1. Jennifer is uncomfortable with just one thing. She tells Sam, "It's Harry. What [should we do] about Harry?" When Sam responds, "Harry? Don't you think about Harry," both Sam and the camera shift ever so slightly screen right so that the rocker–Harry's ghost jumps into the frame.

2. Later in the same room, Sam asks Captain Albert Wiles (the estimable Edmund Gwenn in his fourth and final film for Hitchcock), incredulously, "Well, you haven't dug him up again?" The captain says, "Well, I—" and Hitchcock cuts to the empty closet door opening again, Bernard Herrmann's *faux*-spooky score sounding appropriately ghoulish. As they leave to bury Harry a *third* time, the empty closet door opens once more.

By the time the film ends, the trouble with Harry hints at never ending, for we see his body put back in exactly the same place we had first seen it, shot from ground level with its feet and colored socks in the foreground, pants in the distance. Harry has twice been shot this way, bookending the film, and Hitchcock, Hayes and Story are most certainly telling us that we must all die at least a little in order to grow. Yacowar made this same point another way: "The dead complete and shape the living, but the living ... make their own use of the dead" (1977, p. 262). In this film at least, the now deceased object known as Harry, it seems, has had both the first and last word.

The Man Who Knew Too Much (1956)

> Hitchcock is here developing the theme of communication, emphasized by the constant use of the telephone. Fifteen calls are either made or attempted in [this film]. If a call is completed, it is not good news; if not complete, frustration has cut off the possibility of comfort. From *Rebecca* to *Frenzy*, the telephone has this ironic function in Hitchcock's films. It is a modern device which ordinarily fails the user and sends more bad news than good [Spoto, 1976, p. 274].

The opening of Hitchcock's second *Man Who Knew Too Much* immediately shows us one of the major "players" in our narrative—music itself—in the form of an orchestra in performance. More specifically, we are listening and watching the "Storm Cloud Cantata" being performed, composed by Australian Arthur Benjamin (adapted and conducted by Bernard Herrmann). Bass drums are pounding away on the soundtrack in portent of the coming suspense. At the end of this anxiety-inducing credit sequence, the following words appear onscreen: "A single crash of Cymbals and how it rocked the lives of an American family." As Steven C. Smith, Herrmann's biographer, rightly tells us in the 2004 DVD bonus feature "The Making of *The Man Who Knew Too Much*," more than "any of the other Herrmann-Hitchcock collaborations, music is almost a character in *The Man Who Knew Too Much*.... It's very important. It's right there in the opening titles, letting us know that music is going to be key to this story."

Hitchcock's Objects as Subjects

Similarly, lights and lighting yet again "speak" loudly, illuminating major points. When Louis Bernard (French actor-director Daniel Gélin) asks to use the McKennas' hotel room phone, and he speaks into it, Hitchcock shoots him from behind standing against a blank wall. His is a dark and foreboding figure backlit by an eerie green light coming from all the jade-covered lamps in the room. Food, too, conspires against the McKennas' during dinner, as James Stewart's character Dr. Benjamin McKenna struggles to eat his Moroccan meal with only two fingers and the thumb of his right hand, a total frustration to his happiness.

Extreme close-ups of telephones and ears trying to listen take center stage several times in this film. The way Hitchcock uses them, they typically prevent rather than provide access to hearing for characters in the film and us, the audience. (See, especially, *Secret Agent* and *Topaz*, too.) Early on, we see Bernard whisper his secret about an assassination in an extreme close-up of his mouth and Dr. McKenna's ear. The unknown (at this point) stranger who warns Ben not to share that knowledge speaks into his phone from a hidden spot behind a large, high-backed chair. Hitchcock cuts to another extreme close-up of McKenna's ear as it hears the warning about his son, a visual that immediately takes us back to Bernard's whisper. Later, we are not permitted to hear one of the spies speak into a pay phone at the airport due to overhead noise. But when heroine Jo McKenna (Doris Day) begs her young son Hank (Christopher Olsen) on the hotel phone to tell her where he's being hidden, another overhead plane drowns out *his* voice, stymying all of our hopes. In these cases, Hitchcock's genius lay in his ability to thwart sounds that would normally be heard in a sound picture via telephone conversations in a purely silent film manner.

Likewise, the taxidermist scene (precursor by four years to Norman's avocation in *Psycho*) is one of Hitchcock's great silent-film slapstick numbers. The elder Ambrose Chappell (English actor George Howe) is first seen next to a brightly lit and imposing stuffed pelican, while his son Ambrose Chappell, Jr. (English character actor Richard Wordsworth, who is the great-great-grandson of the poet William Wordsworth!), is shot alongside a darkly shadowed, bare-toothed tiger. Dr. McKenna will shortly get his arm stuck in the tiger's mouth during

The Man Who Knew Too Much (1956)

a fight that finds the elder Chappell saving a swordfish from almost certain destruction.

Patricia Hitchcock O'Connell, the Hitchcocks' daughter, rightly reminds us of the importance of location in all the director's films on that same 2004 DVD bonus feature mentioned above: "He and my mother really enjoyed traveling ... so he would find a place, and then he would see how he could incorporate it into the story."

Smith, discussing the power of Herrmann's music in this film, said: "When Jimmy Stewart is going to the taxidermist, there's a wonderful kind of music that Herrmann could write to suggest the anxiety that people were feeling in this situation as well as to make that anxiety be felt in the audience as well."

At the actual Ambrose Chapel the congregants are seen singing the dirge-like "From whence these dire portents abound," our worst fears made choral. Later, spellbound by the "Cantata" at Albert Hall, Jo stands frozen, as the song is sung by the orchestra's large choir. The powerful character of music itself sings out throughout this film.

At one point, even a pastoral painting in juxtaposition with different individuals highlights the distinction between villains and heroes. First, as the ambassador's second in command argues with Mrs. Lucy Drayton (British Brenda De Banzie) over the murder, the lovely landscape painting is centered behind them, idylls threatened. Later, when Hank hears Jo's singing voice in the same room wafting up from far below, we again see the painting over Mrs. Drayton's shoulder, but its image rings hopeful this time. The camera, too, searches for the boy:

> In tracing the journey of Jo's voice to the ears of her stolen son, the camera becomes the projection of her desire and of the power of her art and, perhaps, of art itself. It goes up to awaken and recover the sleeping, captive Hank and to make whole again the broken family. Like the Prince coming to kiss Sleeping Beauty, it restores, with the same action, the integrity of a society as well [Brill, 1988, p. 130].

In other words, the object of the camera itself helps bring hopefulness up the stairs to Hank as it *literally* follows her voice. Getting closer the further it travels, Jo's song gets fainter and fainter the more we move and it moves from her. But the camera also carries our wishes for his

Hitchcock's Objects as Subjects

rescue upon this whisper of a tune on the soundtrack ... Louis Bernard's secret perhaps not yet stilled.

The Wrong Man (1957)

> With Hitchcock in *The Wrong Man*, you could feel the height of the camera ... the duration of the shot, [it] was that precise. The scene with [Henry] Fonda in the jail cell was a subjective shot, but it's taken from an objective point of view [Paul Sylbert, "Guilt Trip: Hitchcock and The Wrong Man," 2004 *Wrong Man* DVD special feature].

Shot on location in the real Stork Club at the beginning of the film, the empty purposelessness of masses of anonymous dancers is highlighted by oppressively hanging balloons, yawning waiters, bored musicians, and the incessantly stark and spare Bernard Herrmann score. All these so-called individuals are just going through the motions, Hitchcock seems to be saying. Likewise, recalling the cities in both *Shadow of a Doubt* and *Rear Window*, "[the] roar of the subway past the victim's apartment evokes the crushing and carriage of bodies, and souls, of which the prison system is no more than an intensification; while the hazards of ill-luck are part of the city's nature, its brutal mixture of movement and confinement, of junctures and solitudes, of crowds and cells" (Durgnat, 1974, p. 277).

Christopher Emanuel "Manny" Balestrero, played by Henry Fonda with easily the most low-keyed "everyman" acting in all of the director's oeuvre, embodies that nondescript quality tenfold in *The Wrong Man* as he relentlessly and, seemingly, hopelessly seeks a dignified subjectivity throughout the film. Nothing he does—except, finally and ironically, prayer—will accomplish that reality for him. In this film made just over a decade after the end of World War II, Manny (in real life and onscreen) embodied one of the millions of second-generation Italians (and Germans, and Greeks, and many other immigrants) quietly trying to assimilate themselves and their families into American culture to achieve some kind of promised, middle class living. "And the actual locales of the film were shot with an interpretive fidelity to detail and

The Wrong Man (1957)

a sense of the loss of identity that city living means for many" (Spoto, 1976, p. 288).

When we first spy Manny playing bass in the Stork Club, we are clearly meant to think "how dull" his life and all the dancers' lives are. "The suggestion of death-in-life is ... extended to Manny's own home, and again the score contributes to the effect: the double-bass, Manny's own instrument, seems to stalk him down his hallway..." (Mogg, 1999, p. 139).

The screenplay by Pennsylvania-born Maxwell Anderson and the British-born Angus MacPhail quietly works counter to this oppressive feeling. According to his wife Rose early in the film, we hear about Manny's saving grace notes through his comments about how lucky he is to be in love with her, how they have two bright boys, a job he likes, and how he will make "everything all right again." Portrayed in an extraordinarily sad and intensely restrained manner by Vera Miles (in her first of two Hitchcock films), Rose ironically becomes the literal embodiment, by film's end, of an object, not a person.

Likewise, in the Life Insurance office scene, the three women workers' fears prevent them from giving Manny the benefit of human doubt—a God-given American right. Not real people, they act more like dehumanizing, impersonal objects in reaction to a situation; masses, again, without any empathy. Intensifying the feeling of inhumanity, Hitchcock hides Manny's face from them in the same way he hid Larrue's from Father Logan in *I Confess*. Frequently seen in profile, the policemen themselves are immobilized into objectivity, too. In fact, profile shots provide a motif, objectifying many characters that way. If people are treated like blank walls in this film, inscrutable, their objective must be to bar others from connecting to real human beings, too.

A trapped animal in the jail cell after incarceration, Manny *finally* begins to show some strength of character when we see him make fists in a close-up, harkening back to Jonathan's hands similarly shot near the end of *Stage Fright*, or Bruno's throughout *Strangers*. This scene occurs right before the camera subjectively asserts itself in a swirling and dizzying shot of his head that art director Paul Sylbert discussed in the opening quote of this chapter. Both Manny's hands and the camera are objects that fully represent his struggles.

Like the frozen, inhuman faces staring back at us from Mount

Hitchcock's Objects as Subjects

Rushmore in *North by Northwest*, the thoughtless cops do not even call Manny by his real name, using the assumed nickname "Chris" rather than empathetically asking him how he would prefer to be addressed. Again, Hitchcock has Fonda play Balestrero as nondescriptly passive as possible so he can be easily mistaken for anybody, or nobody. Poor Rose never had to think for herself, another abandoned "object," apparently.

Exhausting and nightmarish, Manny's trials drain the life out of him as he is driven all over town by the police, repeatedly but falsely tagged as the thief by strangers.

> First there is the confrontation with witnesses: under the dull stares of the office workers or the slightly curious ones of the shopkeepers before whom he is paraded, he is reduced to anonymity, becomes something that has to be identified. The idea [deals with] the fundamental *abjectness* of a human being, who once deprived of his freedom is no more than an object among other objects ... [Rohmer and Chabrol, 1957, pp. 146–147].

In seeking help, Manny and Rose find that all of his alibis have died. Rose starts to lose any grip on reality she may have had. Hitchcock shoots her in still profile at one point, just like a figurine object or the in-profile (and profiling) police in their squad car, when Manny was bookended between them as they drove all over town. Rose shortly falls into her own private "cell" by the second half of the picture—a bare bedroom space at home and, later, the institution bedroom—as Hitchcock's enforced feelings of passivity continue to unnerve us.

Due to a juror so bored by Manny's trial that he exclaims, "Why bother?" a mistrial forces everyone through the whole experience once again. Still treated like an object, Manny finally likens himself to one, saying, "It's like being put through a meat grinder." And even when the "right" man is finally caught, this new person's cries—he is not an object but has his own family and children—are the ones that now fall on the deaf ears of inhumanity.

Vertigo (1958)

The swirl of Kim Novak's hairdo is similar to the swirl in the hairdo of Carlotta Valdes, and also becomes a meta-

Vertigo (1958)

phor throughout the film from the very opening credits, [for] the kind of spiral that leads someone down, the kind of dizziness that occurs through vertigo ... leads you ... downward through a spiral over an abyss [William Friedkin, 2008 *Vertigo* DVD audio commentary].

Colors, too, particularly on clothing and via lights, play their parts alongside hair spirals in this film. Near the start, the art studio of Midge Wood (Barbara Bel Geddes) bears a striking resemblance to Jeff's apartment in *Rear Window*, for they both have colored blinds and are about the same size and feel. In the restaurant known as Ernie's, Hitchcock ups the brightness of the red light behind Madeleine's face for an instant. (Madeleine Elster and Judy Barton are both played by actress Kim Novak.) This heightens the contrast of her blond hair and bright green dress for both Scottie and us. She is also treated in this scene less as a human and more as an object.

> Madeleine is presented in terms of the "work of art," which is precisely what she is. Her movement through the doorway suggests a portrait coming to life, or a gliding statue; when she pauses and turns her head into profile, the suggestion is of a cameo or silhouette, an image that will recur throughout the film. As a work of art Madeleine is at once totally accessible (a painting is completely passive, offering itself to the gaze) and totally *in*accessible (you can't make love to a picture) [Robin Wood, cited in Deutelbaum and Poague, 1986, pp. 227–228].

As she and Gavin Elster (Tom Helmore in his second Hitchcock film) leave Ernie's (she is his supposed wife, but really a plant), we catch a distant glimpse of their doubles in a mirror, a clear portent of the ruse Elster has already begun playing with Scottie. In the next scene, Madeleine gets into a green car and takes Scottie on a languorous trip through the city (starting out via an implied wrong direction down a conspicuously placed ONE WAY sign); he follows behind in his own. Wearing a pale green dress, she stands out again and again in a flower shop and cemetery among all the colors, often red. The circular bun in her hair, as noted by William Friedkin at the top of this chapter, echoes the vertiginous spirals created by designer Saul Bass during the opening credits. (This was the first of Bass' three films for the director.) It also recalls Patsy's kiss curl from Hitchcock's first film, *The Pleasure Garden*.

HITCHCOCK'S OBJECTS AS SUBJECTS

The winding staircase of the bell tower at the mission; Carlotta Valdes' single lock of spiraling dark hair and, in imitation of that, Madeleine's (and later Judy's) hair; the spiraling downward journey of the two cars on San Francisco's hilly streets ... it is significant that the action occurs in San Francisco, a city of steep hills, of sudden rises and falls, of high climbs and dizzying drops ... the rings of the tree trunks in the Sequoia forest; the camera's spiraling around Judy as she composes the letter to Scottie—all these movements induce in the viewer the sensation of vertigo with which Scottie is afflicted [Spoto, 1976, pp. 300, 302].

After Madeleine is fished out of San Francisco Bay, a reversal of colors occurs back at Scottie's apartment when he puts on a green sweater and hands her his red dressing gown. Hitchcock seems to be saying that he represents life now, and she, danger. Even his front door is painted red in contrast with the soft green curtains next to it and green plants below.

> [The set dresser] is in charge of what is the most vital element of the décor, the atmosphere. Instead of being a set dresser he should almost be a writer, because he ought to know the character of the person who lives in that room.... In *Vertigo*, Stewart was playing a retired detective who went to law school and who lived in San Francisco. So I said to the photographer, "Go to San Francisco, find out where a retired detective lives, make sure he went to law school, and go in and photograph his house. Get all the detail and bring it back and dress the set that way" [Hitchcock, 1972; cited in Gottlieb, 2003, p. 97].

The importance of specific colors on other essential objects occurs during their walk through the Sequoia forest, when Scottie proclaims that the trees are "always green, ever living." This comment is reinforced by Wood when he says that the trees represent a "complex thematic and emotional deepening" (1965, p. 72) of these people and their relationship to each other. Madeleine disagrees: "I don't like them." Scottie: "Why?" Madeleine: "Knowing I have to die." Judy's head board on her bed, and the apartment's hallway walls, are also painted green—for danger, for the challenges of living and growing.

The gray feel of fog as obstructing protagonist relentlessly plays its part in this film, too. It recalls any number of smoke-filled scenes from *Mr. and Mrs. Smith, Shadow of a Doubt, Stage Fright, I Confess* and others.

> For many of the film's day scenes, Robert Burks used fog filters of varying density. He also devised special diffusion filters to lend Madeleine a

Vertigo (1958)

magical greenish glow for certain scenes. In both cases—and this was the film's rationale for the famous gray suit—Hitchcock wanted to suggest that Madeleine had materialized out of the San Francisco fog and that she might soon vanish again. (Throughout, she is constantly disappearing around corners and out of rooms [like Mrs. Danvers].) [Mogg, 1999, p. 141].

When Midge confronts Scottie with her own painted version of Carlotta, with Midge herself as Carlotta, we see him enter and leave her apartment behind a wall of blinds similar to the ones that opened *Rear Window*. The blinds are lit from behind in such a way that Scottie's body is almost completely obliterated, and anticipate the dreamlike quality of Madeleine's re-emergence from Judy via Scottie's make-over. Back in his home, *his* blinds, while pulled down, are twisted open horizontally, in concert with the same kinds of lines etched into his broad fireplace. Both are in sharp, right-angle contrast to the vertical folds on the curtains behind Madeleine, as well as a large lampshade screen left, another major protagonist in this film.

As Madeleine lies to Scottie about having never seen the San Juan Bautista Mission, Hitchcock films them in six extraordinarily executed, alternating four-second shots, each appearing to be sitting in the same position under that huge lampshade. Posed in the same way, too, the shots tell us that Scottie is Madeleine and Madeleine Scottie, interchangeable characters. The lamp's glow also spotlights their heads with a bright halo above each of them. On the sixth and final shot, Scottie moves to comfort her but we're suddenly surprised by his movement because Hitchcock has him pass *behind* the lamp's base to join her on its other side, a brilliantly clever use of the lamp to further force our identification with these two. "The camera moves with Scottie as he goes to Madeleine's side. On his words 'You're going to be all right now, Madeleine,' the lamp momentarily eclipses Scottie in the frame, a quintessentially Hitchcockian effect" (Rothman, 1988, p. 156).

Later, in Judy's apartment, a conspicuous fan hanging from two lamps on a wall can be spotted. The first time we see it, when Scottie makes his first moves toward her, they are unlit, the fan seeming to try to flame their love. The second time, when their ardor begins to burn, we see that the fan is now brightly lit by the turned-on bulbs, another subtle Hitchcock touch.

Hitchcock's Objects as Subjects

Buildings and edifices loom large as powerful protagonists in this film, too, stand-ins for people. Their final kiss foregrounds another halo effect with one of the many Mission arches framing Madeleine's head. She then runs through one of them, off to enact her false death.

> Despite his breakdown, Scottie continues to be presented as an authority figure. Earlier in the film his authority was established visually and sexually by repeated low-angle shots framing him with phallic towers (the landmark Madeleine uses to find his apartment is Coit Tower) which represent both his official and sexual authority and his domination by ideals beyond his control (as Norman Bates, sitting among his stuffed birds, will be presented at once as their analogue and their prey) [Leitch, 1991, p. 205].

Scottie revisits Ernie's where he had spied Madeleine for the first time and retraces her steps in reverse. Moving past the same earlier mirror in the restaurant, perhaps he is hoping for its doubling effect to occur again. Of course, throughout the city he keeps seeing women who look just like her and are similarly dressed. Finally, he does spot Madeleine on a street; she is now Judy, her real self, but he (and we) know she's the same woman, for Hitchcock frames her in the same profile that he and we had first seen her in Ernie's—full circle.

When Judy says yes to dinner, Hitchcock exaggeratedly bathes the entire scene in a deep and passionate red light. Of course, as she relives the murder of the real Madeleine Elster, the one she helped perpetrate, she is wearing a dark green dress. Increasing the tension of this scene, the bedposts in her room are colored green and her suitcase is red. "The fact is that Hitchcock is one of the few filmmakers for whom color is an auxiliary and not a shackle, who keeps it from being a servile imitation of painting.... [Color] is not an end but a means of providing a particular object with a supplementary degree of reality. It is to this that we owe the sharp sense of the concrete" (Rohmer and Chabrol, 1957, pp. 131–132).

Judy writes her note of explanation to Scottie for the murder, and Hitchcock shoots her half hidden behind a small lamp, preventing us and her from a fully confessional absolution:

> As she writes her letter the camera half circles her, and the shade on her table lamp fills a large area of the screen, at one point obliterating her. The image recalls the scene where Madeleine came to Scottie at dawn

to tell him her dream. She sat at his writing table, leaning forward in the light from his table-lamp as she described her terror of "darkness." The effect was of the pitiful inadequacy of human illumination to combat the enveloping metaphysical darkness (compare the flashbulbs in *Rear Window* and the torch in *The Birds*). By linking the two scenes through this image (the lamp and shade get great visual emphasis in both), Hitchcock links Judy's present situation and her inability to cope with Madeleine's "darkness" [Wood, 1965, p. 93].

That night, as they return to the Empire Hotel, her room is bathed in an eerie green light from an outside neon sign. When they enter, we see her profile again against that bright suffusion. "Cinematographer Robert Burks carried out Hitchcock's color schemes of reds and greens and used fog filters to create a dreamlike atmosphere" (*Obsessed with Vertigo*, 2004 DVD bonus feature).

At the clothing store, Judy and Scottie are shot before yet another mirror, clear representation of the double lives they are now fully leading. "Here again they're reflected in these mirrors, the duality of each character now as they see the exact copy of the dress" Scottie compels her to wear (William Friedkin; 2008 *Vertigo* DVD audio commentary). And when her transformation into Madeleine is complete, she walks towards Scottie and the camera as if out of a dream. "[T]his rejection of life for an unattainable Idea is something fundamental in human nature.... The tendency in relationships to form an idealized image of the other person and substitute it for the reality is relevant here" (Wood, 1965, p. 94).

Does such a perfect image of anyone treat that person like an object, or does it (merely) objectify him or her? Especially in *Vertigo*, perhaps the answer to both questions is "yes."

North by Northwest (1959)

I love the way Hitchcock has James Mason light the scene gradually by darkening [the room], then throwing himself in profile that way with the lamp. He's back lit, [and it] makes him appear slightly sinister. That's an elegant Hitchcock touch [Ernest Lehman; 2004 *North by Northwest* DVD audio commentary].

Hitchcock's Objects as Subjects

The rapidity of the dialogue that comprises the first five minutes of *North by Northwest* keeps pace with the speed of the crowds scurrying about the New York City streets. Rushing to get everywhere (shades of similar openings in *The Lodger* and *Rich and Strange*), but neither the patter of their feet nor the spoken word reveals any more character than the frenetic life in the fast lanes. Like Larita in *Champagne*, Roger "The O stands for nothing" Thornhill, our businessman about town played by Cary Grant in the fourth of four films for Hitchcock, "relies above all on the exterior trappings of modern civilization ... for protection" (Wood, 1965, p. 101). The man latent within the trappings of the city will spend this whole film fighting towards health.

Since the twenties, Hitchcock had been wanting to make a film that was all about the character of just such a city. Its title, unsurprisingly, would be *Life of a City*: "The story of a big city from dawn to the following dawn. Hitchcock: "This is something I've wanted to do since 1928. I want to do it in terms of what lies behind the face of a city—what makes it tick—in other words, [the] backstage of a city.... It must be done in terms of personalities and people, and with my technique, everything would have to be used dramatically" (Bogdanovich, 1963, p. 46).

As a visit to the fictional George Kaplan's hotel room is filmed in mostly objective, medium distance shots for nearly four and a half minutes, the city as character, versus humans, plays itself out. After a few quick cuts to the closet, a pair of pants and the telephone, the latter suddenly rings and, as Roger goes to pick it up, Hitchcock's camera moves in with a slow twenty-second zoom, finally resting forebodingly over his head. Long shots and overheads of interiors and exteriors of buildings and apartments like this one proliferate in this film, further reducing characters to objects that are often moved around like chess pieces.

Sympathetic Mrs. Finley (Madge Kennedy) is given the last word during the CIA's group-think on the fate of the imaginary Kaplan when she says, "Goodbye, Mr. Thornhill, wherever you are." Cut to yet another long shot of people-as-chess-pieces zipping by in the cavernous Grand Central Station. Hitchcock's camera peruses the crowd scene for a full fifteen seconds before letting us glimpse Grant, he's so (deliberately) hidden by the masses. "America has become a place, the

North by Northwest (1959)

film continually reminds us, where human beings and works of art alike are reduced to objects bought and sold. [Even] Eve is treated as a piece of sculpture, and statues also are denied their souls" (Rothman, 1988, p. 175).

After the hustle and bustle of the New York City streets, Grand Central, and Chicago's train station, the wide open fields where Thornhill is eventually deposited by bus feel downright frightening. Who would have thought crop fields where there are no crops could be such unnerving characters? "Here you have the big city man, the cosmopolitan man, all alone in the middle of nowhere, everything that makes him feel safe and confident stripped away" (Curtis Hanson, "*North by Northwest*: One for the Ages," 2009 DVD bonus feature).

When Thornhill-Kaplan miraculously escapes the field and returns to Eve's Ambassador Hotel room in Chicago, all the lampshades and pillow cases and wallpaper and clothing are colored in a drab, lifeless gray—including Grant's tie and the spare Japanese tree and limbs drawn on the wall above her bed. Only Eve's floral red and black dress, created by the brilliant costume designer Edith Head, stands out, the black widow spider outfit she has unwillingly embodied hung on her own limbs.

Hitchcock loved to turn his sound features into silence, and does it once again as the professor and Thornhill walk towards the plane taking them to Rapid City, South Dakota, home of the huge Mount Rushmore carvings.

> The monument is an elaboration of the huge god's head, aloof and implacable, in *Blackmail*. If there is no defense from chaos in the afternoon crowds of New York, or the civilities of the Plaza's bar, or the diplomatic immunity of the United Nations lounge—all early scenes of chaos in this film—then there is no defense, either, in an open field or at a national monument [Spoto, 1976, p. 344].

Even the Mount Rushmore cafeteria is filmed in long shot, making yet another building feel gargantuan next to, and much more powerful than, the tiny world of these humans and their busy-ness. As Hitchcock's camera pans left with Thornhill across the cafeteria's wide expanse, it pauses ever so slightly at a table he will bring his coffee to, conveniently dead center in the room and onscreen. Even an object as simple as a table seems to upstage people in this film.

Hitchcock's Objects as Subjects

Psycho (1960)

> The mirror imagery is no accident. The story concerns a pathologically split personality, and the constant presence of mirrors suggests that the other characters are similarly split.... Because the camera forces our identification first with Marion and then with Norman, and because the ubiquitous mirrors reflect them out towards us, it becomes impossible to separate ourselves emotionally or psychologically from their moral descent.... [It] is only by fully confronting a reflection of ourselves that psychic healing is possible [Spoto, 1976, pp. 357–358].

The vacuity of the city in *North by Northwest* is followed by an exploration of the vacuity of individuals in *Psycho*. Several earlier films are recalled and referenced at its beginning. As Saul Bass's title design and Bernard Herrmann's title music are seen and heard at breakneck speed, the previous film's initial pace is mimicked (those two artists worked on that picture too). Throughout an early office conversation, Marion is repeatedly seen foregrounding a huge photograph of a desert, perhaps the setting outside of Morocco at the start of the second *Man Who Knew Too Much*. With Marion wearing a black bra and panties in her bedroom, Hitchcock's camera slowly zooms in to an extreme close-up of the stolen $40,000, Herrmann's hypnotic music working on Marion's mind and reminding us of the vertiginous streets of San Francisco in *Vertigo*. In a two-shot with a photo of her scolding parents looking over her shoulder, Marion bites the bullet and stuffs the money in her handbag.

Mirrors wend their way through this film in ways that were only hinted at in *The Wrong Man*, and more overtly used in *Vertigo*. When Marion goes into the ladies room at the car dealership and takes out $700 to trade in her car, Hitchcock jumps to his classic overhead shot with her image doubled in a mirror. Upon entering the Bates Motel office, she is again duplicitously shot in a wall mirror, her present and future selves uneasily standing side by side.

Marion thanks "Mr. Bates" (the great Anthony Perkins in his only Hitchcock film) for setting her up in Cabin One, conveniently right next to the office, and he corrects her with, "*Norman* Bates." Hitchcock

Psycho (1960)

immediately cuts to a close-up right profile of Marion uncomfortably doubled in yet another wall mirror for an awkward and, in this case, sexually charged five seconds. Adorning the motel wall behind them, five drawings of inquisitive birds look on. And, when Norman brings the tray of milk and sandwiches down from his home—"the house, looking like a huge skull, is lit from within its window-eyes" (Spoto, 1976, p. 366)—he walks into his own two-shot reflection in right profile to Marion's left, reversing their previous face-off. In this extraordinary shot, we can just make out part of *his* reflection doubled in an outside window, but this one is a ghostly half image, incomplete. "Each being has need of the mirror of somebody else's conscience: but in this universe, where salvation shines only when illuminated by the light of Grace, he sees in that mirror only his own deformed and exposed image" (Rohmer and Chabrol, 1957, p. 114).

Later, in another stunning shot, Marion's sister Lila Crane (actress Vera Miles in her second of two Hitchcock films) quietly inspects Mother's room and gasps aloud as she spots her own *tripled* image in *two* mirrors. Shot by Hitchcock in such a way that the camera simultaneously sees two images of herself from both in front of and behind her, the scene stops us in its tracks, for we think for a split second there is actually someone else in the room with her.

> Lila's reflection is framed within the mother's mirror, which in the past framed Mrs. Bates' reflection; standing before this mirror and looking into it, Lila occupies the mother's place. In Lila's vision and in her reflection, Mrs. Bates momentarily comes to life, as in Lila's view of the hands. But has Lila taken possession of Mrs. Bates, or has Mrs. Bates taken possession of Lila? We do not know who the being framed in the mirror really is. Nor can we say whether, in this vision, our gaze really represents Lila's or Mrs. Bates's gaze [Rothman, 1982, p. 322].

In fact, the entire house practically lives and breathes (like *Rebecca*'s Manderley), fully standing in for both Norman Bates and his mother:

> Lila's exploration of the house is an exploration of Norman's psychotic personality. The whole sequence, with its discoveries in bedroom, attic and cellar, has clear Freudian overtones. The Victorian *décor*, crammed with invention, intensifies the atmosphere of sexual repression. The statue of a black Cupid in the hall, the painting of an idealized maiden

disporting herself at the top of the stairs, a nude goddess statuette in the bedroom, are juxtaposed with the bed permanently indented with the shape of Mrs. Bates' body (the bed in which, we learn later, she and her lover were murdered by Norman), the macabre cast of crossed hands on her dressing table, the stifling atmosphere of stagnation: one can almost *smell* [the house] [Wood, 1965, pp. 119–120].

Likewise, "meals are often significant in Hitchcock. We hear in Mother's harangue her association with food and ugly appetite with sexuality," states Stephen Rebello on the 2004 *Psycho* DVD audio commentary. Marion and Norman's very intimate conversation over sandwiches in the parlor—total strangers, really—builds to an intensity that charges the air around them, especially with Herrmann's music deliberately withheld from the soundtrack. Hitchcock cuts back and forth between them a full forty times, but with twice its length on Norman than Marion. The director is subtly but insistently shifting our identification to him. When Marion says, "You know, if anyone ever talked to me the way I heard, the way she spoke to you," Hitchcock cuts to a typically audacious, up-under privileged close-up shot of Norman. This is immediately followed by twenty-eight more alternating, powerful cuts in the narrative. The intensity of this scene makes us feel that we are in the room with Marion and Norman and, equally disturbing, rapidly shifting our identification between them as characters.

> Throughout *Psycho*'s shooting, Hitchcock insisted that a 50mm lens be used so as to approximate the normal field of human vision. Script supervisor Marshall Schlom explained: "He wanted the camera *being* the audience all the time, to see as if ... with their own eyes." Clearly, then, that's *our* eye that peers at Marion through a hole in the wall of Norman's office. Equally, those are our own hands that mop and towel away all last flecks of blood in the bathroom after Marion's death [Mogg, 1999, p. 154].

Birds as objects proliferate in this film, too. Not as often as in *The Birds*, obviously, but certainly enough to catch our eye. Norman Bates eats candy corn and tilts his head just like a bird, and Cabin One and the Bates Motel parlor are stuffed with pictures of sparrows and stuffed birds of prey, especially an owl. Hitch's camera often assumes an extreme tilted angle, especially from that startling up-under position the director favors for menacing shots. And yes, that's as much a feed

Psycho (1960)

store as a hardware store that Sam Loomis (actor John Gavin) works in.

This film is, after all, a true dark comedy, as Hitch himself often said. Immediately after one of the most horrific murders in screen history occurs in the viewers' minds (remember, the knife never penetrates the body), Sam is seen in close-up writing a hopeful love letter to (the now deceased) Marion. Hitchcock's black, black humor comes to the surface, unlike Marion's now sunken car, as he dollies back to a patron perusing a box of insect killer. She says, "I've tried many brands. So far, of those I've used, I haven't had much luck with any of them. Let's see what they say about this one. They tell you what its ingredients are and how it's guaranteed to exterminate every insect in the world. And I say, insect or man, death should always be painless."

"Painless," of course, is the one word that *does not* apply to Marion's gruesome killing, nor to that of detective Arbogast (wonderful character actor Martin Balsam). When he visits the Bates Motel for the first time and accurately identifies Marion's handwriting in the register, Hitchcock's camera is fixed on an extreme close-up of Perkins' shadowed face for a solid fifteen seconds. Leaning in to see the signature, Norman is shot at such an awkward camera angle that we palpably feel creeped out, a bird of prey exposed at extreme close range to our eyes.

Upon Arbogast's return to the motel, Hitchcock shoots his entrance to the Bates home with quickly edited shots of what he sees—hallways, stairs, a parlor door, and the stairs again—alternating with objective medium shots of himself. Herrmann's violins quietly hint of menace on the soundtrack, and we can just discern the earlier-mentioned hallway sculpture of Cupid aiming his bow and arrow up the stairs.

After Arbogast's murder by Mother, Hitchcock cuts to Lila and Sam back at his store, impatiently waiting for his promised return. Sam tells Lila to stay a bit longer as he heads out to check on things, and Hitchcock's humor erupts again as the camera moves in for a close-up on Vera Miles' darkened head and torso. Foregrounding four fanned-out rake heads, each with eight doubled hooks like a scarecrow's halo, darned if Herrmann's music doesn't play a variant of Harold Arlen's music for *The Wizard of Oz* (1939). More black humor ensues when the sheriff's wife deadpans, "I helped Norman pick out the dress [Mrs. Bates] was buried in. Periwinkle blue."

When Norman walks up the stairs to tell Mother she must hide in the fruit cellar for a few days, Hitchcock's camera follows him up on a crane that twists counter-clockwise 180 degrees as it passes the upper landing to look back down on him. It's shot in that same awkwardly angled, up-under feel that Norman was viewed in extreme close-up earlier; we again queasily feel the camera's movement at this moment in the same sickening way as the previous one. "The camera fixes its living subjects, possesses their life. They are reborn on the screen, creature of the film's author and ourselves. But life is not fully breathed back into them. They are immortal, but they are always already dead" (Rothman, 1982, p. 341).

As Sam and Lila approach the Bates Motel office one last time, the lone tree in the motel courtyard shows only a few stray leaves barely clinging to its branches. (Shades of the opening of *Spellbound*.) Birds, we will soon be reminded, often sit on such tree branches ... watching and waiting.

The Birds (1963)

> This leads to the next logical step when I reduced the human element still further in *The Birds*. Now *there* are some actors I would call cattle! You have heard of actors who insist that their names be above the title; these demanded that they be the title! [Hitchcock, 1965, cited in Gottlieb, 1995, p. 57].

The early and humorous pet shop scene sets the tone for Melanie Daniels (Tippi Hedren in her first of two Hitchcock films) as both an embodiment of birds and her complacency as a human being; not fully human, really, but quite birdlike.

> [When Mitch] gets the bird from under his hat he says, "Let's put Melanie Daniels back into her gilded cage, shall we," and that's his way of telling the girl he knows who she is. The pay-off on that one line comes much later ... when the center of the town is attacked by seagulls and the girl seeks refuge in a phone booth—it's glass-walled—and she

The Birds (1963)

can't get out. I take high shots and you see birds beating all around. The gulls are the people now, you see, and she's the bird [Hitchcock, 1963, cited in Gottlieb, 2003, p. 50].

Just like in that early scene, her drive to Bodega Bay is also played for laughs as the love birds Melanie improbably hauls sixty miles north from San Francisco (for Mitch's younger sister Cathy) lean left and right with her careening car. "If Melanie is like a bird, then birds are also treated like people. Mitch tells Melanie he is looking for a pair of lovebirds that are 'not too demonstrative [but] not too aloof [either]'" (Leitch, 1991, p. 228).

With only the sound of her speeding car's revving motor, screeching tires on curves, and aggressive gear shifting juxtaposed with extreme long shots of the California cliff roads (shades of Roger Thornhill's drunken drive in *North by Northwest*)—and not a musical note on the score, just electronically enhanced bird sounds supervised by Bernard Herrmann—Hitchcock manages to suffuse the light-hearted scene with an underlying sense of menace, too.

And we must take our time, get absorbed in the atmosphere before the birds come. Once more, it is fantasy. But everything had to be as real as possible, surroundings, the settings, [and] the people. And the birds themselves had to be domestic birds—no vultures, no wild birds of any kind [Hitchcock, cited in Bogdanovich, 1963, p. 45].

The white Bodega Bay schoolhouse when first spied in long shot is of the foreboding Victorian variety, more than a little reminiscent of Norman's home from *Psycho*. And our next shot of the schoolhouse, with its shuttered green upstairs windows, powerfully frames actress Suzanne Pleshette's dark hair and red sweater after her character Annie Hayworth and Melanie jealously banter over Mitch (Australian actor Rod Taylor).

With the film's headlong narrative presented in the first, mostly humorous twenty-five minutes, Hitchcock almost makes us forget about any coming terror. After Melanie steals into the Brenner home with the love birds, we palpably feel the sexual anticipation in Melanie's eyes as she returns in her boat across the bay to a smiling Mitch waiting on the dock. The pleasurable anticipation we are meant to feel now between these two is the exact moment Hitchcock strikes us full-force with a gull that swoops down and pecks at Melanie's head. "And this seems to me the function of the birds: They are a concrete embodiment of the arbitrary and unpredictable, of whatever makes human life and human relationships precarious, a reminder of fragility and instability..." (Wood, 1965, p. 126).

When Mitch comes to the rescue, we realize that her earlier fey attitude has now been deeply marred as he pulls her little outboard alongside a larger boat, its name FAY MAR clearly visible on the stern.

Mitch's absent father's portrait—recalling Lina's painting of her hovering father in *Suspicion*—watches over Melanie as she plays piano after dinner in the living room. His is the love Mitch's mother Lydia (British-American stage and film actress Jessica Tandy) misses so much, and it is wholly irretrievable.

> [The portrait] is alluded to by Melanie and Mitch during Lydia's phone conversation with Brinkmeyer and visible merely in portions during Melanie's conversation with Cathy at the piano. It is seen fully and at an angle only after a bird attack in the Brenner living room. It assumes significance in a later attack on their home when Mitch rests on the piano bench under the portrait as Lydia sits in [a] chair next to him [Margaret M. Horwitz, cited in Deutelbaum and Poague, 1986, p. 287].

Unlike Norman's mother, the often hysterical Lydia will eventually let go, accept, help and even (physically) embrace Melanie. But it is the shrill sound of her truck as it tears away from the dead Dan Fossett's home, his eyes horribly pecked out by the antagonistic birds, which will far outdo even Lydia's agitation.

> The screech of the truck engine starting off conveys her anguish.... In the previous scene we had shown that the woman was going through a violent emotion, and when she gets into the truck, we showed that this was an emotional truck, not only by the image, but also through the sound that sustains the emotion. It's not only the sound of the engine you hear, but something that's like a cry. It's as though the truck were shrieking [Hitchcock, cited in Truffaut, 1967, p. 224].

Back at the Brenner home, the small figurine on the piano of a woman combing her hair embodies the domesticity of a happy family life missing in this household—and only hinted at down the road, possibly, by the end of the picture—since Mitch and Cathy's father died

Marnie (1964)

four years earlier. Later, that little sculpture sits next to Cathy and seems to echo her sentiments when she asks Melanie if she likes them or not, a brief but deeply poignant moment.

After Melanie returns to Annie's, their complicated rivalry banter over Mitch, turning finally into a kind of grudging, mutual respect, is exacerbated by the ever-so-subtle chirping of birds sounding slowly but perceptibly louder on the soundtrack. Annie lights a cigarette in the middle of their joust, her lighter flaming up a full three inches (worth of jealousy). Shortly, Mitch and Melanie's more serious conversation takes place on a hill (as does Michael and Sarah's conversation two films hence in *Torn Curtain*), a brief respite but clear portent of the imminent gull attack below them during Cathy's birthday party.

A truly frightening scene occurs in the apparent comfort of the Brenner living room shortly after dinner. Just prior to dozens of sparrows swarming down the chimney, the house is filmed as a dangerous antagonist itself, for the "shots are angled and framed so that the ceiling seems to press down on them" (Wood, 1965, p. 146).

Objects in this room, like the birds, have begun to take over and even supplant these people's lives, representatives for all of humanity in this apocalyptic film. First, in *Psycho*, Hitchcock made it impossible to take a shower without locking one's bathroom door. In *The Birds*, even a home is not safe (as in *Shadow of a Doubt*). A dozen years after *The Birds*, Steven Spielberg will scare us away from the ocean.

Marnie (1964)

> Unbroken rows of tall ugly brick houses ... give us a sense of imprisonment [and] claustrophobia, all possibility of freedom and openness shut out; at the end, the ship loom[s] up ominously, as if blocking the exit. When we first see the image it is not precisely explicable, but it conveys admirably ... the intolerable constriction of Marnie's life [Wood, 1965, p. 151].

The film credits unfold like the pages of a book, only backwards. The beginning of the soundtrack by Bernard Herrmann uses rousing music, prepping us for a wild ride. (In fact, at one point Mark Rutland, the character played by actor Sean Connery on hiatus between the "Bond ... James Bond" films *From Russia with Love* [1963] and *Goldfinger* [late 1964], speaks to that very idea.)

Abruptly, Herrmann's racing tune stops. In silence except for the clicking of high heels walking, the first sequence of the film starts with an extreme close-up follow shot of a bright yellow handbag tightly clutched in the crook of the left arm of a woman wearing a gray coat. She will turn out to be Margaret "Marnie" Edgar, although she assumes several different (false) identities throughout the first part of the picture. She is played in an extraordinary, long underappreciated manner by "Tippi" Hedren (born Nathalie Kay Hedren, 1930). In one take and for exactly one minute she walks away from the camera along a yellow warning line on the outdoor platform of a train station. "She carefully walks along the yellow 'caution' line, and that is a paradigm of her whole life" (1976, p. 412), Spoto notes. No one else is around.

Muted yellows and greens and grays and browns and soft, dull pastels are the primary colors for this film, all the better, we will soon find out (but not understand, for most of two hours), to sharply contrast with Marnie's flashbacks, when the screen becomes suffused in a startlingly bright red. "We tried to minimize the main color of the film and kind of neutralized color until we would accentuate it in her vision of red" (Robert Boyle, set designer, "The Trouble with Marnie," 2000 *Marnie* DVD bonus feature).

When Strutt, who describes Marnie the thief with stereotypically objectifying adjectives, remarks to Mark that he should remember her, he inhumanely refers to her *à la* Bond with "Oh, that one, the brunette with the legs." Withholding our view of Hedren's lovely face for a full six minutes, Hitchcock finally reveals her in a gorgeous close-up immediately after she washes black dye out of her hair and flings her head back to look straight into the camera for a stunning three seconds. She is no object to us now but a beautiful human, but it will take nearly this entire film full of enormous emotional struggles, many of them initiated by Mark, for her begin to *treat* herself as one. In this film, as in so many others, subjects as objects—the reverse phrase of this book's title—press in hard upon our sensibilities. Interestingly, as in the long opening scene, Hitchcock cuts to more and more shots of her back, an object unavailable to us.

Marnie (1964)

Later, as she walks away from the camera again at a bus station, two huge suitcases are clasped in her hands. We see her place them in a locker and Hitchcock zooms in on her locking them up. In tight close-up now, the camera stays glued on the locker key in her hand, echoes of the classic crane shot descending to an extreme close-up of the Unica key in Alicia's hand in *Notorious*. Spotting a floor grate for water drainage, Marnie walks over to it as Hitch stays on a close-up of the key a moment longer until she drops it to the floor, then kicks it between the metal bars, lost forever. An afterimage of Bruno's nearly lost cigarette lighter down a similar drain from *Strangers on a Train* comes to mind. Another key, yet again, will play its own part later in this film.

Marnie arrives in Baltimore for a visit to her mother Bernice Edgar (a rich, underrated performance by Louise Latham). The huge backdrop painting at the end of her street reveals a towering ship that figuratively bars the route between mother and daughter intimacy and true love.

Inside Mrs. Edgar's house, the bright reds of her gladiolas not only contrast sharply with the rest of the subdued colors used in the film but also trigger the screen's recurring red suffusion for three seconds—the same length of time we were permitted to see Hedren's freshly washed face for the first time. As with the large portrait of two loving dogs highlighted in the background of the torture scene of Van Meer in *Foreign Correspondent*, a similar portrait of two calm, domesticated canines frequently hovers in counterpoint on the wall behind Marnie and her mother. As represented by the picture of these happy dogs, their uncomfortable conversation reinforces the lack of love between them.

Rutland and Company's parking lot is shot from high above, its car lanes painted in a perfectly designed zigzag pattern that anticipates a coming thunderstorm full of streaked lightning. In his office, Mark remarks to Marnie (the names read and sound fitting together, like Mark and Margot in *Dial M for Murder*) about the meanings of two kinds of objects in the room. The pre–Columbian art in a large glass case is all that he still owns of his dead wife. On his desk is a scary-looking photo of a Jaguarondi, a South American wildcat, that prefers solitude and is shy and reclusive—like Marnie. He notes that the Jaguarondi was stalked and tamed by him. As if they were still alive, both the pre–Columbian art and the wildcat will shortly be protagonistic objects to reckon with.

Hitchcock cuts to a medium three-shot of Mark and Marnie flanking a huge lamp and its wide shade. As shot from somewhat of a distance, it strikes the even wider gulf between them at this point in the film. Famed female screenwriter Jay Presson Allen's sharp dialogue captures the essence of their relationship for much of the story. Mark tells Marnie that the paper he wants her to type up "deals with the instincts of predators, what you might call the criminal class of the animal world. Lady animals figure very largely as predators," he notes about Sophie (the name for his Jaguarondi), but he is really referring to the woman before him.

During the lightning storm, Marnie's frightening red suffusion washes over the screen several times. Hitchcock cuts to a medium long shot of the large office windows, their translucent curtains drawn closed. As lightning rapidly flashes, two starkly silhouetted sculptures of stalwart men on tall pedestals stand symmetrically between an erect coat rack and the earlier lamp—four guards or infantrymen threateningly marching towards Marnie. Seemingly on cue, as shot from one of Hitchcock's inimitable and always startling high overhead shots, a huge tree branch crashes through the window, demolishing the glass cabinet that held all the pre–Columbian figurines, the final vestiges of Mark's wife's legacy.

Mark moves to comfort Marnie and cannot help but kiss her full on the forehead, then moves down to her mouth in an intensely intimate extreme close-up that even Hedren herself, on the 2000 DVD bonus feature "The Trouble with Marnie," said was one of the most sensual-looking kisses she had ever seen in a film. Although there are any number of other Hitchcockian screen clinches that certainly qualify as most intimate—Devlin and Alicia in *Notorious*, John and Francie in *To Catch a Thief*, and Lisa and Jeff in *Rear Window*, to name just three—Hedren was right, it's a delicious moment.

Animals as protagonists continue to impact scenes. When pressed by Mark to admit whether she loves anything, Marnie states that horses (like the Jaguarondi, and the dogs and foxes in an upcoming hunt) are the only things in the world that are beautiful—certainly not people. Mr. Rutland, Mark's father (English actor Alan Napier, who soon played Alfred the butler in the 1960s *Batman* TV series), confirms her assess-

Marnie (1964)

ment: "Best thing in the world for the inside of a man or woman is the outside of a horse." On their so-called honeymoon cruise, Hedren does an excellent imitation of a feral cat pacing back and forth in their stateroom, unable to escape the traps that keep appearing in her life.

Later, as Marnie approaches Mark's office desk, the key to the office drawer where the safe's lock combination is hidden is given another brief close-up in her hand. As she makes her way to the safe with the combination firmly in her memory, she again looks like a cat seeking its prey, ever alert to the danger of discovery and capture. After Mark does, indeed, "capture" her, Jay Presson Allen reinforces all the animal action with more pertinent dialogue in the car. Note how Mark's words treat her like an object, a trophy, much more than as a person.

MARK: Whatever you are, I love you.
MARNIE: You don't love me. I'm just something you've caught. You think I'm some kind of animal you've trapped.
MARK: That's right, you are. And I've caught something really wild this time, haven't I? I've tracked you and caught you and, by God, I'm gonna keep you.

In fact, they each talk about and subsequently treat her as if she is his "legal possession." Marnie similarly complains about nuptials in the following way: "I didn't want to get married. It's degrading. It's animal!" And when Mark thinks out loud about a plan to pay remunerations to all the people and places she's robbed, Hedren again prowls the room as if she's caged. Soon after this point in the picture, she must literally kill her beloved horse Forio—the only object she believed, wrongly, had any intrinsic or earned beauty, including herself, Mark, and her mother. As with so many Hitchcock heroines and heroes, Marnie must find a way to move past this (false) assumption about life if she is to have a chance at redemption and happiness.

As another stand-in for things she "loved," the safe lock back at Rutland's is lovingly rendered in three rapid-succession extreme close-ups shot from three different angles. The safe is treated by Hitchcock as the only home of that false path to happiness for Marnie: money. After she unlocks it, Hitchcock first cuts to a close-up of her hand turning the handle of its right door, but then quickly cuts to a close-up of just that door magically opening all by itself (shades of *Rear Window*'s opening blinds, or the empty but assertive closet door in *The Trouble with Harry*). Because of the way the safe is shot in this scene, and the lack of muscle strain on her face, I believe we are meant to feel not so much that her hand is pulling the door back but that it indeed is opening out of love for her! And after it opens (by itself), Hitchcock shoots the door silently and almost delicately in a pose (repose?) screen left next to her screen right face.

Mark creeps up behind her and tries to help her grab the loot. It's hers now, after all, so she's entitled to it, he tells her. Cut to several close-ups from various angles of her shaking hand and his firm one, both unable to move forward or backward, once again caught in a place she can neither escape from nor progress toward.

As he takes her to Baltimore to confront her mother, pouring rain and thunder and lightning again predict the final battle between Mrs. Edgar and her daughter. Marnie finally remembers the horrible murder she herself committed at the age of five in protecting her prostitute mother from an apparent (but accidentally misunderstood) advance by a sailor john, played in a brief cameo by a young Bruce Dern. It is the calm after the storm that reveals the final object of so many that motivated people in this film. Mrs. Edgar says, "You know how I got you, Marnie? There was this boy—Billy. And I wanted Billy's sweater. I was fifteen. And Billy said, if I let him, I could have the sweater. So I let him.... I still got that old sweater. And I got you, Marnie."

In *Marnie*, it seems that objects themselves turn out to have been the primary driving force that moved the story forward, especially affecting the lead protagonist, who was almost wholly unable to control any person or thing in the film, especially herself.

Torn Curtain (1966)

Red has [a] hellish connotation because of its association with fire, which is in fact the major image in the film. The credits appear against a flame, and faces emerge from gray smoke on the [right]. Throughout, Gromek's cigarette lighter does not work for him (although it does for Michael just after the murder). Lindt lights several cigars with a large flame, and Mr. Jakobi, the leader of the freedom bus,

Torn Curtain (1966)

lights a cigarette for another "passenger," and so distracts the police from recognizing Michael and Sarah. The final fire imagery appears in the ballet sequence [Spoto, 1976, p. 418].

Extreme close-ups of disembodied hands and faces, as if separated from their bodies—harbinger of their ubiquity throughout *Topaz*—are the objects that transfer one of *Torn Curtain*'s two MacGuffins early on in this film: the book with the π symbol. In a sudden close-up, we are privy via three hands touching a note with a bookstore address and, shortly, the transfer of the actual book between the hands of Sarah Sherman (Julie Andrews, fresh off *Mary Poppins* and *The Sound of Music*) and Michael Armstrong (Paul Newman). Later, their bodyguard Hermann Gromek's (German actor Wolfgang Kieling) legs are treated similarly, legs that will stand in for his entire being immediately after the farmer's wife whacks them with a large shovel at the beginning of his horrific murder.

When their plane lands in East Berlin, Sarah tries to spot her fiancé Michael but Hitchcock's milling passengers, rushing to retrieve their carry-ons, completely block her view. Same problem during the press conference. Sarah is dwarfed and crowded out by the press, who congregate all about Michael. Even as they walk down a hall together after his public "defection," she does not really have access to him due to the crush of reporters and politicians. Hitchcock even shows Gromek himself having trouble breaking through the mass of bodies, a portent of his coming impotence, perhaps.

There is a running gag—one that we will quite literally gag on after the German's murder—with Gromek's inability to light all his cigarettes with his lighter throughout the film. (Conversely, his boss, Hugh, and Professor Lindt never have trouble keeping their Cubans lit.) Gromek tries three times to light one, all unsuccessful, before he falls prey to the ultimate irony, a gas oven, which most certainly is turned on. Only after his death does his lighter work, flicked on by his murderer Michael himself. In addition, the red flame that a match or gas oven requires to be lit is an important objective motif throughout the picture.

In contrast, the drab, washed-out gray colors throughout this film, most notably on everyone's clothing but especially all of the buildings and via the lighting upon their arrival in East Berlin, are of particular note for this Cold War palette. Sarah's dull brown overcoat and dress also now dampen any ardor Michael and she had for each other at the start of the film. The mottled gray marble walls of their hotel's halls—empty, high-ceilinged and oppressive—further keep the tone of the film muted.

> When we did *Torn Curtain*, we set up a rule: The moment we got into East Germany, we'd go to gray and beige tones only. No bright colors—except a spot of red now and again which would reflect the red of the uniforms worn by the Vopos. That was a decision we made, coordinated with the costume designer [Hitchcock, 1967, cited in Gottlieb, 1995, p. 306].

Sarah's room, also filled with gray shadows, barely allows the diffuse late afternoon sunlight to penetrate its space. In the similar gray of the morning, her bright red nightgown is a welcome, perhaps hopeful sign of how she might affect positive change to their nightmare. "Hitchcock's use of color throughout this first third of the film, in which warm colors are associated with Sarah's anguished love and cool colors with the East Germans and their country, is so elegant and painterly that the film suggests the visual style of Antonioni, not a director from whom Hitchcock often borrowed" (Leitch, 1991, p. 233).

In an effort to escape Gromek's tail, Michael alights on his own from the hotel's elevator in a signature high overhead shot, the sounds of scrubbing floors, of all things, on the soundtrack. A crane shot pulls back and further up to reveal first one, then two, then three, and finally four cleaning women on their hands and knees in the hotel foyer—reminiscent of the four cleaning women in a similar position from *Waltzes from Vienna* thirty-three years earlier—and then moves precipitously down into a startling close-up of Gromek chewing his ever-present gum, ever vigilant and suspicious. In total silence but for the footsteps of hard-soled shoes (which recall Marnie's high-heeled walk at the beginning of *Marnie*), Michael's escape from Gromek through the cavernous, wholly empty Berlin Museum is yet another brilliantly suspenseful Hitchcockian scene. Shot in an extreme long shot from overhead at one point, Michael pauses in a huge hall with a marble floor, a pattern of eight possible paths in the design below his feet. He picks one out to pass along as we cut back to the museum's imposing Greek columns standing guard outside.

Torn Curtain (1966)

After Michael's arrival and discovery by Gromek at the farmhouse, Hitchcock gives us four separate extreme close-up shots from a bit up under of yet one more knife in his oeuvre as the woman of the house silently stalks Gromek, arm held high as in the *Psycho* shower scene. On the fifth and sixth extreme close-ups, Hitchcock cuts to her directly facing the camera, arm and knife raised at our faces. On the seventh, she lunges right at us, her mouth silently screaming in a wide, frightening close-up. Cut to a close-up of the knife breaking off right above Gromek's heart, blood spreading on his white shirt in the same way Juanita's dark purple dress billows out on the floor during her murder in Hitchcock's next film *Topaz*. Also in close-up, we now see the woman smash Gromek's knees with the abovementioned shovel four times in rapid succession, its dull, echoing clang resounding hollowly in the silence of the farmhouse. Unlike the murder in *Psycho*, there is no music on the soundtrack for this one. Hitchcock cuts to a quick extreme close-up of Gromek's legs buckling, an echo of Marnie's in front of the Rutland safe when he caught her.

Gromek's murder takes a full four minutes of anguished and hor-

Torn Curtain (1966): **Michael Armstrong (Paul Newman) is dwarfed by the Berlin Museum in the same way Tracy was by the British Museum in *Blackmail*, Mrs. de Winter by Manderley in *Rebecca*, and Roger Thornhill by the United Nations and Mount Rushmore in *North by Northwest*.**

rific screen time; his flailing hands, shot from above, are all that we see of him as he spastically releases Michael's neck. The gas oven hisses him to lifelessness. As horrid a character as he is in this film, even we may feel some reluctant sympathy for this German who dies in his small gas chamber twenty-one years after the end of World War II. Or do we? Interestingly, John Kander and Fred Ebb's *Cabaret*, itself a clear-eyed examination of the Nazis coming to power in the thirties, arrived on Broadway the same year as *Torn Curtain*.

> I thought it was time to show that it was very difficult, very painful, and it takes a very long time to kill a man. The public is aware that this must be a silent killing because of the presence of the taxi driver on the farm. Firing a shot is out of the question. In line with our old principle, the killing has to be carried out by means suggested by the locale and the characters. We are in a farmhouse and the farmer's wife is [helping with] the killing. So we use household objects: the kettle full of soup, a carving knife, a shovel, and, finally, the gas oven [Hitchcock, cited in Truffaut, 1967, p. 234].

In close-up, we see the shovel in the farm wife's hands mime digging Gromek's grave, another image all too relevant to Nazi atrocities. Hitchcock immediately shows us Michael lighting Gromek's lighter for the first time, hope illuminating the film, perhaps, at this ultimately ironic moment.

Back at German headquarters, another hint of hope springs to life in Sarah's now spring-green dress, the only color bursting forth among the increasingly oppressive grays in the room. Bombed-out gray buildings of the city are also visible behind everyone through the windows, one small and forlorn green-leafed tree and one bush hinting at life in the rubble. Shortly, sadly, Sarah's next outfit screams that she may be coming over to the Communist side. It's light gray, and buttoned up all the way to her neck; she is suddenly a cold and closed-off individual *à la* Marnie on her wedding night. Edith Head's costumes provide just the right amount of ambiguity within Hein Heckroth's deliberately muted production design.

When Sarah is asked for information by the East German authorities, Hitchcock slows down her reaction so much that we cannot read her face at all until she blurts out that she will *not* answer any questions. Climbing a hill like the one Melanie and Mitch stood upon during their

Topaz (1969)

intimate reveals to each other in *The Birds*, Michael and Sarah are seen in an extreme long shot, no sound of their conversation available to us. Only the hill is privy. Upon reconciliation, Michael pulls her into the first and only lush green hedge we have seen in this film for a momentarily private, deliciously intimate kiss. As embodied by that hedge, verdant love finally will out.

Their discovery by a ballerina amidst the German crowd at a ballet concert is yet another perfect example of Hitchcock's use of settings to drive the narrative forward.

> A rule that I've always followed is: Never use a setting simply as a background. Use it one hundred percent. For example, in *Torn Curtain*, Paul Newman goes to a ballet. Who discovers him? A ballerina, in the middle of her dance. How does he get the idea to shout "Fire!"? From a scenic fire on the stage. You've got to make the setting work dramatically. You can't use it just as a background. In other words, the locale must be functional [Hitchcock, 1967, cited in Gottlieb, 1995, p. 313].

Likewise, their escape is carried out, in part, through a long montage using public transportation. Hitchcock explains how he treated those movable objects as subjects, too: "I directed that whole scene by imagining the bus to be a character of the film. We have a good bus, which is going to help our couple to escape. And a few hundred yards behind them is the bad bus, which is threatening the good one" (Hitchcock, cited in Truffaut, 1967, p. 234).

Again, the importance of objects as protagonists cannot be overstated in Hitchcock's films. The immobilized ones such as lighters and knives and hedges and museums and hotel rooms find ways to emotionally move the storyline along, while the mobile ones like ballet crowds and buses and legs do the same via their actual ability to transport.

Topaz (1969)

[The color] red associated with the Russians in Red Square is also associated with the real danger of their military might. When André shows Juanita how the Geiger counter works, a red lamp on the bedside table warns against using it. Red is associated with danger most obviously when, as in *Marnie*, it is figured as brilliant blood, often on a white background: when the Mendozas are apprehended because of the wife's bleeding wound, when André's son-in-law is shot, when Jarre is found on the roof of his car, and when blood seeps from under Juanita's body [Brill, 1988, p. 189].

Huge masses of bodies as a single character open *Topaz*. We're reminded of the crowded audience at *Torn Curtain*'s ballet, but this time they are in the thousands and hundreds of thousands, not the dozens or hundreds. Communists at a Cold War rally marching military style to one drum, Hitchcock's mindless crowds are finally taken to the nth degree here.

The ever-so-somber grays from *Torn Curtain* continue in many of these buildings, too, while all the lamps throughout the first two-thirds of the film are turned off and dark, their shades black. No illumination seems possible in *Topaz*, beginning with André Devereaux's (Czech-born actor Frederick Stafford) meeting with his Russian and French counterparts. Only the defector's daughter, Tamara Kusenov (Swedish actress Tina Hedström), is permitted to wear a bright yellow blouse above a cheery red and black skirt, as she plays piano in the safe house. Her mother, too, is briefly seen being fitted for a lovely pine-green, full-length outfit, but all the politicians wear nothing but blacks and grays. Devereaux's wife Nicole begs him to leave all political machinations behind, wishing to go back to Paris from Washington, D.C. Hitchcock cuts to a verdant green landscape painting prominently displayed on the wall over André's left shoulder, but her hope for that kind of life is almost immediately dashed by the complex narrative.

Hitchcock's perverse humor erupts with the mannequin heads constructed as camouflage for the defecting Kusenov family. Their visages are eerie and unnerving, especially the one of Tamara that she holds in her hands for a moment directly facing the camera. More black humor, and religious to boot, comes out when African American actor-director Roscoe Lee Browne's character Philippe Dubois, a flower shop owner, turns to a worker and says, "Benny, work on this cross. And don't brighten it up too much." Even flowers are not permitted their normally optimistic tone. In fact, they're downright oppressive in *Topaz*. "Every set is ablaze with floral arrangements. And the image

Topaz (1969)

Topaz (1969): Tamara Kusenov's (Tina Hedström) outfit represents one of the few colorful, hopeful sights in a film full of greys.

suggests a ubiquitous and massive funeral, since each locale has the faint redolence of death.... The rooms in Cuba are banked with flowers, as are the rooms in Paris" (Spoto, 1976, p. 430).

Food, too, plays its subversive part during the stolen briefcase scene. (Food will act with black humor vengeance in Hitchcock's next film, *Frenzy*.) We are meant to think Rico Parra (Canada-born actor John Vernon) is looking for his briefcase when, in fact, he's searching for a document he wants copied; it lies beneath a half-eaten hamburger that has soiled the sought-after document with grease. Of course, it is birds carrying food—filmed twice from screen left to screen right— that give away the old couple's hiding place, their spying cameras hidden in the chicken sandwich bread for their lunch "picnic."

> Hitchcock's use of food and flowers [represent] hypocrisy and the compromise of personal loyalties. When Rico Parra interrupts Devereaux's last night alone with Juanita, she offers him some dinner, and Devereaux praises the chicken, not mentioning that earlier that day it had been used to conceal a camera which took pictures of the Soviet military hardware [Leitch, 1991, p. 237].

Body parts representing the whole person rear their heads again, an extreme close-up of Parra's left ear appearing in a scene when Mrs.

Hitchcock's Objects as Subjects

Carlotta Mendoza (Nicaragua-born Anna Navarro) whispers the name of Juanita de Cordoba (German-born actress Karin Dor) into it during her torture. As with similar extreme close-ups in other Hitchcock films, most notably in *Secret Agent* and *Vertigo*, we are palpably revolted by this violating intimacy. Hitchcock cuts immediately to a close-up of Parra's hands sliding up his trouser legs, reminiscent of other hands from *Torn Curtain* and Bruno Anthony's murderous ones from *Strangers on a Train*.

For the first time with Hitchcock, elevators drive the narrative forward (contemporary versions of staircases?), for they are all out of order in this film. We end up instead seeing people running up and down staircases, shades of films from as far back as *The Lodger* and *Downhill* through *Psycho*, *The Birds* and even the final shot of *Family Plot*.

Frenzy (1972)

> Covent Garden is a herbivorous rather than a carnivorous food-market, but the equation corruption = corpses = food is carried through to food = money. Blaney storms out of a pub and a job over his supposed theft of a drink. Later a customer complains over the stench of an outdated Scotch egg [Durgnat, 1974, p. 296].

The picture opens with two minutes worth of a lovely helicopter view in long shot, traveling up the Thames River in London. Right after the director's name flashes onscreen as the final credit, black smoke from a tugboat blots out the sky, warning of hazards to come.

Our first shot of the murderer Bob Rusk, perversely and, typically for Hitchcock, charmingly played by English actor Barry Foster, shows him eating a green apple plucked from the Garden of Eden; specifically, Covent Garden market, where he owns a stall. Shades of the damning lighter from *Strangers on a Train* (and Gromek's, from *Torn Curtain*). Look fast to spot Hitchcock's camera quickly showing us Rusk's necktie pin. Often used to disgustingly pick at food between his teeth, it will be the object that finally implicates him for the murders.

Frenzy (1972)

The first half-hour of the film is awash with Covent Garden colors, until Rusk visits Brenda Blaney (actress Barbara Leigh-Hunt) at her matchmaker's office, where all the lighting suddenly turns the look into a drab and cold gray (recalling *Torn Curtain* and *Topaz*). Hitchcock intersperses Rusk's horrific rape of Mrs. Blaney with many shots of her hands reaching for the phone, legs writhing in protest (recalling the legs of Marnie and Gromek), fingers aflutter like Gromek's, and an extreme close-up on his tie pin. After recovering from his sickening consummation, two oval pictures on Mrs. Blaney's mantelpiece stare back at him and the camera like accusing eyes as he picks up another green apple to take a bite. "Food, in *Frenzy*, is a basic visual metaphor for the devouring abuses of man-against-man. Potatoes, fruit (particularly grapes), and gourmet delicacies appear on the screen and in dialogue with increasing frequency as the film progresses.... [Indeed], food is almost the 'main character' in the film!" (Spoto, 1976, p. 436).

Because the rape and murder of Mrs. Blaney is so horrible in its close-up details of hands and legs, Hitchcock shows us nothing but a blank wall as we wait for the discovery of her death. The wall itself easily imprints the afterimages of her passing in our memory.

> From the moment Monica [Mrs. Blaney's secretary] enters the building, for a painstaking 23 seconds, we wait for her to react to what we are well aware she will encounter upstairs. Hitchcock makes this enormous delay more unendurable by showing us nothing but, literally, a blank wall. He thus reveals a singular, anti-voyeuristic phrase in cinema language: the power of not showing that which can be imagined [Sharff, 1991, pp. 194–195].

For the murder of Babs, Blaney's girlfriend, in Rusk's second floor apartment, Hitchcock mischievously—no, maliciously, gleefully—increases our tension by taking more than twice as long (fifty-two seconds) to pull the camera back down the curving stairs, through the hallway, and out the door into Covent Garden marketplace. Hitch shows us not one bit of Babs' (English actress Anna Massey) murder, for the events we know are about to happen occur completely in our minds. And it is the camera itself this time as object, not a blank wall, which carries the painful empathy we feel for this innocent and sympathetic woman back down the director's signature stairway. "The significance of these repeated shots (on the stairway) cannot be overestimated.... In addition to giving unity to the film and heightening the drama, they are a personal kinesthetic statement of Hitchcock, to whom stairways are always a central, almost architectural pivot for a film" (Sharff, 1991, p. 218).

The only objects that are symmetrically balanced when we visit the home of Inspector Tim Oxford (Alec McCowen) and his studious but gastronomically incompetent Mrs. Oxford (Vivien Merchant), as she serves up a ghastly soup de poisson, are the candles on the table and the lamps on the walls. When the inspector sits down to (hysterically) gag through the first course, Hitchcock's camera shifts clockwise to place him in ridiculous contrast to the inedible food, perfectly framed between two pairs of warmly lit lamps on the wall behind him. It is a deliberate counterpoint image of marital bliss that is nonexistent in their scenes together.

Mrs. Oxford returns to the kitchen to fetch the next frightening course and a cut puts her dead center in the background, two gently burning candles on the foregrounded dinner table now framing her. Upon her return with a serving of barely cooked quail, she sits across from him while the camera swings clockwise to pan back and bring into view for the first time a large table lamp perfectly centered between both candles and spouses. "She keeps giving him the most repulsive and inedible meals," screenwriter Anthony Shaffer says on the 2000 DVD special feature, "The Story of *Frenzy*." Hitchcock adds one of Shaffer's blackly comic spoken lines to the inspector at the precise moment his fork and knife fruitlessly stab at the sauce-drenched bird: "We've got to find [the rapist killer] before his appetite is whetted again."

After Rusk dumps poor Babs' body into a potato truck and returns to his flat, we can just make out two women's portraits in *faux*-paradise, Gauguin-style staring him down as he moves screen left to screen right to lie down below them, exhausted, on his horrid-colored orange couch. When he realizes he lost his teeth-picking tie pin with the letter "R" embossed on it when Babs tried to fight him off, the soundtrack shifts from a lovely dance-like passage to a frantic chase theme.

The search for the pin, clasped tightly in the girl's hand in a bag full of potatoes, is played for very dark laughs as one of Babs' feet kicks him twice, hard, square on the face while the potato truck, now jostling about on the highway, flings him, tons of potatoes, and the dead body all around. And when Richard "Dick" Blaney (Jon Finch)

Frenzy (1972)

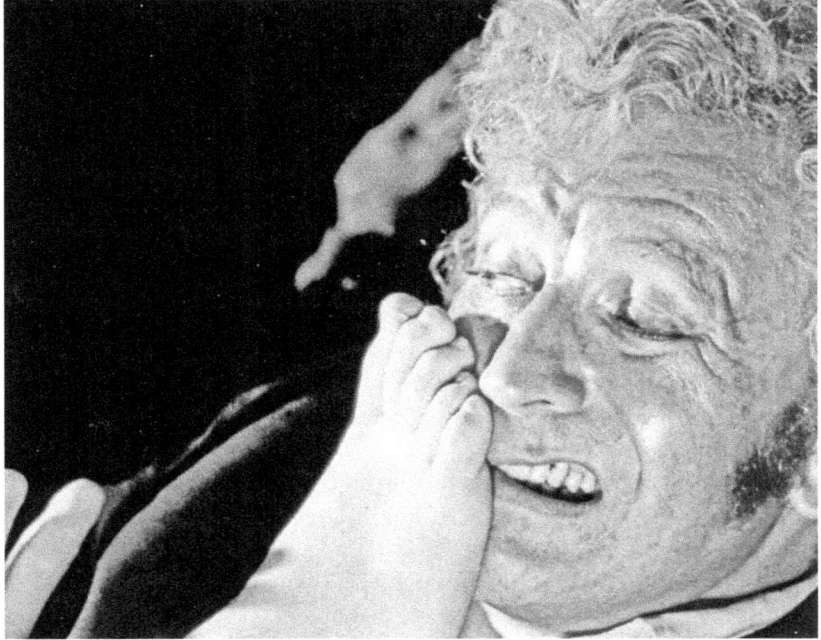

Frenzy (1972): Just like David in *Rope* and Harry in *The Trouble with Harry*, the dead continue to affect the living as Babs' (Anna Massey) lifeless foot kicks Bob Rusk (Barry Foster) in the face.

holes up at Rusk's flat, thinking he's got at least one safe night ahead of him—he doesn't, of course, because Rusk is setting him up for the killings—Hitchcock shoots Rusk once again with those two portraits accusingly looking back at him and us, perfectly framed between them in medium shot as he goes on about how sweet his "ol' mum" is. Blaney is told to help himself to the booze, and as he moves to get some, we see that it sits on a dresser directly below a painting of flamenco dancers living it up, yet another ironic contrast to his continually harrowing life.

"There's a texture which you can get by using humor and giving it to the blackest character in the piece," Barry Foster (Rusk) says in the 2000 *Frenzy* DVD commentary. Truer words were never spoken in this horrible little tale of unquenchable appetites, and food that never satisfies.

Hitchcock's Objects as Subjects
Family Plot (1976)

> As we have seen in earlier films, jewelry is always for Hitchcock a symbol of spurious value, of the apparent versus the real. As such, it was a major prop in *The Ring, Shadow of a Doubt, Lifeboat, Under Capricorn, Stage Fright, To Catch a Thief, Vertigo,* and *Frenzy* [Spoto, 1976, p. 450].

In *Family Plot*, Hitchcock's 53rd and final film, the deeply satisfying irony that transparent diamonds have been hidden throughout the film in a large, all-glass, brilliantly radiant chandelier—revealed at the very end via the seemingly telepathic, all-seeing spiritualist Blanche Tyler (Barbara Harris)—is a fitting end to this director's themes of illumination and extinction.

Again, lamps may or may not brighten circumstances, but they can and do affect proceedings in unanticipated ways. Right from the start, Julia Rainbird (Cathleen Nesbitt) and Blanche, the spiritualist, are seen dwarfed by two towering lamps, themselves just a small part of the conspicuous consumption on display in Mrs. Rainbird's extravagant home full of expensive, and meaningless, *objets d'art*. She wishes for Blanche (and her boyfriend, George Lumley, played by Bruce Dern in his second film for Hitchcock) to find the illegitimate child of her daughter that she gave away years ago, so that she may "give him every-thing—*everything*" that he never had. At the end of this ten-minute séance scene, Hitchcock dollies back to a long shot of the two of them surrounded by Mrs. Rainbird's spoils of wealth. As with a focus on the meaninglessness of money as early as his first film, *The Pleasure Garden*, in the character of Jill, Hitchcock brings that sentiment full circle fifty years later!

Blanche, white as a ghost (via makeup) in the back seat of George's cab (in typical Hitchcock fashion, Dern successively plays a cab driver, detective, and lawyer), perfectly reflects the dead spirits she has (falsely—or is it honestly?) claimed to have recently contacted. Even her name suggests paleness personified, as in the word "blanch," meaning to "remove color" (the French word for "white" is *blanc*). She will look pale as a ghost several times in this film, nowhere more clearly than at the end of the picture, when she actually finds the stolen diamonds.

Family Plot (1976)

Hitchcock loved to give his audience more information than the screen characters, so that we might more easily identify with them in their search for the knowledge we already have. At the twenty-three–minute mark, he shows us the final solution to the many mysteries in this movie, shooting the chandelier in plain sight with the stolen jewels hidden among its glittering crystals. And if we might not have gotten the hint as to the whereabouts of his final MacGuffin, he shows us a close-up of Arthur Adamson-Eddie Shoebridge (actor William Devane) reaching for some Scotch tape in a drawer and then standing alongside that chandelier on the stairway. In a canon full of lamps, this final, gloriously lit chandelier sparkles for our attention.

When George plays detective, he is always seen wearing an absurdly large Sherlock Holmes–type pipe in his mouth, a humorous stereotype for the sleuthing he does throughout the film. At one point, Hitchcock shares a little in-joke, a portent of bad things to come, when Fran (Karen Black) walks past a sign that says Bates Avenue. Now that was one mean house.

Conclusion

Alfred Hitchcock, it is important to remember, was all about "charging the screen with emotion" in ways that could best move his audience. Narrative, human characters, montage, *mise en scène*, costumes, colors, sizes and shapes of images and, yes, objects were all tools for the director to deliberately and carefully place onscreen, in juxtaposition with and relation to each other, in order to powerfully affect us. Such was his primary goal.

Through the exact placement and movements of his highly mobile camera, objects as well as people appeared to move by themselves as if they were also human beings with character and motivation. Lamps, smoke (and steam), staircases, chairs, eyeglasses, candles, figurines and statues, tables, clothing, buses, national monuments, boats, the ocean, signs, food, animals (especially birds), mirrors, cigarettes, crowds (masses of bodies), bottles, the camera itself, clocks, cities, buildings, keys, lighters, books, bottles, telephones, dead bodies, and even body parts such as hands and feet all took on protagonistic qualities in a Hitchcock film. Like the human actors that performed for Hitch's audience, these objects played their parts equally as well.

Studying the objects and the parts they play does not detract from one's enjoyment of Hitchcock's films; in fact, they augment that enjoyment, as we try to see and understand how objects contribute to the action, the story, our engagement. There are more characters onscreen than we may have believed possible in his movies, and treating these details as if they can affect the other actors as well as ourselves, the viewing audience, can only increase one's pleasure and emotional response.

Bibliography

Barr, Charles. (1999). *English Hitchcock*. Moffat, Scotland: Cameron and Hollis.
Bogdanovich, Peter. (1963). *The Cinema of Alfred Hitchcock*. Garden City, NY: Doubleday.
Brill, Lesley. (1988). *The Hitchcock Romance: Love and Irony in Hitchcock's Films*. Princeton, NJ: Princeton University Press.
Deutelbaum, Marshall, and Leland Poague (eds.). (1986). *A Hitchcock Reader*. Ames: Iowa State University Press.
Durgnat, Raymond. (1974). *The Strange Case of Alfred Hitchcock, or the Plain Man's Hitchcock*. Cambridge: MIT Press.
Gottlieb, Sidney (ed.). (1995). *Hitchcock on Hitchcock: Selected Writings and Interviews*. Berkeley: University of California Press.
Gottlieb, Sidney (ed.). (2003). *Alfred Hitchcock Interviews*. Jackson: University Press of Mississippi.
Leitch, Thomas M. (1991). *Find the Director, and Other Hitchcock Games*. Athens: University of Georgia Press.
Mogg, Ken. (1999). *The Alfred Hitchcock Story*. London: Titan Books.
Pomerance, Murray. (2004). *An Eye for Hitchcock*. New Brunswick, NJ: Rutgers University Press.
Rohmer, Eric, and Claude Chabrol. (1957). *Hitchcock: The First Forty-Four Films*. (Trans. Stanley Hochman). New York: Frederick Ungar.
Rothman, William. (1982). *Hitchcock—The Murderous Gaze*. Cambridge: Harvard University Press.
Rothman, William. (1988). *The "I" of the Camera: Essays in Film Criticism, History, and Aesthetics*. Cambridge: Cambridge University Press.
Sharff, Stefan. (1991). *Alfred Hitchcock's High Vernacular: Theory and Practice*. New York: Columbia University Press.
Spoto, Donald. (1976). *The Art of Alfred Hitchcock: Fifty Years of His Motion Pictures*. Garden City, NY: Doubleday.
Spoto, Donald. (1983). *The Dark Side of Genius: The Life of Alfred Hitchcock*. Boston: Da Capo Press.
Truffaut, François. (1967). *Hitchcock*. New York: Simon & Schuster.

Bibliography

Weis, Elisabeth. (1982). *The Silent Scream: Alfred Hitchcock's Sound Track*. Rutherford, NJ: Fairleigh Dickinson University Press.
Wood, Robin. (1965/1989). *Hitchcock's Films Revisited*. New York: Columbia University Press.
Yacowar, Maurice. (1977). *Hitchcock's British Films*. Hamden, CT: Archon.
Yanal, Robert J. (2005). *Hitchcock as Philosopher*. Jefferson, NC: McFarland.

Index

Numbers in ***bold italics*** indicate pages with photographs

apartments 11, 50, 67, 68, 88, 95–97, 123, 137, 139, 140–143, 146, 157–160, 162
artworks 9, 21, 28, 31, 45–47, 53, 85, 86, 97, 117, 135, 139, 140, 150, 153, 157, 163, 173, 174, 188

The Birds 5, 7, 8, 11, 22, 27, 42, 78, 90, 98, 100, 114, 147, 161, 166, ***168–171***, 181, 184
Blackmail 6, 9, 23, ***44–47***, 54, 73, 78, 82, 87, 88, 100, 132, 133, 163, 179
body parts 10, 11, 23, 43, 46, 62, 77, 82, 107, 131, 148, 183
buildings 1, 4, 9, 11, 20, 45, 54, 58, 64, 72, 96, 106, 117, 129, 131, 133, 137, 160, 162, 163, 177, 180, 182, 185, 190

candles 4, 8, 9, 52, 75, 76, 86, 87, 103, 115, 120, 123, 125–127, 135, 186, 190
cars 1, 4, 84, 158
Chabrol, Claude 18, 113, 123, 127, 137, 143, 156, 160, 165
chairs 1, 4, 27, 36–38, 43, 57, 68, 69, 76, 79, 80, 89, 101, 109, 111, 114, 118, 135, 140, 144, 147, 150, 152, 170, 190
Champagne 35, ***39–40***, 49, 83, 84, 89, 98, 109, 114, 162
cigarettes 16, 17, 21, 30, 42, 66, 71, 86, 89, 90, 99, 109, 111, 115, 118, 119, 133, 136, 141, 171, 173, 176, 177
cities 2, 18, 19, 64, 74, 77, 94, 95, 105, 112, 128, 143, 146, 154, 155, 157, 158, 160, 162–164, 180
crowds 10, 18–20, 25, 26, 32–34, 37, 44, 46, 48, 53, 54, 60–65, 67, 70–72, 74, 75, 78, 80–82, 86, 88, 89, 92, 98, 99, 103, 104, 109, 112, 118, 127, 132, 137, 147, 154, 162, 163, 177, 181, 182

Dial M for Murder 9, 18, 49, 65, 108, ***137–142***, 173
doors 2, 5–7, 18, 19, 28, 42–44, 48, 50, 51, 57, 59, 64, 75, 79, 87, 89, 98, 102, 107, 111, 115, 117, 128, 129, 136, 137, 141, 144, 150, 157, 158, 167, 171, 172, 175, 185
Downhill 7, 8, 17, ***26–27***, 47, 49, 184

Easy Virtue 10, 16, 21, ***27–31***, 36, 39, 49

Family Plot 10, 39, 49, 114, 145, 184, ***188–189***
The Farmer's Wife 8, ***36–39***, 43, 177, 180
flowers 89, 91, 118, 132, 145, 147, 157, 182
food 2, 37, 59, 64, 83, 84, 86, 98, 109, 120, 122, 125, 152, 166, 183–187
Foreign Correspondent 9, 42, ***92–96***, 97, 121, 148, 173
Frenzy 7, 18, 83, 114, 117, 128, 132, 151, 183, ***184–187***, 188

glasses 4, 19, 23, 35, 39, 41, 47, 67, 74, 75, 77–79, 83, 85, 98, 99, 102, 113, 120, 122–124, 129, 132, 134, 135, 139, 144, 147, 168, 173, 174, 188, 190

hands 10, 11, 23, 44, 49, 53, 56, 64, 73,

Index

77, 88, 98, 99, 123, 124, 130, 132, 144, 148, 155, 165, 166, 173, 177, 180, 184, 185
hearth 36, 38, 43, 50, 51, 87, 91, 114

I Confess 7, 13, 22, 25, 42, 44, **134–137**, 149, 155, 158

Jamaica Inn 29, 41, 44, 51, 83, **86–88**, 89, 90, 101, 120, 130
Juno and the Paycock **47–51**, 138

The Lady Vanishes **82–86**, 98
lamps 1, 4, 8–10, 20, 21, 23, 50, 51, 53, 70, 77, 79, 89, 91, 94, 95, 103–105, 111, 112, 114, 117, 118, 120, 122–125, 132, 135, 137–145, 147, 152, 159–161, 163, 174, 181, 182, 186, 188–190
legs 10, 11, 18, 23, 41, 61, 77, 107, 131, 134, 172, 177, 179, 181, 184, 185
Lifeboat 4, 28, 49, 56, 73, 90, **108–110**, 117, 137, 188
The Lodger 6–8, 11, 15, **17–26**, 28, 32, 43, 46, 51, 64, 78, 82, 162, 184

The Man Who Knew Too Much (1934) 51, **60–66**
The Man Who Knew Too Much (1956) **151–154**
The Manxman 8, **41–44**, 90
Marnie 49, 88, 96, 107, 113, 121, 131, **171–176**, 178, 179, 180, 182, 185
mirrors 34, 50, 81, 90, 102, 119, 121, 125, 129, 130, 157, 160, 161, 164, 165
Mr. and Mrs. Smith 42, 49, **96–99**, 130, 158
Murder! 17, **50–51**, 78

North by Northwest 3, 10, 11, 15, 27, 47, 49, 62, 65, 68, 93, 103, 133, 156, **161–163**, 164, 169, 179
Notorious 9, 10, 17, 27, 30, 41, 65, 70, 72, 86, **113–120**, 126, 135, 145, 173, 174
Number Seventeen 50, 54, **57–59**, 67, 70, 85, 87, 88, 94, 128

The Paradine Case 8, 9, 49, 79, 88, 94, 100, 104, **120–123**, 138, 141, 142
The Pleasure Garden 7, **15–17**, 29, 49, 51, 82, 89, 157, 188

Psycho 4, 7, 8, 62, 112, 130, 138, 152, **164–168**, 169, 171, 179, 184

Rear Window 35, 59, 108, **143–146**, 157, 159, 161, 174, 175
Rebecca 9, 49, **88–92**, 94, 99, 100, 114, 117, 121, 127, 135, 149, 151, 165, 179
Rich and Strange 40, 49, **53–57**, 59, 107, 162
The Ring 21, 30, **31–35**, 38, 42, 56, 75, 82, 104, 134, 158, 188
Rohmer, Eric 18, 113, 123, 127, 137, 143, 156, 160, 165
Rope 11, 87, 94, 108, **123–125**, 137, 138, 149, 187

Sabotage 9, 17, 62, **73–78**, 79, 87
Saboteur 11, 34, 47, 93, **103–105**, 106
sculptures 1, 25, 28–31, 79, 97, 104, 113, 114, 144, 148, 163, 167, 171, 174
sea 44, 54, 55–57, 65, 75, 78, 79, 86, 87, 90, 91, 109, 168
Secret Agent 7, 10, 34, 40, 56, **69–73**, 74, 84, 93, 104, 146, 152, 184
Shadow of a Doubt 7, 10, 40, 42, 43, 85, 98, **105–108**, 117, 130, 131, 135, 136, 144, 154, 158, 171, 188
The Skin Game 49, **51–53**, 94, 138
smoke 30, 42, 43, 58, 59, 73, 87, 89, 98, 106, 111, 129, 130, 135, 136, 158, 176, 184
Spellbound 8, 9, 65, 67, 79, 97, 102, **110–113**, 117, 137, 168
Stage Fright 17, **128–131**, 132, 136, 155, 158, 188
stairs 1, 4, 6–8, 17, 20–23, 27, 31, 39, 43–47, 58, 60, 64, 66, 70, 72, 83, 87, 89, 94, 97, 99, 101, 104, 107, 112, 113, 118, 119, 128, 129, 135–137, 147, 153, 158, 166–169, 184, 185, 189, 190
statues 11, 30, 47, 93, 104, 120, 126, 157, 163, 165, 190
Strangers on a Train 67, 79, 107, 130, **131–134**, 144, 146, 147, 173, 184
Suspicion 9, 48, 49, 58, 79, **99–102**, 113, 117, 121, 135, 140, 170

tables 1, 24, 25, 33, 34, 37, 44, 59, 64, 75, 77, 78, 83, 85–88, 98, 99, 103, 104, 106, 115, 118–120, 122, 125, 130, 138,

Index

142, 147, 160, 163, 166, 181, 186, 190

The 39 Steps 49, 50, 57, **66–69**, 88, 131

To Catch a Thief 37, 49, 117, **146–149**, 174, 188

Topaz 9, 22, 28, 102, 147, 152, 177, 179, **181–184**, 185

Torn Curtain 23, 47, 64, 81, 87, 88, 114, 133, 171, **176–181**, 182, 184, 185

The Trouble with Harry 9, 94, 125, **149–151**, 187

Under Capricorn **126–128**, 188

Vertigo 8, 9, 22, 46, 67, 70, 100, 117, 122, **156–161**, 164, 184, 188

Waltzes from Vienna **59–60**, 94, 178

The Wrong Man 22, 25, 81, **154–156**, 164

Young and Innocent 41, **78–82**, 90

www.ingramcontent.com/pod-product-compliance
Ingram Content Group UK Ltd.
Pitfield, Milton Keynes, MK11 3LW, UK
UKHW042010140426
5217IPUK00015B/1079